Marketing and
Society
THE CHALLENGE

AMA Reprint Series
Editor John J. Wheatley

Marketing and
Society
THE CHALLENGE

Edited for the
AMERICAN MARKETING ASSOCIATION
by

ROBERT J. LAVIDGE
President, Elrick and Lavidge, Inc.

and

ROBERT J. HOLLOWAY
Professor of Marketing
University of Minnesota

FOR MARKETING KNOWLEDGE

AMA Reprint Series
1969

Richard D. Irwin, Inc., Homewood, Illinois
Irwin-Dorsey Limited, Georgetown, Ontario

First Printing, June, 1969

Library of Congress Catalog Card No. 73-83124

Printed in the United States of America

PREFACE

The editors of this volume share the view that marketing people must give increased consideration to the effects of our actions and inactions on society. We believe it is vital that attention be given to the ways in which marketing contributes, or can contribute, to society as well as to societal issues which relate to advertising, labeling, and other marketing functions. Greater recognition of our responsibilities and opportunities hopefully will have an effect in raising ethical standards in the field and in stimulating actions which will benefit society as well as advance the discipline. This suggests the purpose of the volume.

Considering the opportunities he has and the concerns and conflicts he must face, what are the challenges which confront the marketing man? On what standards should he base his responses to these challenges? These questions are raised throughout the entire volume, which is composed of readings taken from American Marketing Association publications, conferences, and reports.

No final answers are provided to the difficult question: What are the marketing man's social responsibilities? It is our hope that these readings will help direct attention to this question and to related questions for which each individual must seek his own answers. The volume is intended to provide a framework for lively and meaningful discussion as well as individual reflection. Toward this objective, conflicting opinions are presented.

For their encouragement and assistance, the editors are grateful to Professor John J. Wheatley, Reprints Editor, and Professor Stephen A. Greyser, Publications Board Chairman. We are most indebted, of course, to the authors of the articles appearing in this volume.

May, 1969   ROBERT J. LAVIDGE
                                                     ROBERT J. HOLLOWAY

TABLE OF CONTENTS

Part I

MARKETING'S ROLE IN SOCIETY

What is marketing's role in society? The readings in Part I present varied answers to this question.

Marketing people clearly have a role to play in the distribution, promotion and sale of goods and services. Within the past decade, a great deal of attention also has been focused on the key role played by marketing in planning the goods and services which will be made available by the business firm. Marketing's relationship to society as a whole has been discussed largely in the context of unethical practices, especially in advertising and pricing. Marketing people, as well as others, have given inadequate attention to the role of marketing in economic development and in bringing, or failing to bring, the benefits of our economic system to the disadvantaged.

A. Two opposing views

The first two readings in Part I present diametrically opposed views of the role and the importance of marketing. Peter F. Drucker states that the development of marketing, "above all others, makes possible economic integration and the fullest utilization of whatever assets and productive capacity an economy already possesses. It mobilizes latent economic energy. It contributes to the greatest needs. . . ." He focuses on the critical role of marketing in the development of the "underdeveloped" countries.

At the other end of the spectrum, Richard N. Farmer argues that marketing, as it is practiced, "is unethical, and that marketing is irrelevant." He presents a challenge to those involved in marketing to recognize and act upon what he sees as the differentiation between what marketing's role in our society might be and what it is.

1

1. MARKETING AND ECONOMIC DEVELOPMENT*

Peter F. Drucker

MARKETING AS A BUSINESS DISCIPLINE

The distinguished pioneer of marketing, whose memory we honor today, was largely instrumental in developing marketing as a systematic business discipline:

> In teaching us how to go about, in an orderly, purposeful and planned way to find and create customers;
> To identify and define markets; to create new ones and promote them;
> To integrate customer's needs, wants, and preferences, and the intellectual and creative capacity and skills of an industrial society, toward the design of new and better products and of new distributive concepts and processes.

On this contribution and similar ones of other Founding Fathers of marketing during the last half century rests the rapid emergence of marketing as perhaps the most advanced, certainly the most "scientific" of all functional business disciplines.

But Charles Coolidge Parlin also contributed as a Founding Father toward the development of marketing as a *social discipline*. He helped give us the awareness, the concepts, and the tools that make us understand marketing as a dynamic process of society through which business enterprise is integrated productively with society's purposes and human values. It is in marketing, as we now understand it, that we satisfy individual and social values, needs, and wants—be it through producing goods, supplying services, fostering innovation, or creating satisfaction. Marketing, as we have come to understand it, has its focus on the customer, that is, on the individual making decisions within a social

_____

*Journal of Marketing, January, 1958, pp. 252–59.

Editor's Note. This is the text of the Parlin Memorial Lecture, presented to the Philadelphia Chapter of the American Marketing Association on June 6, 1957. The annual lecture, given since 1945, is in memory of Charles Coolidge Parlin, for many years Director of Commercial Research at the Curtis Publishing Company, and frequently referred to as the founder of modern marketing research. The Parlin Memorial Award is presented each year to a lecturer chosen for his ability to make a distinguished contribution to the science of marketing and for outstanding achievement in the marketing field.

Although *The Journal of Marketing* ordinarily does not publish speeches as such, an exception is made in this case, because of the great significance of Mr. Drucker's remarks.

structure and within a personal and social value system. Marketing is thus the process through which economy is integrated into society to serve human needs.

I am not competent to speak about marketing in the first sense, marketing as a functional discipline of business. I am indeed greatly concerned with marketing in this meaning. One could not be concerned, as I am, with the basic institutions of industrial society in general and with the management of business enterprise in particular, without a deep and direct concern with marketing. But in this field I am a consumer of marketing alone—albeit a heavy one. I am not capable of making a contribution. I would indeed be able to talk about the wants and needs I have which I, as a consumer of marketing, hope that you, the men of marketing, will soon supply:—a theory of pricing, for instance, that can serve, as true theories should, as the foundation for actual pricing decisions and for an understanding of price behavior; or a consumer-focused concept and theory of competition. But I could not produce any of these "new products" of marketing which we want. I cannot contribute myself. To use marketing language, I am not even "effective demand," in these fields as yet.

THE ROLE OF MARKETING

I shall today in my remarks confine myself to the second meaning in which marketing has become a discipline: The role of marketing in economy and society. And I shall single out as my focus the role of marketing in the economic development, especially of under-developed "growth" countries.

My thesis is very briefly as follows. Marketing occupies a critical role in respect to the development of such "growth" areas. Indeed marketing is the most important "multiplier" of such development. It is in itself in every one of these areas the least developed, the most backward part of the economic system. Its development, above all others, makes possible economic integration and the fullest utilization of whatever assets and productive capacity an economy already possesses. It mobilizes latent economic energy. It contributes to the greatest needs: that for the rapid development of entrepreneurs and managers, and at the same time it may be the easiest area of managerial work to get going. The reason is that, thanks to men like Charles Coolidge Parlin, it is the most systematized and, therefore, the most learnable and the most teachable of all areas of business management and entrepreneurship.

INTERNATIONAL AND INTERRACIAL INEQUALITY

Looking at this world of ours, we see some essentially new facts. For the first time in man's history the whole world is united and unified. This may seem a strange statement in view of the conflicts and threats of suicidal wars that scream at us from every headline. But conflict has always been with us. What is new is that today all of mankind shares the same vision, the same objective, the same goal, the same hope, and believes in the same tools. This vision might, in gross over-simplification, be called "industrialization."

It is the belief that it is possible for man to improve his economic lot through systematic, purposeful, and directed effort—individually as well as for an entire society. It is the belief that we have the tools at our disposal—the technological, the conceptual, and the social tools—to enable man to raise himself, through his own efforts, at least to a level that we in this country would consider poverty, but which for most of our world would be almost unbelievable luxury.

And this is an irreversible new fact. It has been made so by these true agents of revolution in our times: the new tools of communication —the dirt road, the truck, and the radio, which have penetrated even the furthest, most isolated and most primitive community.

This is new, and cannot be emphasized too much and too often. It is both a tremendous vision and a tremendous danger in that catastrophe must result if it cannot be satisfied, at least to a modest degree.

But at the same time we have a new, unprecedented danger, that of international and interracial inequality. We on the North American continent are a mere tenth of the world population, including our Canadian friends and neighbors. But we have at least 75 per cent of the world income. And the 75 per cent of the world population whose income is below $100 per capita a year receive together perhaps no more than 10 per cent of the world's income. This is inequality of income, as great as anything the world has ever seen. It is accompanied by very high equality of income in the developed countries, especially in ours where we are in the process of proving that an industrial society does not have to live in extreme tension between the few very rich and the many very poor as lived all earlier societies of man. But what used to be national inequality and economic tension is now rapidly becoming international (and unfortunately also interracial) inequality and tension.

This is also brand new. In the past there were tremendous differences between societies and cultures: in their beliefs, their concepts, their ways of life, and their knowledge. The Frankish knight who went on Crusade was an ignorant and illiterate boor, according to the standards of the polished courtiers of Constantinople or of his Moslem enemies. But economically his society and theirs were exactly alike. They had the same sources of income, the same productivity of labor, the same forms and channels of investment, the same economic institutions, and the same distribution of income and wealth. Economically the Frankish knight, however much a barbarian he appeared, was at home in the societies of the East; and so was his serf. Both fitted in immediately and without any difficulty.

And this has been the case of all societies that went above the level of purely primitive tribe.

The inequality in our world today, however, between nations and races, is therefore a new—and a tremendously dangerous—phenomenon.

What we are engaged in today is essentially a race between the promise of economic development and the threat of international world-wide class war. The economic development is the opportunity of this age. The class war is the danger. Both are new. Both are indeed so new that most of us do not even see them as yet. But they are the essential economic realities of this industrial age of ours. And whether we shall realize the opportunity or succumb to danger will largely decide not only the economic future of this world—it may largely decide its spiritual, its intellectual, its political, and its social future.

SIGNIFICANCE OF MARKETING

Marketing is central in this new situation. For marketing is one of our most potent levers to convert the danger into the opportunity.

To understand this we must ask: What do we mean by "under-developed"?

The first answer is, of course, that we mean areas of very low income. But income is, after all, a result. It is a result first of extreme agricultural over-population in which the great bulk of the people have to find a living on the land which, as a result, cannot even produce enough food to feed them, let alone produce a surplus. It is certainly a result of low productivity. And both, in a vicious circle, mean that there is not enough capital for investment, and very low productivity of what is being invested—owing largely to misdirection of investment into unessential and unproductive channels.

All this we know today and understand. Indeed we have learned during the last few years a very great deal both about the structure of an under-developed economy and about the theory and dynamics of economic development.

What we tend to forget, however, is that the essential aspect of an "under-developed" economy and the factor the absence of which keeps it "under-developed," is the inability to organize economic efforts and energies, to bring together resources, wants, and capacities, and so to convert a self-limiting static system into creative, self-generating organic growth.

And this is where marketing comes in.

Lack of Development in "Under-Developed" Countries

1. First, in every "under-developed" country I know of, marketing is the most under-developed—or the least developed—part of the economy, if only because of the strong, pervasive prejudice against the "middleman."

As a result, these countries are stunted by inability to make effective use of the little they have. Marketing might by itself go far toward changing the entire economic tone of the existing system—without any change in methods of production, distribution of population, or of income.

It would make the producers capable of producing marketable products by providing them with standards, with quality demands, and with specifications for their product. It would make the product capable of being brought to markets instead of perishing on the way. And it would make the consumer capable of discrimination, that is, of obtaining the greatest value for his very limited purchasing power.

In every one of these countries, marketing profits are characteristically low. Indeed the people engaged in marketing barely eke out a subsistence living. And "mark-ups" are minute by our standards. But marketing costs are outrageously high. The waste in distribution and marketing, if only from spoilage or from the accumulation of unsalable inventories that clog the shelves for years, has to be seen to be believed. And marketing service is by and large all but non-existent.

What is needed in any "growth" country to make economic development realistic, and at the same time produce a vivid demonstration of what economic development can produce, is a marketing system:

A system of physical distribution;

A financial system to make possible the distribution of goods; and

Finally actual marketing, that is, an actual system of integrating wants, needs, and purchasing power of the consumer with capacity and resources of production.

This need is largely masked today because marketing is so often confused with the traditional "trader and merchant" of which every one of these countries has more than enough. It would be one of our most important contributions to the development of "under-developed" countries to get across the fact that marketing is something quite different.

It would be basic to get across the triple function of marketing:

The function of crystallizing and directing demands for maximum productive effectiveness and efficiency;

The function of guiding production purposefully toward maximum consumer satisfaction and consumer value.

The function of creating discrimination that then gives rewards to those who really contribute excellence, and that then also penalizes the monopolist, the slothful, or those who only want to take but do not want to contribute or to risk.

UTILIZATION BY THE ENTREPRENEUR

2. Marketing is also the most easily accessible "multiplier" of managers and entrepreneurs in an "under-developed" growth area. And managers and entrepreneurs are the foremost need of these countries. In the first place, "economic development" is not a force of nature. It is the result of the action, the purposeful, responsible, risk-taking action, of men as entrepreneurs and managers.

Certainly it is the entrepreneur and manager who alone can convey to the people of these countries an understanding of what economic development means and how it can be achieved.

Marketing can convert latent demand into effective demand. It cannot, by itself, create purchasing power. But it can uncover and channel all purchasing power that exists. It can, therefore, create rapidly the conditions for a much higher level of economic activity than existed before, can create the opportunities for the entrepreneur.

It then can create the stimulus for the development of modern, responsible, professional management by creating opportunity for the producer who knows how to plan, how to organize, how to lead people, how to innovate.

In most of these countries markets are of necessity very small. They are too small to make it possible to organize distribution for a single-product line in any effective manner. As a result, without a marketing organization, many products for which there is an adequate demand at a reasonable price cannot be distributed; or worse they can be produced and distributed only under monopoly conditions. A marketing system is needed which serves as the joint and common channel for many producers if any of them is to be able to come into existence and to stay in existence.

This means in effect that a marketing system in the "under-developed" countries is the *creator of small business,* is the only way in which a man of vision and daring can become a businessman and an entrepreneur himself. This is thereby also the only way in which a true middle class can develop in the countries in which the habit of investment in productive enterprise has still to be created.

DEVELOPER OF STANDARDS

3. Marketing in an "under-developed" country is the developer of standards—of standards for product and service as well as of standards of conduct, of integrity, of reliability, of foresight, and of concern for

the basic long-range impact of decisions on the customer, the supplier, the economy, and the society.

Rather than go on making theoretical statements let me point to one illustration: The impact Sears Roebuck has had on several countries of Latin America. To be sure, the countries of Latin America in which Sears operates—Mexico, Brazil, Cuba, Venezuela, Colombia, and Peru—are not "under-developed" in the same sense in which Indonesia or the Congo are "under-developed." Their average income, although very low by our standards, is at least two times, perhaps as much as four or five times, that of the truly "under-developed" countries in which the bulk of mankind still lives. Still in every respect except income level these Latin American countries are at best "developing." And they have all the problems of economic development—perhaps even in more acute form than the countries of Asia and Africa, precisely because their development has been so fast during the last ten years.

It is also true that Sears in these countries is not a "low-price" merchandiser. It caters to the middle class in the richer of these countries, and to the upper middle class in the poorest of these countries. Incidentally, the income level of these groups is still lower than that of the worker in the industrial sector of our economy.

Still Sears is a mass-marketer even in Colombia or Peru. What is perhaps even more important, it is applying in these "under-developed" countries exactly the same policies and principles it applies in this country, carries substantially the same merchandise (although most of it produced in the countries themselves), and applies the same concepts of marketing it uses in Indianapolis or Philadelphia. Its impact and experience are, therefore, a fair test of what marketing principles, marketing knowledge, and marketing techniques can achieve.

The impact of this one American business which does not have more than a mere handful of stores in these countries and handles no more than a small fraction of the total retail business of these countries is truly amazing. In the first place, Sears' latent purchasing power has fast become actual purchasing power. Or, to put it less theoretically, people have begun to organize their buying and to go out for value in what they do buy.

Secondly, by the very fact that it builds one store in one city, Sears forces a revolution in retailing throughout the whole surrounding area. It forces store modernization. It forces consumer credit. It forces a different attitude toward the customer, toward the store clerk, toward the supplier, and toward the merchandise itself. It forces other retailers to adopt modern methods of pricing, of inventory control, of training, of window display, and what have you.

The greatest impact Sears has had, however, is in the multiplication of new industrial business for which Sears creates a marketing channel.

Because it has had to sell goods manufactured in these countries rather than import them (if only because of foreign exchange restrictions), Sears has been instrumental in getting established literally hundreds of new manufacturers making goods which, a few years ago, could not be made in the country, let alone be sold in adequate quantity. Simply to satisfy its own marketing needs, Sears has had to insist on standards of workmanship, quality, and delivery—that is, on standards of production management, of technical management, and above all of the management of people—which, in a few short years, have advanced the art and science of management in these countries by at least a generation.

I hardly need to add that Sears is not in Latin America for reasons of philanthropy, but because it is good and profitable business with extraordinary growth potential. In other words, Sears is in Latin America because marketing is the major opportunity in a "growth economy"— precisely because its absence is a major economic gap and the greatest need.

THE DISCIPLINE OF MARKETING

4. Finally, marketing is critical in economic development because marketing has become so largely systematized, so largely both learnable and teachable. It is the discipline among all our business disciplines that has advanced the furthest.

I do not forget for a moment how much we still have to learn in marketing. But we should also not forget that most of what we have learned so far we have learned in a form in which we can express it in general concepts, in valid principles and, to a substantial degree, in quantifiable measurements. This, above all others, was the achievement of that generation to whom Charles Coolidge Parlin was leader and inspiration.

A critical factor in this world of ours is the learnability and teachability of what it means to be an entrepreneur and manager. For it is the entrepreneur and the manager who alone can cause economic development to happen. The world needs them, therefore, in very large numbers; and it needs them fast.

Obviously this need cannot be supplied by our supplying entrepreneurs and managers, quite apart from the fact that we hardly have the surplus. Money we can supply. Technical assistance we can supply, and should supply more. But the supply of men we can offer to the people in the "under-developed" countries is of necessity a very small one.

The demand is also much too urgent for it to be supplied by slow evolution through experience, or through dependence on the emergence of "naturals." The danger that lies in the inequality today between the few countries that have and the great many countries that have not is much too great to permit a wait of centuries. Yet it takes centuries if we depend on experience and slow evolution for the supply of entrepreneurs and managers adequate to the needs of a modern society.

There is only one way in which man has ever been able to short-cut experience, to telescope development, in other words to *learn something.* That way is to have available the distillate of experience and skill in the form of knowledge, of concepts, of generalization, of measurement —in the form of *discipline,* in other words.

THE DISCIPLINE OF ENTREPRENEURSHIP

Many of us today are working on the fashioning of such a discipline of entrepreneurship and management. Maybe we are further along than most of us realize.

Certainly in what has come to be called "Operation Research and Synthesis" we have the first beginnings of a systematic approach to the entrepreneurial task of purposeful risk-taking and innovation—so far only an approach, but a most promising one, unless indeed we become so enamored with the gadgets and techniques as to forget purpose and aim.

We are at the beginning perhaps also of an understanding of the basic problems of organizing people of diversified and highly advanced skill and judgment together in one effective organization, although again no one so far would, I am convinced, claim more for us than that we have begun at last to ask intelligent questions.

But marketing, although it only covers one functional area in the field, has something that can be called a discipline. It has developed general concepts, that is, theories that explain a multitude of phenomena in simple statements. It even has measurements that record "facts" rather than opinions. In marketing, therefore, we already possess a learnable and teachable approach to this basic and central problem not only of the "under-developed" countries but of all countries. All of us have today the same survival stake in economic development. The risk and danger of international and interracial inequality are simply too great.

Marketing is obviously not a cure-all, not a paradox. It is only one thing we need. But it answers a critical need. At the same time marketing is most highly developed.

Indeed without marketing as the hinge on which to turn, economic development will almost have to take the totalitarian form. A totalitarian system can be defined economically as one in which economic development is being attempted without marketing, indeed as one in which marketing is suppressed. Precisely because it first looks at the values and wants of the individual, and because it then develops people to act purposefully and responsibly—that is, because of its effectiveness in developing a free economy—marketing is suppressed in a totalitarian system. If we want economic development in freedom and responsibility, we have to build it on the development of marketing.

In the new and unprecedented world we live in, a world which knows both a new unity of vision and growth and a new and most dangerous cleavage, marketing has a special and central role to play. This role goes:

Beyond "getting the stuff out the back door";
Beyond "getting the most sales with the least cost";
Beyond "the optimal integration of our values and wants as customers, citizens, and persons, with our productive resources and intellectual achievements"—the role marketing plays in a developed society.

In a developing economy, marketing is, of course, all of this. But in addition, in an economy that is striving to break the age-old bondage of man to misery, want, and destitution, marketing is also the catalyst for the transmutation of latent resources into actual resources, of desires into accomplishments, and the development of responsible economic leaders and informed economic citizens.

2. WOULD YOU WANT YOUR DAUGHTER TO MARRY A MARKETING MAN?*

Richard N. Farmer

Lack of growth, sluggish changes in the curriculum, and a generally uninspiring future seem to characterize education in the field of marketing.[1] And there is every possibility that the situation may get much worse before it gets better.

The fault is not so much with the teachers or the curricula, but in the very nature of American marketing philosophy. The whole world, including the United States, appears to be moving in a direction in which marketing is decidedly *not* prepared to go. Unless this trend is recognized for what it is, and unless marketing scholars finally face up to the essential and basic questions in marketing, the entire field of marketing is in for considerable difficulty.

No amount of improvement in the curricula, intensive research in traditional marketing problems, or concern about the fate of business schools will serve to avoid the two basic issues. And the teachers and practitioners of marketing, for all of their success in so many ways, have never really come to grips with either of these issues.

Journal of Marketing, Vol. 31 (January, 1967), pp. 1-3.

[1] In this connection, see David J. Luck, "Is Marketing Education Driving or Drifting?" *Journal of Marketing*, Vol. 29 (April, 1965), pp. 22-24.

If the marketing people manage to do so, the field of marketing will prosper. If not, it will be regarded as an interesting cultural quirk of the mid-twentieth century, which temporarily attracted the attention of some very intelligent people.

The two basic issues which have to be faced are that *marketing is unethical,* and that *marketing is irrelevant.*

MARKETING IS UNETHICAL

For the past 6,000 years the field of marketing has been thought of as made up of fast-buck artists, con-men, wheeler-dealers, and shoddy-goods distributors. Too many of us have been "taken" by the tout or con-man; and all of us at times have been prodded into buying all sorts of "things" we really did not need, and which we found later on we did not even want.

In itself, this can be looked on as a problem of personal gullibility. Yet marketing men who conduct serious studies of how to persuade more people to buy more products and services will continue to be in ethical difficulties.

When one examines physical distribution, channel theory, or similar kinds of distribution problems, this point does not hold. After all, the production-oriented side of marketing does offer a great deal to a human race which has never been efficient enough to give all persons their material due.

But when we turn to advertising, sales-promotion, and other techniques and studies calculated to "push" goods on uninterested individuals, that is another question. This is perhaps the major reason why marketing departments often attract inept students.

One can point to many refutations of the above point, most of which are believed by marketing men and persons involved in sales work.[2] Any group of intelligent and able people working in an exciting and technically demanding field can convince themselves of the value of their work. But the real question is: *Does anybody else believe it?*

Unfortunately, too few of the intellectually important people do. It is true that some surveys have indicated a certain satisfaction with advertising;[3] but the 80% or so who feel satisfied may be typically those whose opinions will not count in the future. The scholars, opinion-makers, intellectuals, clergymen, and others whose words will count

---

[2]Examples are in Steuart Henderson Britt's *The Spenders* (New York: McGraw-Hill Book Co., 1961).

[3]Raymond A. Bauer, "Some Insights Into the Support and Criticism of Advertising," paper delivered at the 1965 Annual Meeting, American Association of Advertising Agencies, pp. 2–4.

continue to remain skeptical, or simply bored about the present state of sales promotion.[4]

Elaborate surveys are not needed to verify this point. Merely follow some student discussions in the coffee shop or in other uninhibited surroundings. Observe the concern of so many businessmen over the fact that so many college graduates are going into nonbusiness fields. Read some of the nonadvertising publications that do not give a sop to advertisers.

What is "visible" about marketing is not the intriguing, truly exciting research work in a variety of behavioral and technical areas. Instead, it is the picture of some pitchman selling hair spray on television!

MARKETING IS IRRELEVANT

The United States is the only nation both wealthy enough and inept enough to operate consistently below potential output-capacity most of the time.

Except for the war-years, this country has not operated up to economic potential since 1910. Only in 1917–1918, 1927, 1942–46, 1953, and 1956–57 has unemployment been below 3%.[5] In 1964, a year of extremely good economic performance, some $27 billions of output was lost through the full-employment gap.[6] The American economy could have produced this much more if all resources (land, labor, and capital) had been fully employed. Not only were many men unemployed, but factories and fields also were not used to capacity, largely because the demand for such goods and services did not exist.

While the reasons for this failure to obtain full utilization of productive potential are exceedingly complex, the output of our economy rarely exceeds 90% of potential capacity, and more often operates around the 80 to 85% level.

The sales-promotion aspects of marketing have reached full flower in this country. In most other countries sales-promotion activities do not flourish because everything produced is almost immediately consumed. Production, not marketing, is the key factor around which the economy turns.

For this reason the American concept of organizing the firm around marketing possibilities is almost incomprehensible to many foreign man-

[4]Same reference as footnote 3. Also, see Colston E. Warne, "Advertising—A Critic's View," *Journal of Marketing*, Vol. 26 (October, 1962), pp. 10–14.

[5]Lance E. Davis, Jonathan R. T. Hughes, Duncan M. McDougall, *American Economic History* (Homewood, Ill.: Richard D. Irwin, Inc., 1961), p. 95.

[6]Council of Economic Advisers, *Economic Report of the President, 1965* (Washington, D.C.: U.S. Government Printing Office, 1965), pp. 82-83.

agers. Such orientation implies that the firm can always produce more than the market can absorb, which can happen generally only in an economy operating below potential capacity.

To operate at less than capacity implies that there is always more than the consumers can afford. In this situation competition, even "cut-throat" competition, becomes very real indeed.

TWO ETHICAL QUESTIONS

Two kinds of ethical questions arise here.

First, is it right to prevent people from consuming when you obviously can produce the goods, but when the consumers do not have the necessary income?

Second, if you can produce more, and if someone somewhere is in want, is it ethical to allow any factories and farms to produce at less than full capacity?

With some two-thirds of the world in perpetual poverty, is it right to try to move up the American average propensity to consume from its present 92% of disposable income to 93%? Intensive marketing promotion may be able to induce more consumption out of available income, but it might prove more desirable to utilize savings for more socially useful ends.

CALVINISM AND TRADITION

The feeling that marketing is largely irrelevant is by no means restricted to people in other countries. In one sense, a great many Americans are Calvinists; and our country was built on a doctrine of self-denial, plus concern for hard labor and good works. In the older American tradition, consumption meant survival but not necessarily enjoyment. A lot has been done in marketing to make people forget their guilt feelings about consumption, as they drive along in anodized chariots or sit beside their swimming pools.

But curiously, the trend today is back to the old ethic. There are problems of economic development, of urban renewal, of poverty, and of racial conflict; but for the most part marketing people have avoided such issues.

Even though they enjoy the fruits of marketing, most of the rest of the world, and certainly many Americans, see the basic irrelevance of marketing quite clearly.

Harsh words? Not really. Anyone can convince himself and his colleagues that what he is doing is important and relevant. But marketing, especially as viewed by many young people today, appears to be a trivial activity indulged in by trivial people. For a group that has been so brilliant in selling and distribution as have American marketers, this is sad.

Perhaps marketing men have sold everybody everything, except themselves and the significance of marketing.

THE OTHER SIDE OF THE COIN

Marketing *can* be both ethical and relevant, although unfortunately the image presented by American practitioners does not suggest that this could be the case. In a world largely preoccupied with production problems, questions of distribution and product-mix can prove intractable without proper utilization of marketing techniques; and many Communist and Socialist countries have learned this to their dismay.[7]

The growing complexity of the world's economies leads inevitably to the need for more efficient marketing methods and tools. As soon as the questions of the supply of basic food, shelter, and clothing have been solved for the majority of the world population, questions of what to do next will require the services of marketing experts of the highest caliber. Moreover, in spite of the annoying amount of "noise" produced by some promotional activities, advertising and sales promotion do produce some quite tangible benefits.[8]

But too many marketers in the United States create an image of vulgar hucksters, unable to share in the most important part of the world's work. The tragic part of this preoccupation with the less important parts of marketing is that relatively few of the long-run distribution problems ever get the attention they deserve.[9]

SO WHAT?

Do you want your son to study in a modern American school of business? Lord, no! (I teach in one of the best, too, but even it is not good enough.) And if he majored in marketing, I would cut him off without a cent.

If that nice young man who has dates with your daughter turns out to be a marketing major, what would you do? I would chase him off the premises fast. Who wants his daughter to marry a huckster?

Nobody knows the troubles we are going to see if we do not face up to certain essential and basic issues, and soon.

---

[7]Barry M. Richman, *Soviet Management: With Significant American Comparisons* (Englewood Cliffs, N.J.: Prentice-Hall, Inc., 1965), pp. 108–131.

[8]Martin Mayer, *Madison Avenue, USA* (New York: Pocket Books, Inc., 1959), pp. 312–28.

[9]Reavis Cox, *Distribution in a High-Level Economy* (Englewood Cliffs, N.J.: Prentice-Hall, Inc., 1965), pp. 230–31.

B. A call for maturity

William M. Borton discusses marketing's contributions to society as well as its shortcomings. In discussing the former, he focuses on marketing functions, especially those related to effective and efficient communication to and from the marketplace. Then he addresses attention to marketing sins, those of omission as well as of commission. He challenges those in marketing to foster the development of their discipline from short-term selfish concerns toward increased attention to societal values.

3. RESPECTABILITY FOR MARKETING?*

William M. Borton

The distribution of goods has rapidly grown to giant stature in our society. If an inclusive definition is used, something like one out of four gainfully employed persons in the United States is now engaged in marketing.

In addition to its essential delivery and clerical functions, marketing bears increasingly important communication responsibilities. As the number of persons between the producer and the consumer has grown, and the number and complexity of products has increased, consumers have been obliged to rely more and more upon middlemen and advertising for information and assistance in buying and using goods. Increasingly producers depend upon people engaged in marketing for reports of consumer needs and preferences, to guide decisions about what to design and produce.

Marketing also wields enormous influence upon our goals and values —upon our beliefs and assumptions as to what and how much is good, important, worth doing, or worth working for. Business firms spend over $11 billion a year in advertising, in addition to "publicity," which is often not recognized as promotion. The cumulative effect of all these appeals upon our society's values, wants, and behavior is not readily measurable. Even more elusive is the influence exerted by marketing upon our beliefs and activities through the editorial policies of mass-communication media, which depend upon advertising for most of their revenue.

Journal of Marketing, October, 1959, pp. 47–50.

OPPORTUNITIES FOR USEFULNESS

Marketing people have unsurpassed opportunities for usefulness to others, and for making the American system more beneficial and attractive. The final outcome of the contest between free enterprise and Communism will not be decided by bombs or missiles, but by the judgment of the peoples of the world as to which system yields more genuinely satisfying lives for the least economic and emotional costs.

Marketers can do much to increase the satisfactions of living, and to reduce the costs. Industrial marketers can help manufacturers to reduce the economic costs of consumer goods. And consumer marketers can increase satisfactions by more precisely offering particular goods to the kinds of people who will derive most satisfaction from them . . . by increasing the effectiveness of the use of products . . . by discovering unfilled needs and wants . . . by considering which of all the possible new products, designs, and features should yield the truest satisfactions . . . and by reporting these needs, and encouraging the design and production of these goods.

Consumer marketers can lessen economic costs by reducing physical delivery and routine costs of distribution . . . by devoting less effort to trying to sell goods to the kinds of people who will derive less satisfaction from them . . . and by reducing the amount of ineffective advertising.

Consumer marketers have great opportunities for reducing the emotional costs of distribution by using methods and appeals which cause less inconvenience, annoyance, fear, or uneasiness to both purchasers and non-purchasers—and to salesmen and others engaged in marketing. And they can stimulate behaviors, create wants, and shape goals and values which are most genuinely rewarding.

But instead, many critics point out that much marketing activity does little good, and that some results in disappointment, offense, or even injury to others. They call attention to the marketing of goods designed with little attention to consumer wants and usage; useless drugs and cosmetics, even harmful products; insufficient inspection, inadequate instructions; high-pressure, high-cost selling efforts to sell goods to people who do not want them; advertising which irritates or bores, emphasizes insignificant product differences, creates misimpressions through clever wording and effects, or channels the desire for social approval into competitive consumption of fashion goods.

Certainly society's judgment of the usefulness of marketing is not very favorable. Opinion surveys consistently show little respect for advertising, selling, middlemen's functions, and other marketing activities. Naturally, responsible people engaged in these kinds of work are disturbed. Some are baffled or even jealous of the prestige which recognized professions enjoy, even though "they don't require more intelligence or make more money."

Some of the criticisms of marketing relate to waste, mistakes, lack of theory and know-how. Most marketing men have been trained to think in the terms and assumptions of conventional, "scarcity" economics. But economic theory affords inadequate explanations of how business-men behave, and why, and it accounts even less satisfactorily for cur-rent consumer behavior.

MARKETING CREEDS

While marketing is criticized for lack of knowledge, more penetrating opinion surveys generally reveal that it is condemned more for its objec-tives and ethics, or lack of them. Since pre-Biblical days, the motives and morals of traders and merchants have been suspect, often for good reason. What objectives, codes, expectations govern marketing behavior in the United States today?

Money-making is usually held up as the attraction and model for careers in marketing. Businessmen generally assert that they conform to the classic economic assumption that a business is devoted to the pursuit of profits, and that competition will insure that the public inter-est is best served. However, businessmen frequently place more emphasis on increasing *sales.* Many marketing teachers and writers see their func-tion as that of helping the individual business to increase its sales, or profits (at the expense of other firms).

Business associations and many marketing men attempt to reconcile the public interest with increased sales by *all* firms, through equating welfare with the sheer bulk of goods consumed, or even with the total price of goods bought. Marketing is then assigned the responsibility for "maintaining employment"—so that people can consume the maximum amount of goods. However, problems of obesity and discussions of current automobiles are evidences that, past a certain point, quantity of goods consumed bears little relationship to human welfare. Value of goods bought is an even less satisfactory index. By this criterion, human welfare can be increased simply by managing to sell goods at higher prices.

Economists generally attempt to reconcile consumer and business interests by demanding better "adjustment" through greater "knowledge" and "rationality." Apparently, both consumer and businessman should strive to behave more like an "economic man"!

The efforts of more thoughtful businessmen to reconcile private, ma-terial interests with social responsibility or with religion are reflected in many speeches, and in numerous articles in the *Harvard Business Review* and other publications.

The "Sales Manager's Creed" of National Sales Executives, Inc., is confined to relations between employers and salesmen.

Statements of still other marketing men and the cognomen of the American Marketing Association—"an association for the advancement of science in marketing"—emphasize the means rather than the end toward which the means are to be applied.

In the ninth of the Association's listed objectives, and increasingly in discussions of marketing objectives, "sound, honest practices" and "marketing work on a high ethical plane" are mentioned. However, frank avowal of responsibility for the welfare of "outsiders," which is the core of the codes of respected professions, is notably absent.

Marketing may be thought of as a socially adolescent giant, anxious for approval, but at odds with himself as to whether he is supposed to be mainly seeking his own welfare or that of others . . . and as to whether his own well-being is more closely related to sales, profits, or social approval.

INDICATIONS OF MARKETING MATURITY

There are several indications that marketing will mature socially, and that marketers will devote themselves increasingly to the welfare of others, and will scrutinize more closely the relationship of goods to human satisfaction.

One indication is the *passing of scarcity*—of essentials, conveniences, even comforts. The principle of diminishing returns must apply to the satisfactions to be derived from still more, bigger, more-rapidly-obsoleted goods with more chrome and cellophane. Profits, as a means of purchasing these goods, should become a less effective reward and incentive for marketers, compared with social approval.

Another factor is the *growing technical and productive capacity of Russia,* which forces reconsideration of superiority based upon quantity of production alone.

A third indication, already mentioned, is the growing expression of *concern by marketers about the social status and obligations of marketing.*

A fourth consideration is the *increasing influence of psychology, sociology, and other behavioral sciences* upon American marketing theory, methods, and morality. These sciences are bringing increased realization that neither consumers nor businessmen are "economic men," seeking more goods and profits, consistently and rationally. Instead, they are seekers of safety, physical well-being, approval and affection, driven by emotions, possessed of mechanisms by which they perceive, learn, and form habits.

Research methods of the behavioral sciences are supplying marketing men with more effective techniques. But many social scientists feel that the ability to influence others also carries with it the responsibility for the use of that power, and that marketing people should exert their influence in ways that are most genuinely beneficial.

To be sure, the present state of knowledge permits honest disagreement as to what constitutes human welfare, and of the relationship of goods to it. But any conception of human welfare is adequate to disallow certain products and practices, and to raise doubts about others. Efforts to apply this criterion should result in better definition, and more especially of the relationship of goods to welfare.

A provocative question, concerning a marketing proposal, is, "Would an intelligent individual, raised in some other part of the world, regard this as socially beneficial?" Another is, "Would an informed person (possessing the relevant technical and competitive information) accept this?" Still another is, "If all persons obtained it, would it still be desirable?" Clearly, air-conditioning would be desirable, whether others had it or not, but it is not likely that human satisfaction would be increased by supplying every man with an automobile one foot longer than his present one.

Business practitioners, teachers, and writers may choose to combat, ignore, recognize, or promote tendencies toward the assumption of more social responsibility by marketing. Sales and marketing executives and others who wish to increase respect for marketing can advocate business policies and decisions which they believe will contribute most genuinely to human welfare, even if inconsistent with short-term sales or profits. And they can expect others to adhere to a similar code.

In many cases, executives will find superiors, stockholders, subordinates ready to accept this philosophy—which is compatible with steady growth and dividends—and respectful of the individual who takes the lead. In other cases, short-term economic sacrifice by the company or individual will be more than repaid by longer-term economic rewards. This restraint, possibly better described as enlightened or institutionalized self-interest, typifies the respected professions. Laws and licensing relating to them are merely formalizations of certain expected reciprocal behaviors between members of these professions and society.

Adoption of a more mature code or set of expectations for marketing neither leads to a "static society," lessens incentives to innovation, nor entails reduction in either the amount or vigor of marketing effort. Perhaps somewhat less of the total effort would be devoted to "creating" or "developing" wants. Certainly these efforts would be applied more responsibly.

More effort would be directed to the service functions of marketing —*to better filling then-existing demands*—which will continue to change under the impact of ongoing social and technological changes.

Marketers would be making full use of their opportunities for increasing the satisfactions and reducing the economic and emotional costs of living under the American system, and should enjoy approval comparable to that accorded any occupation or profession. The young marketing giant will then have matured into a most helpful, effective, and respected member of society.

C. The rush to regulate

E. T. Grether focuses on some of the implications of the drift in our economy away from the market as a regulator, away from the philosophy of "let the buyer beware" toward increasing government regulation of marketplace activities and the philosophy of "let the seller beware." He emphasizes the need for a: "deeper and wiser understanding on the part of both government and private enterprise as to the realistic nature of competitive functioning under modern technologies" and under diverse market structures.

4. FROM CAVEAT EMPTOR TO AN EMERGING CAVEAT VENDITOR: WHITHER?*

E. T. Grether

The ancient maxim caveat emptor, "let the buyer beware," was enunciated in the 16th Century in a horse trade: "If he be tame and have ben rydden upon then *caveat emptor.*"[1] Undoubtedly, many a buyer in a horse trade has lamented that this minimum warranty had not been enough.

CAVEAT EMPTOR AND THE COMPETITIVE MARKET ECONOMY

The enunciation of *caveat emptor* was an important opening phase in establishing what came to be the competitive system of free enterprise and free consumer-buyer choice, or the market-type economy. Eventually, but gradually, most of the resources of some western societies, including even the services of human beings, and basic natural resources came to be organized, coordinated and allocated through the

---

*From *Changing Marketing Systems,* American Marketing Association, December, 1967, pp. 174–77.
[1]See W. H. Hamilton, "The Ancient Maxim Caveat Emptor," *Yale Law Journal,* Vol. 40 (June 1931), p. 1136.

competitive market system. And, from Adam Smith on, formal economic analysis both rationalized and expressed the presumed rationale of this system. There have long been economic theories of competition.

Now there are those nowadays who deny both the rationalization and the rationale of the competitive market system. In other words, the market, like some conceptions or visions of God allegedly is dead.[2] If this be true then also we have returned full circle, from *caveat emptor* to a *caveat venditor* in which sellers are no longer subject to the discipline of the competitive market but instead to social forces and values expressed largely through governmental regulations, and through their own conceptions of social responsibility. To state things so simply and clearly is to expose the error in the view that the market is now dead. But it may well be that there is an inexorable drift away from the market as a regulator, i.e. that we are moving away from the free market *caveat emptor* to an emerging nonmarket *caveat venditor*.

Clearly, the simple required warranty "if he be tame and have ben rydden upon" is not enough for our modern industrial societies. Many, perhaps most, products and services in our complex, high level economy cannot be appraised by simple inspection or often even through ordinary use-experience. Automobiles, some university instruction, airline transportation, antibiotics, color TV, plastics, guided missile systems, electronic computers, synthetic materials, the sizes and contents of some packaged goods, inadequately explained credit terms, etc., etc., are beyond the ken of many or most users. Hence, traditional simple expressed or implied warranties have had to be extended either voluntarily or under public regulation.

But this extension has been in a legal environment, at least in the United States, that also requires independent rivalry and action. Hence, one cannot appraise business behavior in making and selling the enormously varied offerings of goods and services in our markets merely in terms of traditional ethics and mores. From this standpoint things would be much simpler if enterprises in the United States could join forces in cartels and work out group arrangements and controls as in some other parts of the world, or, if a governmental bureaucracy made the decisions for consumer-buyers, or, set strict rules for business behavior, or, if there were only one monopoly outlet for sale (as in the case of alcoholic beverages in some states). But by the same token things would be much duller, the offerings to consumer-buyers would be less varied, and most likely would include a lot more shoddy than now.

Our insistence upon our basic national economic policy of competition inevitably affects behavioral patterns and results in marketing. Since

---

[2]See e.g., A. A. Berle, *The American Economic Republic* (New York: Harcourt, Brace & World, Inc., 1963); J. K. Galbraith, *The New Industrial State* (Boston: Houghton Mifflin Co., 1967).

enterprises must go it alone, product innovation and product differentiation, and branding and trade-marking are greatly enhanced. Consequently, also, brand sales promotion and especially advertising become the key elements in an organic process of new product development and of independent rivalry. Actually, of course, this is not in itself new, but the modern technological and industrial and social environment makes a difference in degree almost one of kind. The branded products and myriad services in our markets today cannot be compared directly to the simple, staple "commodities" of yesteryear with its low standard of living. Originally, goods were branded—literally—for identification in shipment. So too, were they packaged for protection in handling and storage. They were marked too, so that the worker who produced shoddy could be traced and identified. Modern brands and trademarks, and packages, still, of course, identify and help protect users. But the primary role of the modern trademark and brand in the United States is to allow the seller in independent rivalry, to channel a large portion of the benefits of his innovations—aggressive or defensive, and of his expenditures in building and holding markets—to himself. Of course, in cartelized markets, much of this expenditure can be saved, especially the defensive expenditures to hold market positions and market shares. But this is not our way of doing things in this country. Consequently, there tends to be an enormous proliferation of products, outlets, alternatives for choice and especially of brands in our markets. Consequently, both the alternatives for consumer-buyer choices as well as the difficulties of making wise choices are enhanced.

Clearly, in this context, it is of utmost importance that consumer-buyers be given accurate and adequate information about products and services to guide choices. "If he be tame and have ben rydden upon" obviously is not enuf. Clearly, too, when health and safety are at issue and intelligent choices cannot or will not be made by users, and competitors either independently or through acceptable programs of self-regulation (as F.T.C. Trade Practice Conferences or other lawful means) cannot or do not provide adequate warranties and information, then it is necessary under public auspices to spell out at the very least, the minimum standards essential to protect users, especially ordinary householders. But such requirements in our society, should not, except in very unusual situations, be extended to the point of becoming detailed prescriptions governing the production, marketing and sale of products and services. To do so, is to turn backwards towards the types of onerous detailed regulation out of which the competitive market system evolved.

This conclusion in no sense points away from appropriate governmental regulation. Markets have never been entirely "free" or "unregulated." There is always the continuous interaction between the governmental or other external constraints, intended to "regulate" markets and the regulatory, disciplinary forces of competitive markets themselves. The market system is not a mechanical closed mechanism but an open ended system more largely biological in character than mechanistic. Hence, the basic issue for us today, as in the past, is the character of required public constraints appropriate to our needs and times. This assumes that one does not go along with those who hold that the rule of competition is over[3] or on the contrary, that we accept fully the dictum of the United States Supreme Court that "subject to narrow qualifications, it is surely the case that competition is our fundamental national economic policy, offering as it does the only alternative to the cartelization or governmental regimentation of large portions of the economy."[4] In my view, Mr. Justice Brennan erred when he stated that the qualifications on the rule of competition are only "narrow." On the contrary, the combined burden of public and private qualifications of competitive functioning are so heavy, as to lend some support to the views of those who hold that the market is dead and that antitrust enforcement of the policy of competition is a charade.[5] But it is sounder public policy to assume that free consumer choices and independent competition, among sellers, are or can be made, so acceptably effective as to be preferable to alternatives.[6]

But to accomplish this end, two basic requirements must be reconciled that can be in conflict. First, the complexities of many products, and the enormous variety of alternative brands and services require that accurate information be available to assist buyers. But second, our insistence upon independent, competitive rivalry makes it essential to allow play for the aggressive promotion and proliferation of brands, including the "puffing" of the merits of the branded goods.

Present laws and regulations, federal, state and local, on the whole are adequate for curbing outright misrepresentation and falsehood, given the will and resources for enforcement. It will be recalled that the Wheeler-Lea Amendment to the Federal Trade Commission Act gave the Commission authority to proceed against "unfair or deceptive acts" without reference to injury to competition. Over half of the enforcement funds of the Commission are used to halt deceptive practices in advertising.

The gray zone of "puffing," however, and confusion created by brand proliferation produce much more difficult and subtle problems from a

---

[3]Cf. Galbraith, *op. cit.*, p. 49.

[4]*United States* v. *Philadelphia National Bank*, 374 U.S. 321, 372 (1963).

[5]Galbraith, *op. cit.*, p. 197 and see footnote 6 below.

[6]See, e.g., the seminar discussion involving Galbraith, W. Adams, W. F. Mueller and Donald F. Turner, on "Are Planning and Regulation Replacing Competition in the New Industrial State," Select Committee on Small Business (Washington, D.C.: U.S. Government Printing Office, 1967).

regulatory standpoint than outright deception, or a *per se* violation of antitrust. The issues here are not so much those of actual misrepresentation but of confusion and good taste. In this area it is essential that public regulation tread softly and deftly because the requirement of independent pursuit of business objectives makes product differentiation, branding and brand promotion as of the essence. But in this great area, there are tremendous, additional unutilized opportunities for self-regulation without violating the *per se* rules of antitrust. It is in this area too, that social critics find abundant opportunity for their criticisms of the impacts of advertising and selling expenditures upon social and aesthetic values and judgments. An endeavor to resolve these issues by detailed oversight and regulation by government would create more serious problems than those resolved, except possibly where measurable health and safety factors are involved.

THE SUPREME COURT OF THE UNITED STATES
AND THE ECONOMIC THEORY OF COMPETITION

One of the paradoxes in public policy in the regulation of competition in the United States has been the lack of application of the economic theories of competition, especially in antitrust enforcement. As late as 1955, the Report of the Attorney General's National Committee To Study the Antitrust Laws hedged the relatively innocuous section of the Report on "Economic Indicia of Competition and Monopoly" as follows:

. . . care must be exercised to recognize that the economists' use of a particular word does not necessarily carry any legal significance. . . . We caution that the theory (as "workable" or "effective" competition) does not provide a standard of legality under any of the antitrust laws. Legal requirements are prescribed by legislatures and courts, not by economic science. . . . This section of the Report is intended as an economic not a legal analysis of competition and monopoly.[7]

In the enforcement of the antitrust laws, economists have been used only to a small degree and typically for the statistical and clerical purposes of the lawyers in charge of cases.[8] And this has been true despite the fact (as noted) that the analysis of competition has been central in economic theory for decades, and that in antitrust research, "much of the most valuable and significant work in the field is . . . done by economists," not by lawyers.[9] The reasons for this state-of-affairs involve both the nature of much of pre-Chamberlinian economic analysis and

---

[7]*Report of the Attorney General's National Committee to Study the Antitrust Laws* (1955), pp. 315, 316.

[8]At one time, even, the use of economists was forbidden in antitrust enforcement.

[9]H. L. Packer, *The State of Research In Antitrust Law*, Walter E. Meyer Research Institute of Law (1963), p. 9.

the inherent conservatism of law and lawyers, and the case-by-case manner in which issues arise and are adjudicated. The tendency in the case-by-case approach is to relate to a slowly evolving body of precedent rather than to a more general body of theory, as in economic analysis. The classifications and distinctions of the economic theories of competition have often been scorned as meaningless or inapplicable (as some are in fact).

We seem, now, however, to be entering a new era in terms of the application of economic analysis in the enforcement of our national economic policy of competition. In the words of one commentator, "Beginning in 1962, . . . the Supreme Court began to recognize explicitly, and to come to grips with the problem of oligopoly power. Antitrust has not been the same since." The same commentator notes that in the *Philadelphia Bank* decision "a rule of law is required to be more consistent with economic theory than with past precedent."[10] Thus, in a sense, Chamberlinian economic analysis, especially small group oligopoly analysis, has come out of the wings to the center of the stage. It will take many more cases and years for the full meaning to unfold. Another commentator has stated that "the discipline called 'economics' has come to antitrust. And all of the signs suggest very strongly that it is here to stay."[11]

IMPLICATIONS FOR AN EMERGING CAVEAT VENDITOR?

If economic analysis, and especially market structure economic analysis, and particularly, oligopoly or competition among the few, continues as a focal point in antitrust enforcement, the impact will be to reemphasize independent rivalry in American markets but in the context of the modern great corporation. Consequently, appraisals and public policies will continue to be in terms of both traditional ethics, mores and standards and the requirements of a pro-competition policy. There would be a relatively smaller application of standards of social performance and social responsibility in favor of tests of effects upon competition and market power, including so-called oligopoly power. In many instances, however, this will put the appraisal of business practices or arrangements in quite a different setting than that of traditional ethics or mores. For example, the ancient practice of reciprocity is viewed now not so much through the lenses of the traditional ethic of professional purchasing executives, or in terms of kinship with commercial bribery, but in terms of whether competition is substantially enhanced or weak-

---

[10]J. F. Brodley, "Oligopoly Power under the Sherman and Clayton Acts—From Economic Theory to Legal Policy," *Stanford Law Review*, Vol. 19 (January, 1967), pp. 288, 298.
[11]Editorial foreword, *Antitrust Law and Economics*, Vol. 1 (July-August, 1967), p. 3.

ened, under the wording of revised section 7 of the Clayton Act. Conglomerate acquisitions and growth by conglomerate diversification allegedly create a form of conglomerate market power or leverage which can be exercised in systematic, organized, coercive reciprocal trading relations.[12]

Many aspects of business policy and decision-making will have to be reexamined and rethought in the market structure framework, including various types of restrictive arrangements, consignment selling and price discrimination. It needs to be noted that the Supreme Court seems to have generalized the presumptions of some economic analysis and of some oligopoly models that oligopoly is "inherently undesirable," and hence it is necessary to stop the trend towards oligopoly.[13]

It is exceedingly interesting to speculate as to the fate of product differentiation and brand promotion and advertising in this setting. There is the possibility that product differentiation will be under even stronger suspicion as a barrier to entry, in accordance with some economic analysis.[14] Inevitably, advertising as the most prominent and public expression of product differentiation and promotion becomes the leading accomplice, especially because in much economic analysis competitive advertising often has been held to be wasteful. In the market structure setting, however, the charge would not be so much waste, as undue success, and hence undue market power and interference with entry and potential competition.

On the other hand, the current emphasis, if it continues, should serve to focus the search light of economic analysis, especially of welfare economics, on the total functioning of competition under diverse market structures much more realistically and in a more revealing manner than in the past. Hopefully, the result will be to sharpen and deepen the level of economic analysis in the great deficit area of oligopoly theory and of actual competitive functioning in our markets, especially with respect to product innovation and development, differentiation and brand promotion. Such an outcome in most fields should point away from highly detailed, positive prescriptions of business behavior in favor of more effective competitive market discipline. But it is likely that this outcome may very well be misinterpreted and sabotaged by some of the chief beneficiaries. Under these conditions, detailed tests of social performance, rather than tests of competitive market structure and performance may become dominant.

---

[12]See Brodley, op. cit., pp. 325–29 and J. D. Narver, Conglomerate Mergers and Market Competition (Berkeley and Los Angeles, Calif.: University of California Press, 1967), pp. 112–14.

[13]Brodley, op. cit., p. 289 and elsewhere and Brown Shoe Co. v. United States, 370 U.S. (1962).

[14]See the classic volume of Joe S. Bain, Barriers to New Competition (Cambridge, Mass.: Harvard University Press, 1956).

FINAL OBSERVATION

From my point of view what is needed is:

1. A deeper and wiser understanding on the part of both government and private enterprise as to the realistic nature of competitive functioning under modern technologies.
2. A willingness on both sides to accept and encourage market structure adjustment when necessary to maintain acceptably competitive market discipline.
3. For private industry to take full advantage of all independent and cooperative opportunities for self-regulation to assist consumer-buyers to make reasonable, efficient choices among alternatives without, however, reducing the vigor of competition.[15]
4. For legislatures and administrative tribunals to resist measures that would prescribe business practices in detail, except where health and safety in a measurable sense are involved, and private industry in competition or in cooperation is unwilling to provide for the necessary protection of consumer interests.[16]

Our insistence upon a policy of effective competition requires that we accept also in our society a certain amount of *caveat emptor* in the purchase of most goods. In most buying situations today, however, "if he be tame and rydden upon" is not enuf. But the requirements upon sellers must not be so burdensome and detailed as to destroy competitive motivation and incentives.

D. Evaluating the role of marketing

The role of marketing in our society has changed with the shift of our economy from product orientation to market orientation. But what is the standard against which the performance of marketing in the society should be measured? Reavis Cox proposes that a proper evaluation of the role of marketing must be considered in terms of the objectives of the total society.

---

[15]See e.g., Jerrold G. Van Cise, "The Hobson's Choice of Industry—Partnership with the Federal Government," 45th Annual Conference of Texas Industry, October 26, 1967.

[16]Senator Philip A. Hart has stated that, "tight economic regulation of any sector of industry is justified only if absolutely necessary," Annual Meeting of the Federal Bar Association, Washington, D.C., May 3, 1967.

5. CHANGING SOCIAL OBJECTIVES IN MARKETING*

Reavis Cox

When Professor Bartels invited me to speak here today, the subject he suggested seemed interesting and not too difficult to handle effectively. Perhaps I was misled by the familiarity of the words into believing that I really knew what they meant. Certainly I fell into the common delusion that meetings of this sort are comfortably far off in the future, so that there will be plenty of time to work through uncertainties and ambiguities before the zero hour arrives.

On both counts I was overly optimistic. What I was asked to talk about has turned out to be extremely difficult to define and formulate. There has not been time to spell out in any detail precisely what we are to mean by "marketing" in this context or by the "social objectives" with which we are to be concerned.

Under some circumstances it might be feasible and useful simply to look systematically at the problems into which one runs when he tries to decide who it is that has social responsibilities in marketing, to whom these responsibilities run, what their precise nature is, and how they have been changing. But the time allotted to me is too short for anything so ambitious, so I firmly put aside the temptation to go into these matters with any substantial degree of thoroughness. Instead I shall plunge directly and without further preamble into a consideration of several changes that have taken place since 1900 or so in our ideas as to what the social functions of marketing are and, therefore, how its social performance can be evaluated. These changes have not so much replaced old ideas with new ones as introduced new ideas to go along with the old or altered the relative emphasis placed upon established ideas.

FROM PRODUCT ORIENTATION TO MARKET ORIENTATION

Consider, for example, the social implications of something we all talk about—the shift from product orientation to market orientation. The precise extent to which those who teach or practice marketing have made this shift is uncertain. We do know, however, that there have been

---

*From an address reprinted in *Emerging Concepts in Marketing,* American Marketing Association, December, 1962, pp. 16–25.

significant changes in the points of view from which many people look at the flows that take place in marketing.

The traditional view is suggested clearly enough by the more or less official definition that says marketing is "the performance of business activities directed toward, and incident to, the flow of goods and services from producer to consumer or user."[1] The impetus for the study of marketing in its early days came from people who had goods to sell. There were the farmers, for example, who wanted to know more than they did about what happens to their products after they leave the country assembly points. Their primary objective was to increase their own share of the ultimate consumer's dollar. Then there were the sales managers and advertising managers, whose function was to move into consumption the goods produced by their employers, preferably in such a fashion as to increase both volume and profit margins. Distributors—wholesale and retail—emphasized their operations as sellers and merchandisers more than their operations as buyers, despite the claims they sometimes made to be purchasing agents for consumers and other users of goods. The basic question to be answered was, "How do we get rid of what we have to sell in satisfactory volume at a satisfactory profit?"

This way of looking at the marketing process has by no means disappeared; but there has been a significant increase in the extent to which marketing is treated as a flow *to* consumers rather than a flow *from* producers—a service of supply for users rather than a system of distribution for makers. The significance of this change for our problem of determining what marketing is supposed to accomplish and how well it does the job is self-evident. It takes us back to the old, familiar but often neglected idea that economic activity is engaged in not for its own sake but because something we call consumption happens at the end of the process. It argues that the true standard against which performance is to be measured is not the profitability of the enterprises that sell what the economy produces, but the quality, variety and quantity of satisfaction created for those who use it.

We can, of course, think of marketing as nothing more than an immensely complicated bridge whose work is done when traffic moves, without regard to what kind of traffic it is. "The function of bridges," says the *Encyclopaedia Britannica*, "may be described as the starting of a stream of human traffic hitherto impossible; the surmounting of a barrier, the linking up of two worlds divided by a gulf."[2] As to the nature and purpose of the traffic, the bridge is completely neutral. So by analogy marketing may be thought of as a system of communication

---

[1]"Report of the Definitions Committee," *Journal of Marketing*, Vol. 13 (October 1948), p. 209.

[2]Article on bridges in *Encyclopaedia Britannica*, Vol. 4 (1948), p. 125.

whose objective is to transmit goods, people and messages without regard to their nature. Performance is to be measured by looking at such factors as the number of "bits" transmitted and the suppression of "noise" that interferes with communication.

In much of our thinking about marketing and its social objectives, however, we do not see it as neutral. We are likely to put a good deal of emphasis upon what is transmitted and with what results for the consumers at the end of the bridge, not merely upon how much is transmitted and how cheaply. In other words, marketing is judged to some extent by the end effects of the complex process of which it is a part. In this context, the social objectives of marketing must be defined to include the serving of socially desirable purposes well, not merely serving well whatever traffic offers itself. It must contribute to the flow of satisfactions reaching consumers, not detract from it.

Even with this definition, the shift of emphasis from product to market orientation does not solve all the problems raised by the evaluation of marketing. Defining the social objective to be attained in terms of satisfactions provided for consumers in general does not set up a schedule of priorities as between different consumers and as between different wants of particular consumers. We are left with a conflict between what have been called the economist's welfare approach and the politician's approach through arbitration or litigation.[3] When an economist guides our judgments as to the performance of marketing he falls back on some concept such as the principle that a society should seek to achieve the greatest good for the greatest number of its members. The politician is more likely to be governed by a desire to work out a viable compromise among conflicting interests and especially among organized pressure groups. In more homely language, he is likely to think of quieting the squeaky wheel.

FROM COST IMPOSED TO VALUE ADDED

We face similar problems of definition when we come to another of the shifts of emphasis we have made of late in our analyses of marketing. This is a preference for thinking of marketing as a process of adding value to goods and services rather than as a process of imposing costs upon those who buy these goods and services. Concentration of interest upon the seller's interest in marketing almost inevitably leads to the attitude that marketing is primarily something to be paid for. At some point, of course, attention must be given to why it is bought and how much it is worth to the buyer; but at least in the beginning

[3]See the discussion of this problem in Donald J. Dewey, "Changing Standards of Economic Performance," *American Economic Review*, Vol. 50, No. 2 (May, 1960), pp. 1–12.

emphasis is likely to be put upon how much must be paid and how to bargain so as to pay as little as possible.

A number of students, and notably Professor Beckman, have argued eloquently in recent years that marketing men do a gross injustice to themselves and to their field of study when they accept without serious question the convention of measuring the performance of marketing in terms of cost. Other sectors of the economy, it is said, are measured by the value they add to goods and services. Why treat marketing differently?

The proposition has much appeal to marketing men, who often find themselves on the defensive. Perhaps we are unduly sensitive to criticism. Perhaps we overestimate the extent of the hostility to marketing and all its works we hear expressed so often. Nevertheless, we shall lose nothing and gain something if we can persuade those who publish statistics about what marketing does, to do so in the same terms they use for statistics about what, say, manufacturing does.

For our purposes here today, the importance of the shift in concepts and in terminology that goes with talking about value added rather than cost lies in the effects it has upon our ideas of what the social objectives of marketing are and how its accomplishments can be measured. If we think of cost, the standard against which to evaluate performance must be some measure of efficiency. Given an output, the best performance by marketing is the one that minimizes cost. Alternatively, given an expenditure for marketing, the best performance maximizes the amount of work done in return. Either way, what we seek is to minimize the ratio of expenditures for marketing to output delivered.

When we think of value added, the standard against which performance is best evaluated becomes productivity rather than efficiency. We think of what marketing does not as a set of undesirable though necessary activities but as the production of worthwhile values. Marketing in the end may still be judged as to whether it wastes resources by using more than it really needs to accomplish its results; but it starts with the assumption that what it does is desirable. So its students and practitioners find themselves under much less pressure to be defensive when they deal with its critics.

There remains, of course, the difficulty of defining and measuring the values marketing produces. The value system implicit in business and in much conventional economic analysis, leaves a great deal to be desired when applied to a social evaluation of marketing. This is true because it tends to encourage concentration upon marketable goods. Macroeconomics takes this point of view when it measures the national product by adding up all the purchases or, alternatively, all the sales made in the economy's markets during a given period.

This method of measuring GNP or its equivalent by-passes or ignores much that must be taken into account in evaluating the performance of the economy. Its limitations in measuring the true value of what is produced lead to pronouncements such as that of Ambassador Galbraith, who urges that strong efforts be made to enlarge the output of "public" as contrasted with "private" goods.[4] Such a shift inevitably would carry with it a reduction in the extent to which the economy depends upon markets and market procedures to direct its operations, as contrasted with governmental or other formal controls.

Whether we should regard this as also constituting a change in social objectives depends largely upon how we define "marketing." We can consider marketing to be merely one of many ways in which a society of specialists organizes the necessary exchange of goods and services. In this view it stands on the same level as reciprocity, redistribution, householding and marketless trade. These are also ways in which nations have organized this work.[5] In such a context its social responsibility is to maximize marketable values. If, on the other hand, we think of "marketing" as a generic term embracing all possible ways of handling exchange and directing the work of economic specialists, then we must correspondingly broaden our ideas as to what its social objectives are. It no longer is bound to the creation of marketable values alone.

WHO IS IT THAT HAS SOCIAL OBJECTIVES?

Thus far we have spoken of marketing as though it is an organized entity of some sort to which social responsibilities have been assigned explicitly. In fact, we assign responsibilities to many different sorts of entities. The narrower the scope of the entity for which we try to set objectives, the more likely we are to accept definitions of its immediate objectives in terms of self-interest. The broader its scope, the more likely we are to insist upon defining its objectives in social rather than personal terms.

The social problem often becomes one of seeing how individual people with their self-centered interests tied into narrowly circumscribed units can be induced to seek social objectives broader than their own immediate wants. Inculcation of moral precepts or religious principles is one way of doing this. Another may be found in reliance upon Adam Smith's doctrine of the invisible hand, which holds that in a competitive society individuals pursuing their own narrow self-interest will drive each other to produce (as a sort of by-product) an overall result that

---

[4] J. K. Galbraith, *The Affluent Society* (Boston: Houghton Mifflin Co., 1958).
[5] See Robert Bartels, *The Development of Marketing Thought* (Homewood, Ill.: Richard D. Irwin, Inc., 1962), pp. 6–9, for a brief description of these various ways of organizing an economy. The discussion by Bartels is derived basically from the writings of Karl Polanyi and his associates.

is good. Yet another way is to use political instruments so as to constrain individuals and coerce them into serving some interest other than their own selfish ones.

Professor Kreps has pointed out how the objectives of economic activity change as we broaden the entity about which we speak.[6] Although he is not concerned specifically with marketing, much of what he has to say is germane to the subject we have under consideration here. He suggests that there are at least four different levels of generalization at which we can make meaningful statements concerning the objectives to be served, for whom the objectives are significant, and the sort of individual to whom we look for leadership.

At the lowest level, we consider individual enterprises. Here we think of the dominant interest to be served as being that of the owner or, in the corporate form of organization, the stockholder. The primary objective normally will be to maximize profit, the monetary income the owners derive from the operation of the business. This primary objective may be modified or supplanted, at least in the short run, by the desire simply to grow larger or to acquire more economic power for its own sake; but the assumption often is that these are merely indirect ways of enlarging profit in the long run. The active leader in all this is the business manager.

At the level of an industry or trade, performance is measured in somewhat different terms. Here the dominant interest is likely to be that of firms organized into more or less formal associations and particularly the larger, more powerful concerns that control such groups. The primary objective now may be to expand the markets of the industry as a whole. Perhaps it will be to make a more effective use of political instruments in the interest of the whole group, as by lobbying for tariffs to shut out foreign competition or for special concessions in some tax law. Its spokesman is the industrial leader or the trade association executive.

At a still higher level, we think of the whole economy. Here is where we take the dominant interest to be served as being that of the ultimate consumer. The objectives we spell out are sometimes mutually reinforcing, sometimes contradictory. We think of such objectives as maximizing the output of consumers goods, of optimizing their assortment or their allocation among consumers. We may emphasize either current output or growth. Perhaps we want to maximize or stabilize employment or to provide economic security at some minimal level for all. The spokesman for such interests as these is likely to be the economist or some comparable observer who stands on the sidelines as an observer

---

[6]Theodore J. Kreps, "Measurement of the Social Performance of Business," *Annals of the American Academy of Political and Social Science*, Vol. 343 (September, 1962), pp. 20–31.

rather than as a participant and evaluates what is happening on the field.

Finally, we can think of the entire nation in all its aspects as the entity whose objectives we want to define. Here the dominant interest to be served is everybody. The primary objectives must be stated in very broad terms indeed—elimination of duress and fraud, protection of the weak against the strong, the preservation and enlargement of human liberties. The spokesman for these interests is likely to be the statesman or, ideally, Plato's philosopher-king.

One of the reasons why we have difficulty in spelling out what we mean by the social objectives of marketing is the fact that we can think of so many different levels of generalization at which to cast our problem. We are caught in what we may call the horseshoe dilemma. The old nursery rhyme tells us that the loss of one horseshoe nail led to the loss of a kingdom. We can say correctly that the function of the nail was simply to hold the shoe to the horse's hoof; but we also can say that its function was to preserve the horse or the rider or to contribute to the winning of the battle. In the broadest sense its function was to support the kingdom.

Much of our concern over the social objectives of marketing grows out of the fact that we are not satisfied as students and observers to confine ourselves to the problem of helping marketing serve as well as it can the narrowest interest of the most narrowly defined entity we can find to talk about—the individual worker or the particular firm. We must at some point subsume our ideas as to the functions of marketing into our ideas of what our whole society is supposed to achieve for us.

MANAGEMENT BY MATHEMATICAL REASONING

In the light of what I have thus far said, we shall find it well worth while to consider one of the consequences flowing from the tremendous development of mathematical approaches to management that have become so conspicuous in recent years. This is a tendency to narrow rather than to broaden our view of marketing and its objectives. In this development we run counter to some of the trends we have already considered.

The nature of the danger to which the use of these techniques exposes us is stated graphically by Professor Rapoport in his comment upon the limitations of science as a guide to social action:

We live in an age of belief—in the omnipotence of science. This belief is bolstered by the fact that the problems scientists are called upon to solve are for the most part selected by the scientists themselves. For example, our Deparment of Defense did not one day decide that it wanted an atomic bomb and then order the scientists to make one. On the contrary, it was Albert Einstein, a scientist, who told Franklin D. Roosevelt, a decision maker, that such a bomb was possible. Today, in greater measure than ever before, scientists sit at the decision makers' elbows and guide the formulation of problems in such a way that scientific solutions are feasible. Problems that do not promise scientific solutions generally tend to go unformulated. Hence faith in the omnipotence of science.[7]

We have reason for concern over the danger that management in marketing also may concentrate its attention upon too small a part of its responsibility by formulating its pay-off matrices, decision rules, probabilities, constraints and all the rest in terms of objectives that make the problems analyzable. Important problems may be left unresolved for no better reason than that they cannot be reduced to analysis by these particular methods. Management's problems grow out of what management has to do, not out of what it can do by applying a specific, limited set of analytical tools.

The resultant danger is not a threat solely against the broad objectives we specify for marketing taken as a part of the social structure. It may threaten what the firm needs to do for itself in its own self-interest. In many particulars competition among firms resembles a game; but it is not really a game. Formulating the problems of the business manager in terms specified by game theory may help him work out answers to his problems but it simultaneously exposes him to serious danger. As has been said of war games used to train officers in the military services, one can sometimes win a war game on points by doing things that would lose the war itself, which does not have imposed upon it the formal definitions and rules characteristic of a game.

CONCLUSION

It should now be apparent why I found the assignment so lightly undertaken one very difficult to fulfill. We are certainly very far from having a well-formulated set of social objectives for the guidance of students, practitioners and regulators of marketing. Whether we can ever have such a thing or whether we should have it, I shall not venture to state. I am willing to predict, however, that at least those of us whose lives are passed in the academic sectors of marketing will continue to try to find it.

---

[7]Anatol Rapoport, "The Use and Misuse of Game Theory," *Scientific American,* Vol. 207, No. 6 (December, 1962), p. R108.

Part II

THE PHILOSOPHICAL BASE

In addition to the proscriptions and prescriptions of the law, what guidelines or principles are there to aid the marketing man in his attempt to formulate a personal code of business behavior? How are the ethical standards which guide marketing practices derived? The readings in Part II relate to these questions.

Within our society, there is growing reluctance to accept monetary profit as the sole objective of business activity. There is corresponding reluctance to accept effectiveness and efficiency as the sole measures of marketing performance. This reflects a changing business ethos.

Business ethics in turn, reflect the value system of the society. They are in a constant state of evolution related to both economic and non-economic expectations as well as to religious teachings, philosophical norms, sanctions and legal requirements.

A. A macro approach

In the final article in Part I, Reavis Cox pointed to the need to consider society's objectives when evaluating the contributions and the short-comings of marketing. In the first article in Part II, Clarence C. Walton again discusses "the interplay of values in a pluralistic society" and dis-cusses the relationships of marketing practices to ethical criteria and societal expectations. To treat questions such as: "What priorities prevail when value systems clash?" he discusses theological norms, philosophical ethics and the business ethos.

6. ETHICAL THEORY, SOCIETAL EXPECTATIONS, AND MARKETING PRACTICES*

Clarence C. Walton

I. INTRODUCTION

Philosophers' condemnations of man's cupidities and theologians' fulmination against human frailties are as old as Plato's *Republic* and as new as Rabbi Finkelstein's now famous *Fortune* blast against the current business ethos.[1] To concede that material affluence is not moral influence, that power is not probity, or economic security the equivalent of safety is to germinate a paradox. The paradox begins to press home when we are told that television has turned the high art of polity into the low cult of personality, and that the marketplace has despoiled judgment, debased tastes, invaded individual sovereignties, and eroded moral fibre.[2] If, indeed, these are the ample symptoms of the working out of a Gresham's law of ethics, then Marx's prophesies of the eventual doom of free-market economies appear readied for fulfillment.[3]

Yet for all its alleged weaknesses, no less an authority than Reinhold Niebuhr holds firmly that the economic realm, above all else, has become the "strategic testing ground of the adequacy and relevance of a religio-moral worldview."[4] The significance of the observation is the more striking when it is realized that traditional religious attitudes reveal an anti-economic bias. "The careful, calculating, economizing way of life is neither prophetic nor poetic. It counts the costs; it asks for reward; it has no fine frenzies; it is humdrum, commonplace, even a little sordid"[5]

*From *The Social Responsibilities of Marketing*, American Marketing Association, December, 1961, pp. 7–24.

[1]Louis Finkelstein, "The Businessman's Moral Failure," *Fortune*, September, 1958, pp. 116 ff.

[2]Vance Packard's name and particularly *The Hidden Persuaders* (London: Longmans, Green, & Co., 1957) come immediately to mind. More devastating criticisms have come from Erich Fromm, *The Sane Society* (New York: Rinehart & Co., 1955), and Will Herberg, *Judaism and Modern Man* (New York: Farrar, Strauss, & Young, 1951), esp. pp. 16–23. The phenomenom is not unique to the United States. Viewing the French scene, Reverend Joseph Thomas bemoaned: "*Matérialisation des hommes, matérialisation du corps social, tel est le jugement qu'on doit porter sur notre société quand on l'étudié objectivement.*" "*Le mieux-être matériel est-il le tout de la vie d'un peuple?*" *Chefs d'Entreprise* V (Octobre, 1961), p. 15.

[3]Karl Marx, *Manifesto* (New York: New York Labor News Co., 1933), p. 15.

[4]Reinhold Niebuhr, *An Interpretation of Christian Ethics* (New York: Meridian Books, 1956), p. 165.

[5]Kenneth Boulding, "Religious Foundations of Economic Progress," *Harvard Business Review*, Vol. XXX (May-June, 1952), pp. 33–41.

—yet the economic way of life becomes the stage where the drama of Everyman is to be worked out. If Niebuhr's observation is correct then the relationship of the business order to society's total value structure —always relevant—becomes crucially important.

The modest objective of this inquiry is to explore such relationships from a general and theoretical framework.[6] Although involved with three basic notions which have been identified as *ethical criteria, societal expectations,* and *marketing practices,* respectively, it is patent that each concept has its own solar system. The following questions are most germane:—what *ought* and *ought not* to be done by the market; what should we *like* the market to do beyond the ethical imperatives; and what *is* the market actually doing. The range moves from the obligatory to preference systems to actual practices. The trilogy, while suggestive of focus, fails to penetrate the heart of the matter which is the interplay of values in a pluralistic society. Involved is the total *social system* by which is meant the observable structure and organization through which basic human needs are satisfied. These needs relate to man's religious, political, cultural, sexual and economic life, and the activities carried out according to socially acceptable norms in order to achieve certain objectives. Since norms embody values, it is evident that the social system is "held together by its internal agreement about the sacredness of certain fundamental moral standards."[7]

As thus construed, the system is geared to accomplish the social good —defined by Newman as less the pursuit of a theoretical absolute and more a choice among warring alternatives. To understand and to achieve the good impose the necessity for effective dialogue between men of different intellectual persuasions but of equal good wills. It assumes that peace and liberty, equity and security constitute the good society.[8] What are our sacred and fundamental values? How are they determined and expressed? What priorities prevail when value systems clash? How are refinements made without injury to the polity?

Three broad categories can be usefully employed to treat of such questions and they may be classified as (1) theological norms, (2) philosophical ethics, and (3) the business *ethos.* The first class involves the

---

[6]Reliance on the generalist view carries an important caveat for it means that in this short treatise certain details will be insufficiently treated—a weakness common to the macro approach. When the occasion warrants, therefore, the author assumes a risk in expressing opinions on trends for which supporting empirical data may be presently inadequate. In such cases note will be made that it is an informed opinion and not an established judgment.

[7]"In an inchoate, dimly perceived, and seldom explicit manner, the central authority of an orderly society, whether it be secular or ecclesiastical, is acknowledged to be the avenue of communication with the realm of sacred value." Edward Shils and M. Lipset and Neil Smelser (eds.), *Sociology: The Progress of a Decade* (Englewood Cliffs, N.J.: Prentice-Hall, Inc., 1961), p. 232. Michael Young, "The Meaning of the Coronation," from the collection by Seymour

[8]Terence Kenny, *The Political Thought of John Henry Newman* (London: Rutledge, 1957), pp. 77–88.

Church where matters of faith and sectarian allegiance influence and guide human behavior; the second category looks to values that can be rationally discovered by all men; and the third embraces a host of commitments and expectations which characterize an advanced industrialized society. While the classifications are less than fully satisfactory, they have merit in permitting the development of important distinctions between the supernatural and the secular orders; otherwise, there is the real danger of developing something akin to social monophysitism.[9]

II. THE BASIC TERMS: LEVELS FOR VALUES

A. *Theological Norms*—may be roughly described as standards for conduct which flow from those basic views of Diety and of man and which are often derived from Revelation; from the point of view of the communicant, such standards remain above the realm of debate. They are fixed values and hold the highest priority because they reflect God's will. Exchange of views is difficult, even when undertaken, because each religion clothes its most subtle values within an elaborate ritual[10] which has profound significance to the adherent and is often meaningless to the outsider. Perhaps Plato was right when he declared flatly in the VIIth Epistle that the really profound insights are not communicable; hence poetry, allegory and myth are always necessary. The religions of the Bible are convinced that their roles in the American Commonwealth are "vastly more than a subordinate sociological datum performing an increasingly peripheral function in society. The religions want to be a source of culture, determining its nature from a point of reference beyond it."[11] Whether the Churches are achieving such an objective is difficult to say in view of the conflicting nature of the data and the contradictory opinions held by theologians themselves. For example, Gerhard Lenski's studies of Detroit offer substantial evidence that religion colors the daily behavior of men at both the personal and social levels. Installment buying, savings, attitudes toward work, and political preferences are influenced by the socio-religious group to which one belongs.[12] Yet others, like Rabbi Finkelstein and John Courtney Murray, are far from persuaded that religion has any appreciable influ-

---

[9]An ancient Christological heresy which held that the divine and human natures of Christ fused to form a distinct third nature even as gold and silver combine to form electrum.

[10]See Lyman Bryson *et al.* (eds.), *Symbols and Values: An Initial Study* (New York: Harper & Brothers, 1954), esp. chaps. 4, 5, 7, 10 and 12.

[11]William Lee Miller, "Religion and the American Way of Life," *Religion and the Free Society* (New York: The Fund for the Republic, 1958), p. 4.

[12]*The Religious Factor* (New York: Doubleday & Co., Inc., 1961). Support of this view is given in the two new volumes edited by James Ward Smith and A. Leland Jamison, *Religion in American Life* (Princeton, N.J.: Princeton University Press, 1961).

ence on American social behavior or institutions.[13] Two factors suggest support for the former view. In the first place there is evidence that business practices are being conditioned by religion and the efforts of Quaker businessmen associated with Walter Lamb is a case in point.[14] Secondly, there are clear signs that the Churches are taking a more positive and direct position on contemporary mercantile issues.[15] There are even small signs of reciprocal interests by the business community. Perhaps it is unlikely that anything will develop to approximate the sixteenth century experience of Tomas de Mercado, a theologian at Salamanca, who was earnestly requested by the Seville merchants (then engaged in making the town the trading center for all the Spanish-American possessions) to provide them with a primer in business morality,[16] but it is worth noting that the committee on business ethics set up under the aegis of the Commerce Department does include clergymen. Looking ahead a decade, businessmen might reflect nostaligically on the easy homiletics of the *Organization Man*—and with a wish to return to the conformities which characterized the fifties.

What conclusions may be drawn so far as religious influences on the market? Clearly, Churches are reaching into the marketplace to make known religious views as they relate to a variety of business problems, including wages and working conditions, Sunday shopping and sympathy strikes, competition and advertising.[17] If this development expands,

---

[13]Finkelstein, *loc. cit.*, and John Courtney Murray, *We Hold These Truths* (New York: Sheed and Ward, 1960).

[14]T. H. Blum, "Social Audit of the Enterprise," *Harvard Business Review*, Vol. XXXVI (March-April, 1958), p. 77 and esp. the now-celebrated article by O. A. Ohmann, "Skyhooks: With Special Implications for Monday Through Friday," *loc. cit.*, Vol. XXXIII (May-June, 1955), pp. 1–9. The most recent attempt to develop empirical data has been reported in part by Rev. R. C. Baumhart, "How Ethical Are Businessmen?" *Harvard Business Review*, Vol. XXXIX (July-August, 1961), esp. p. 168.

[15]See, for example, the report on the 1959–60 steel strike from the Special Committee of the National Council of Churches of Christ in the U.S.A., *In Search of Maturity in Industrial Relations* (New York, 1961), and the sharp critique by James Kuhn, "Piety and Maturity in Labor Management Relations," *Christianity and Crisis*, Vol. XXI (March 6, 1961). This difference of opinion within the "Protestant family" has not paralleled the acerbity of the quarrel over *Mater et Magistra* between liberal Catholics (represented by the Jesuit editors of America) and the conservative Catholics of William Buckley's persuasion as reflected in *The National Review*.

[16]The primer was written in 1569 and entitled *Suma de Tratos y Contratos*. See Bernard Dempsey, *Interest and Usury* (Chicago: Loyola University Press, 1960), for a critical commentary, p. 126.

[17]Encyclicals like *Rerum Novarum* and *Mater et Magistra*, and the studies sponsored by the Federal Council of Churches are clearly concerned with matters that cannot be viewed as strictly related to dogma. See G. C. Tracy, S. J. (ed.), *Five Great Encyclicals* (New York: The Paulist Press, 1939) for the earlier papal encyclicals. The America Press of New York published in 1961 the English text of *Mater et Magistra*. The Protestant study was summarized by Marquis Childs and Douglass Cater, *Ethics in a Business Society* (New York: The New American Library, 1954).

the market faces discipline from external forces for the first time in the century—a development not to be taken lightly by either minister or marketer.[18]

B. *Philosophical Ethics*—is here employed to denote the nature of right and wrong, good and evil as clarified by analysis and discussion. It can employ with equal effect either the deductive or inductive methods but its essential characteristic—as distinguished from religious ethics—is its complete reliance on human reason working with human materials: man's nature and man's institutions. However one views the intricate technical debates between absolutists and relativists,[19] between natural-law theorists and pragmatists, or between those who lament or ignore the decline of a public philosophy,[20] one is driven inexorably to fall back to an image or "model of man" as the ultimate arbiter of such differences.[21]

Now the model of man depends largely on three assessments as these touch on (1) his capability for rational judgment, (2) his capacity for exercising free options among defined alternatives, and (3) his basic motivations. Ever since Freud the whole thrust of psychology has been into examinations of man's irrational impulses. Herbert Simon assures us that "however adaptive the behavior of organisms in learning and choice situations, the adaptiveness falls far short of the ideal of maximizing postulated in economic theory. Evidently, organisms adapt well enough to 'satisfice'; they do not, in general, 'optimize.' "[22] The evidence is however, far from conclusive[23] to suggest abandonment of a theory

[18]This is said because there are substantial differences in ethical approaches to social problems. The differences are brilliantly developed in succinct form by Norman St. John-Stevas, *Life, Death and the Law* (Bloomington: Indiana University Press, 1961), chap. 1. A longer treatment but of equal competence is by Edward Duff, *The Social Thought of the World Council of Churches* (London: Longmans, Green, 1953), esp. pp. 93–106.

[19]That all is not relative in human affairs is argued persuasively by R. L. Humphreys, "Human Nature in American Thought," *Political Science Quarterly*, Vol. XIX (June, 1954), pp. 266–71. We agree with this position.

[20]See Walter Lippmann, *Essays in the Public Philosophy* (New York: The New American Library, 1955), and David Truman, "The American System in Crisis," *Political Science Quarterly*, Vol. LXXIV (December, 1959), pp. 481–93 for contrary views. The nub of the matter in Lippmann's view is that institutions in Western society are unworkable without relevance to a natural law. "Alexander had discovered empirically what Zeno was to formulate theoretically—that a large plural society cannot be governed without recognizing that, transcending its plural interests, there is a rational order with a superior common law," p. 83.

[21]See Richard Bendix, "The Image of Man in the Social Sciences: The Basic Assumptions of Present-Day Research," *Commentary*, Vol. II (1951), pp. 187–92.

[22]Herbert Simon, *Models of Man: Social and Rational* (New York: John Wiley & Sons, Inc., 1957), p. 261.

[23]See Arnold M. Rose, "A Study of Irrational Judgments," *The Journal of Political Economy*, Vol. LXV (October, 1957), pp. 394–402. "True intransitivity (irrationality) in making choice or judgments appears to be a very rare phenomenon, if it exists at all," p. 401. See also Warren J. Bilkey, "The Vector Hypothesis of Consumer Behavior," *The Journal of Marketing*, Vol. XVI (October, 1951), pp. 137–51.

which, flowing from scholastic thought through classical economic theory, underpins representative government, personal responsibility, consumer sovereignty, and the Western legal system.[24] There is postulated therefore, as the first attribute of an ethical act, the capacity for rational decision by seller and buyer on the market; business practices which help or hinder rational choice are tinged with philosophical implications of an ethical nature.

When attention turns to the second problem, the area of individual freedom, the assessment is more difficult. Thirty years ago, John Dewey felt that "personal motives hardly count as productive causes in comparison with impersonal forces"[25] and that the range for individual initiative and action was indeed narrowing to the point of insignificance. Even with this stricture, Dewey allows more latitude than the classical market concept with its assumption of automatic governance by the impersonal forces of supply and demand.[26] There is postulated as the second characteristic of an ethical act freedom to choose. The practical issue is the measure of freedom accorded to producer and to consumer on today's markets.

The third and final problem to be touched upon relates to the purposes of human actions. Is human destiny fulfilled by service to others or to the self? The medievalists put the emphasis on the supernatural order. Man's gaze was firmly fixed on heaven even as his tired eyes and tortured back bent to search the earth's fruit. The Renaissance ruptured this ideal and, later, John Locke and Adam Smith erected a new intellectual structure designed to emancipate man from religious or governmental bondage.[27] If Locke was the forerunner of laissez-faire and Adam Smith its most eloquent spokesman, both were urging a hedonism at variance with the earlier views. Self-interest rather than service was the keyword but the real achievement was the equation of self-interest with public good. Economic justice was to be served in the new dominion not by ethical precept but by impersonal laws of supply and demand.

Yet it must be observed that in the whole school of English classical economics self-interest becomes a dominant factor *only* in economic transactions. What is often forgotten in our concern with the classic *Wealth of Nations* is that Smith earlier rejected the notion that self-

[24]See Anthony Downs, *An Economic Theory of Democracy* (New York: Harper & Brothers, 1957).

[25]John Dewey, *Individualism: Old and New* (New York: Minton, Balch & Co., 1930), pp. 35–36.

[26]See Edward Mason, "The Apologetics of Managerialism," *Journal of Business,* Vol. XXX (January, 1958), pp. 1–11, and Karl Polanyi, *The Great Transformation* (Boston: Beacon Press, 1957).

[27]See C. A. Czajkawski, *The Theory of Private Property in John Locke's Political Philosophy* (South Bend, Ind.: Notre Dame Press, 1941); and Eli Ginzberg, "The Pleasures and Pains of Economic Man," Bryson, *op. cit.,* pp. 427–32.

interest was the primary determinant of historical progress[28]—a conviction shared by Ricardo and John Stuart Mill.[29] What the classicists asserted, therefore, was that a whole range of interests and motives—such as charity or social service—transcended the marketplace but that economic justice was so uniquely promoted by market mechanisms that no outside intervention by either Church or State was necessary.

In the nineteenth century people as intellectually apart as Marx and Leo XIII challenged the beneficiences of the market. Marx denounced self-interest as the "most violent, mean, and malignant passion of the human breast."[30] And Leo XIII, in the 1891 encyclical on labor, felt equally that self-interest had run rampant. Shared in common was a rejection of Smith's invisible hand as the deft manipulator of a just society. Thus was joined the historic debate between those who placed a primacy on self-interest and those who placed emphasis on service, between those who counted the gains and others who measured the cost, between men who relied on self-adjusting market and others who would put constraints upon it. While the classical position of strict laissez-faire has been substantially modified there remains the conviction that a more-or-less freely operating market is preferable if the other extreme involves centralized control over prices, wages, and production. This leads directly to the question: can such a market promote justice? Before responding to the question there is required some rough working definition of justice itself.

Now justice, even in the most mechanistic terms, involves two elements: *equality* and *proportionality*. Equality (exchange of equivalents) has traditionally been the kind of justice to which the market could and should make a major contribution; proportionality or equity (allocating fair shares) has been variously assigned to private philanthropy and to the government. It is the contention here that the market should continue to focus on the former and that equity is not a primary purpose in the exchange function.

The argument, summarily stated, rests on the premise that the market is not exclusively an impersonal and automatic mechanism; that it not only permits but relies on human judgment and choice; and that the market judgment and choice should be properly directed to exchange justice (sic, a transactionalistic ethic) and not to problems of social justice.

---

[28]Adam Smith, *The Theory of Moral Sentiments,* Part VII, pp. 542–611.

[29]A. A. Young, "The Trend of Economics," *Quarterly Journal of Economics,* Vol. XXXIX (Spring, 1953), esp. pp. 175–81.

[30]*Capital,* Vol. I, Introduction, p. 15. For good interpretation see M. M. Bober, *Karl Marx's Interpretation of History* (Cambridge, Mass.: Harvard University Press, 1948), chap. 4. See also the encyclical *On the Condition of Labor* in G. C. Treacy, *op. cit.,* pp. 1–39.

C. *Business Ethos*—It is clear, then, that the transactionalistic ethic limits moral responsibility in the market to "the most fundamental relationship in the business world"—that which prevails solely between buyer and seller.[31] Even within this narrow spectrum, exchange justice was frequently denied its vital principle by total reliance on ruthless competition and rugged individualism. The real danger now is that in attributing a new dynamic quality of personal freedom and responsibility to the exchange function we expect too much. The full range of justices demanded by a complex, twentieth-century, industrialized economy cannot be met by the market; therefore, what might be called market ethics and what is often termed business ethics are not identical and never will be. The business ethic is primarily a problem for management as it seeks to discharge obligations to a variety of claimants such as stockholders, workers, consumers, suppliers, local communities, and to the public at large.[32]

And ethos will embrace value systems and expectations that have been reasonably well-defined and soundly approved. An affluent society may suggest as reasonable expectations fulfillment of ambition to own one's own home, to have quality and variety in clothing, to be able to join a social club or two. A technological society may face problems of chronic unemployment or depressed areas where the ethos will impose upon management responsibilities for retraining workers, or for assuring job security even at the cost of increased profits. In a word, the ethos shifts markedly with time and circumstances and is concerned, more and more, with equity.

The point can be illustrated in terms of business power. How internal disciplines are to be developed and managed provided a spacious arena for debate. Some see in the self-perpetuating oligarchies the emergence of the corporate conscience which presumably would make the new lords temporal the guardians of the larger society.[33] Some see the emergence of ethical behaviour less in terms of ennobled business motives and more in structural changes within the business order itself.[34] Some would go even further to institutionalize both corporate con-

---

[31]Frank Sharp and P. G. Fox, *Business Ethics: Studies in Fair Competition* (New York: Appleton Century Company, 1937), p. 13. Peter Drucker goes beyond this but carefully limits managerial authority to business performance. *The Practice of Management* (New York: Harper & Brothers, 1954).

[32]Manley Howe Jones, *Executive Decision Making* (Homewood, Ill.: Richard D. Irwin Co., Inc., 1957), is philosophically oriented in its treatment of social objectives for business. He is concerned with the company's ideological, political and legal environment and not simply with more narrowly conceived economic ends. See pp. 280-98.

[33]A. A. Berle, *The Twentieth Century Capitalist Revolution* (New York: Harcourt Brace, 1954).

[34]Courtney Brown, *The Businessman of the Future.* Address to Life Insurance Office Management Assoc. (Chicago, November 10, 1961).

science and corporate structure into a formally organized government pattern.[35]

Since it is patent that a whole host of values is being transformed it may be appropriate to suggest wider use of a concept called the *marginalist ethic*.[36] According to this notion, traditional criteria are challenged vigorously when a society enters a period of dynamic change. Thus, in the nineteenth century, employers who provided for workers beyond market wages soon found themselves at a competitive disadvantage with producers who did not. Soon they refused to accept such responsibilities. Such a development represented a decline in business morality from the older acceptance of trusteeship. But the change can be constructive. Accommodating values to affluence may improve traditional ethical standards by according to workers greater participation in decisions affecting the work life, or by providing relief from long hours of fatiguing toil. What is involved in marginalistic ethics, of course, is no ethical standard but a device for appraising change in the value systems of society. It seeks to relate the continuum to change: to insist on certain minimum absolute values while allowing wide scope for pragmatic assessment.

III. SOCIETAL EXPECTATIONS

At a level lower than ethical imperatives and lower than the ethos is a substratum of somewhat inchoate ambitions which can be called *societal expectations*. More specifically, these expectations are generated by knowledge that the traditional theory of scarcity has been modified by affluence, that buy-now-pay-later can be economically prudent (something absolutely alien to the Puritan mentality), that thrift is not always a virtue, that leisure may indeed be more humanly constructive than work, and that property no longer allows untrammeled personal control over its use. Like Gompers' old formula for labor unions, the American consumer wants more.

These expectations have begun to thrust upon the country some disturbing contradictions. We demand efficiency and competition but are uncertain that the traditional alliance between the two is a sound one; indeed, a determination of what constitutes monopoly and what constitutes competition is based less on economic and more on legal criteria.[37]

---

[35]Earl Latham, "The Anthropomorphic Corporation," *American Economic Review*, Vol. XLVII (May, 1957), *Proceedings*, pp. 303–31.

[36]Goetz Briefs claims to have first developed the idea in *Untergang des Abendlandes, Christentum und Socialismus* (Freiburg: Herder Publishing Company, 1920); fuller and more systematic treatment is found in Werner Schoellgen, *Grenzmoral* (Dusseldorf: Bastion Publishing Co., 1946).

[37]Irston Barnes, "Competitive Mores and Legal Tests in Merger Cases: The du Pont-General Motors Decision," *The Georgetown Law Journal*, Vol. XLVI (Sum-

The fact that a high value has been attached to competition does not mean that the concept of itself is an ethical one. While we have not gone nearly so far as Learned Hand who argues that "as a principle of universal application competition defeats itself" since it always leaves the "group worse off than it would be without it," there is a clear ambivalence in our current thinking.[38] Perhaps in basic conviction we are moving toward the Italians who, according to Professor Vito, never rated competition "highly in the general opinion and conviction."[39]

Or let us turn to the contrary pulls imposed on business by a commitment to full employment, and the expectation that the private business sector would assume primary responsibility for its implementation. To achieve full employment involves a per capita increase in Gross National Product which, in turn, can be achieved through increased government expenditures, increased net export, and increased domestic consumption. In a society already at high levels of consumption this means aggressive salesmanship to sell more and more goods if the private sector is to contribute to steady employment. And yet this takes the market perilously close to accepting the wisdom of ultra-special pressure campaignings in advertising and in public relations. It is related to the oft-stated criticism that the market is immoral because it urges man to increase his desires rather than concentrate on his needs.

There is also the expectation of improved products due to technological innovation. Some may see in this expectation a rationale for what Schumpeter called "creative destruction" and still others may feel that the response is planned obsolescence where the product's life is deliberately shortened and the consumer asked—and unethically in this view—to pay hidden costs. The advance of science has proceeded so intensively of late that property and work—the two pillars of economy—have "at length fallen" with consequence for the traditional morality. The problem, we are told, may be to "find people qualified to consume the increasing abundance of goods produced by a declining number of workers" and the "traditional morality," like the "conventional wisdom" appears inadequate for the assignment.[40] And finally, there is a growing expectation that business has financial responsibilities to schools, to

---

mer, 1958), pp. 564–632. As Barnes points out, the Supreme Court itself tried the case as a violation of the Sherman Act for eight years before turning—almost as an afterthought—to section 7 of the Clayton Act.

[38]Learned Hand, *The Spirit of Liberty* (New York: Vintage Books, 1959), p. 29. Even Alfred Marshall admitted that perfect functioning of competitive markets would not yield automatically ethically acceptable results. *Principles of Economics* (London: Macmillan Company, 1948), p. 29 of eighth edition.

[39]E. H. Chamberlin (ed.), *Monopoly, Competition and Their Regulation: Papers and Proceedings of a Conference held by the International Economic Association* (London: Macmillan Company, 1954), p. 57.

[40]Gerard Piel, *Consumers of Abundance* (New York: Center for the Study of Democratic Institutions, 1961), pp. 3, 5 and 7.

hospitals and to community projects in a manner reminiscent of those once assumed by the medieval *casa*. Here, literally, the consumer is being taxed for philanthropies he may actually disapprove of.

The foregoing catalog is more suggestive than exhaustive. Yet, it illustrates some of the basic contradictions being foisted upon the business community and helps to explain why any application of simplistic ethical formula to the market is misleading and why the new business ethos is still so amorphous.

IV. MARKETING PRACTICES

Thus far, two major conclusions may be drawn. The first holds that while the Churches are urging their views upon business with greater vigor than ever before, there is not great likelihood of early agreement among theologians on any practical moral code for business. Even if agreement were reached there is little evidence to suggest a willingness on the part of the business to abide by such norms. The second conclusion relates to the business sector itself. In the face of contradictory demands by society there is grave doubt that the business community will effectively develop a satisfactory ethos on the basis of industry codes, adjustments in federal statutes, advertising or selling practices. To say this is not to deny the possibility of a more rational or ethical ordering of marketing institutions. The question here is simply where initiative for guideposts can be secured.

Yet recent anti-trust cases, congressional hearings on the drug industry, and efforts by a distinguished committee of experts to draft a code of business ethics remind us constantly that the market is being assessed by criteria that transcend the sheer profit-and-loss calculus. So the problem essentially is to give greater logic and clarity to these criteria and it is submitted that philosophical ethics has much to offer. Indeed, as an initial basis for inquiry and assessment, one might ask if the market today is encouraging more rational decision-making and more rational consumer behavior. Is it encouraging greater freedom of choice for seller and buyer—even recognizing that gains for one of these parties may mean losses for the other? Is it promoting the growth of hedonistic culture or is the push for greater consumption justified by need to maintain, for example, high levels of employment and growth? If a judgment must be rendered it is the contention that, on the whole, the ethical dimension is being expanded by current market practices. The conclusion beggars support.

If a simple model of the economy embraces the production and sale of goods and services, and their purchase and consumption,[41] it is

---

[41]William A. Kovisto, *Principles and Problems of Modern Economics* (New York: John Wiley & Sons, Inc., 1957), p. 53.

evident that marketing is concerned with the selling and buying aspects only.[42] Yet the dynamic aspect, missing from such a definition, can be supplied by considering marketing practices as the production of customers (especially regular ones) just as manufacturing is the production of goods. Thus a product improvement designed to attract new customers is a marketing practice. So is a new store, or air conditioning, or a new product or service. Greater convenience in purchasing, and better terms of payment, communication which enhances the customer's knowledge of the product and perception of its value, also fall within this definition.

It should be noted carefully that such marketing practices seek customers who, by definition, are freely choosing agents not coerced into buying. Indeed the distinction between customer and consumer is an important one for the latter suggests recognition of the ethical element of freedom of choice.

But what of those marketing practices which are allegedly designed to blunt judgment and literally "force" a choice? Here advertising becomes the *bête noire*. The advertising fraternity defends itself on grounds that it promotes economic growth and sales while the critics argue that current advertising promotes too much sale of the wrong goods at the wrong prices. Yet both plaintiff and defense rest their cases on what may be a false assumption, namely, the power of advertising itself. This sense of power is overdrawn. A more realistic view suggests that advertising is akin to casting in a stream when the fish are biting. It does not lure fish into hitherto uninhabited waters. Industrial, retail-store, and mail-order house advertising are geared to market receptivity. Only in cosmetics, remedy goods, and so-called luxury items is advertising effective in creating demand but expenditures in this area are only a small amount of the total expenditures for advertising purposes. Viewed in this context there is not really much room for the "hidden persuaders." And since there are luxury items are they not in the area where less careful calculus of the costs is ethically permissible? And is not the responsibility here more the purchaser's than the vendor's?[43] If one adds the realities of modern life (small suburban homes located some considerable distances from the place of work) it would appear that the American male has neither room nor time for extensive luxury purchases. And even the American woman, after completing expenditures on necessary food and

---

[42]Theodore Beckman, Harold Maynard, William Davidson, *Principles of Marketing* (6th ed.; New York: The Ronald Press, 1957), p. 4. Marketing "covers all business activities necessary to effect transfers in ownership of goods and to provide for their physical distribution. It embraces the entire group of services and functions performed in the distribution of merchandise from producer to consumer, excluding only operations relating to changes in the form of goods normally regarded as processing or manufacturing operations."

[43]One of the most thoughtful studies on this aspect has recently been completed by Thomas Garrett, *Some Ethical Problems of Modern Advertising* (Rome: The Gregorian University, 1961), especially chap. 8.

clothing items for herself and children, is not likely to be an overly gullible creature.

If attention is shifted from customer to marketer we note a major development in forecasting that holds promise for greater ethical performance within the market. Forecasting techniques have improved substantially over the past decades and this means ultimately more effective predicting and satisfying of real demand, better control over inventories, and less pressure to create artificial demand or to tamper erratically with prices. From this point one could go on to assert that reasonable expectations make for a more ethical and orderly society and the farther removed marketing practices are from the "oriental bazaar" mentality the more efficaciously does the market perform.[44]

If there is emerging a healthy "plus" factor for believing that both sellers and customers are operating in an institutional framework where rational decision making is more, rather than less, likely, what of the second ethical criterion—the element of free choice? At the consumer level it would be hard to argue that such choice does not, in fact, exist in an affluent society. Of all the cruel prisons to freedom none is worse than the dungeon of poverty. In terms of range of goods, in terms of possibilities for knowing the range, the American customer is really a monarch by contrast to other times and other societies.

The most persistent charge of violation in this regard is in terms of "planned obsolescence." But there is a waste factor built into every dynamic process and some of it is deliberately contrived to achieve other goals. "Built-for-life" is not always a blessing as some of the antiquated dwellings along Riverside Drive amply demonstrate. If product change and product design are part of the culture then some measure of obsolescence is tolerable and necessary. This strikes cruelly at the folklore of thrift and frugality but it is one of the prices society is asked to pay to achieve other things. Given a choice between full employment with planned rapid turnover of products versus the older ethos of thrift and frugality at the cost of unemployment, there is little doubt what option the American people will select.

Now this does not mean a defense of marketing practices which deceive the customer but such offenses can be corrected by guarantees adjusted to the life of the product. If a customer knows that one television set will last five years and a second will last fifteen for double the price, there is no assurance whatever that it is to his best interest to buy the latter—given the state of modern technology and the fashions of modern life.

Finally, what of motivations? Are they basically moving away from

---

[44]Paul Lazarsfeld points out that the "empirical study of individual choices or decisions . . . has remained largely undeveloped." *Social Science Research on Business: Product and Potential* (New York: Columbia University Press, 1959), p. 103.

narrow self-interest toward a loftier plane? The present state of the question is so murky that the best that can be expected are a few reasoned opinions. Plausible arguments have been developed for holding that "Adam Smith's recognition of self-interest as a perennial and durable spring of human conduct is as true today as it was in his time";[45] that the marketplace responds to the ring of coin and not to moralistic preachment. Yet here again institutional changes of first magnitude are in the making. For example, marketing research is showing first signs of losing its special functional identity as it seeks to relate demand to production. If this develops then the marketing specialist becomes less concerned with his specialty and more concerned with the total process. As a generalist he will tend to relate parts to the whole—to be concerned with the totality. And one of the primary attributes of ethical behavior is precisely this kind of view and this kind of concern. Clearly, there is no necessary connection between an "overview" and more ethical behavior but in the context of business today there are sufficient grounds for holding that such a relationship will in fact prevail.

Nor is this the full story. Ours is an "organization life" and in the economic order group life is being influenced more significantly by that large association known as the corporation. By definition, the corporation is a voluntary association and so long as it remains true to its origins it can survive only as it holds the allegiances of a wide variety of clients. Unlike the seller in Adam Smith's view, the corporation looks to a life eternal and its objective tempers and restrains temptations to shortcut either morals or mores. It relies spatially on mass markets and the very impersonality of this market demands stability in pricing, quality of goods and servicing. Hit-and-run tactics are effective with the pirate's ship but impossible for the citadel, and the corporation is the citadel in the modern economy.

V. CONCLUSIONS

Lamentations over the decline of a "traditional morality" which emphasized thrift and labor not infrequently ignore another aspect of the older ethic; namely the conviction that economic practices operated exclusively under their own laws and, hence were immune to, and unaffected by, other ethical considerations. Glorified was the individual with his immediate self-interest. But the glories have been tarnished and many of the old realities dissipated. Corporations, with long-term interest in society at large, have replaced the small seller and the corporation must be, like Caesar's wife, above suspicion. Corporate leaders would agree that "the economic objective of competitive policy in a

---

[45]E. G. Nourse, *Price Making in a Democracy* (Washington, D.C.: The Brookings Institution, 1944), p. 449.

market economy is to promote good performance—good in the sense that resources are used efficiently (if not ideally), that progress through technological change is encouraged, and the economic activity contributes to, or at least does not interfere with the achievement of equally important social and political goals . . ."[46] Motivations may still be largely self-centered and hence "conscience alone, whether of public trustees or of Christian businessmen, is not enough."[47] But the institutional mechanisms are changing to provide wider latitude for personal responsibility. It is a hard skeptic indeed who, given prevailing market conditions, would not view the widening scope for personal responsibility with greater enthusiasm than the old iron law of supply and demand. Then, too, history has a long and grim verdict to pass on the ethical planes which prevailed in poverty-ridden societies. Affluence brings its problems but also its opportunities. Finally, improvements in pricing, forecasting and distribution suggest strongly a more effective and more efficient satisfying of consumer demands. The ideal moral economy of the Ralph Barton Perry vision[48] may not be realized but surely Professor Henry Oliver is correct when he perceives some major "trends toward a new moral philosophy for Business."[49]

B. Pragmatism — past and future

Business leaders often are perceived as reluctant to accept social responsibility. A contributing factor is that they have consistently opposed social legislation, even those laws which subsequently prove to be beneficial to the business community as well as the public at large. Theodore Levitt proposes that what often is being resisted is not the acceptance of social responsibility but, rather, uncertainty and change. He suggests that the actions and inactions of the business community in the area of social responsibility often are based upon pragmatic rather than ideological considerations.

---

[46]Almarin Phillips, "Policy Implications of the Theory of Interfirm Organization," *American Economic Review: Proceedings,* Vol. LI (May, 1961).

[47]William C. Frederick, "The Growing Concern over Business Responsibility," *California Management Review,* Vol. II (Summer, 1960), p. 61. See also Niebuhr, *Interpretation of Christian Ethics, op. cit.,* p. 165.

[48]Ralph B. Perry, *The Moral Economy* (New York: Charles Scribner's Sons, 1909). See also Robert Bartels, *Business Ethics: Compliance or Conviction* (Los Angeles: University of Southern California, 1961).

[49]Henry Oliver, *Business Horizons,* Vol. I (Spring, 1958), pp. 33–43.

7. WHY BUSINESS ALWAYS LOSES: A MARKETING VIEW OF GOVERNMENT RELATIONS*

Theodore Levitt

BUSINESS, THE PERENNIAL LOSER

Ever since 1887, when American business experienced its first major piece of governmental regulation in the form of the Interstate Commerce Act, business has been a persistent and predictable loser in all its major confrontations with government and with the public that has elected and supported government.

Business' perpetually losing posture over the years has had a monotonously repetitive style. Invariably business has been placed in the unedifying role of predictably and vigorously opposing legislation which the general public seems to have viewed as liberating, progressive, and necessary. Business has been the perpetual ogre—the bad guy who is against good things.

Throughout the entire history of the modern corporation in America every proposal for major meliorative and regulatory legislation that has gotten serious Congressional consideration has been predictably passed over business' predictable opposition. Business has generally blamed its failures on so-called opportunist politicians, rapacious bureaucrats, misinformed do-gooders and a duped public. The fault is always with "them," not "us." But let us consider what would be the reaction of a corporation president faced with a division manager who chronically failed to achieve his plans, and invariably explained that failure by blaming the actions of his competitors. The president would surely think that such a chronic loser must have himself to blame. He'd ultimately fire him.

Is it possible that the fault for business' chronic losses lies at least as much with business as with its "competitors"? Perhaps business has made the mistake not of fighting its competition poorly (it is too well practiced in the arts of competition) but of fighting competition when it should more frequently have joined it.

Surely it is not necessary to recount in detail the dismal record of American business' endless record of lost causes. Whether we talk about the Sherman Antitrust Act, or the Federal Reserve Act, or the Federal

---

*From *Marketing for Tomorrow . . . Today,* American Marketing Association, June, 1967, pp. 14–19.

Trade Commission Act, or the National Parks Act, or the Child Labor Act, or the Securities and Exchange Commission Act, or the Wagner Act, or the Wage and Hour Act, or the Old Age and Survivors Insurance, or the Federal Housing Administration Act, or the Marshall Plan, or Aid to Dependent Children, or the Federal Education Act, or the Poverty Program, or Medicare, business as a general rule opposed these and lost. And often it opposed them with such gruesome predictions of awful consequences to our system that one wonders how the makers of such statements can now face themselves in the mirror each morning and still believe themselves competent to make important decisions on major matters even in their own firms.

The unhappy fact is that business has not won or had its way in connection with even a simple piece of proposed regulatory or social legislation in the last three quarters of a century. The only possible exceptions are the Smoot-Hawley Act of 1924 and the Taft-Hartley Act of 1948. Significantly, these were also the only pieces of legislation during this extended period which business did not oppose. The only times it won was when it favored, not opposed, a piece of legislation. Where it opposed, it lost.

Sometimes it has taken time to lose, so that at any given time business may have confidently felt it won, such as when President Truman first proposed national health insurance in 1947. But it was a transient victory. Today we have Medicare and Medicaid, and what we have is only the beginning. We also now are about to get a systematic cleaning of our entire environment, from highway beautification, urban cleanup, air and water cleanup, and probably advertising cleanup.

I believe the thoughtful and fair-minded reader will grant that practically all of the legislation business has opposed, has turned out to be good for our society, and good for business. Business is far better off with the Sherman Act's destruction of the giant trusts—with the fact, for example, that instead of having one huge oil monopoly in the form of the old Standard Oil Company, we have now, as the result of the dissolution decree in 1911, five vigorously independent and effective progeny—SO of NJ, SO of Ind., SO of Ohio, SO of California and Mobil Corporation.

Clearly business is better off with National Parks that provide its employees with low-cost vacations where they can refresh themselves and strengthen their family ties and commitments. Clearly business is better off with the elimination of child labor, so that children may grow into healthy, educated, productive, and amply consuming adults. Clearly business is better off with legitimate and respectable labor unions that increasingly bargain like responsible institutions, help enforce work rules, and produce sensible grievance procedures than it would be if it were dealing with loose bands of anonymous, dissatisfied, and embittered workers. Clearly business is better off with the disclosure require-ments and regulatory activities of the Securities and Exchange Act than if it were back in the dark days of sharpshooting exploitation and mis-trust. Clearly business is better off with the Pure Food and Drug Act which brings all competitors under the same civilized rules rather than letting Gresham's law poison both competition and consumer. Clearly business will be better off with highway and urban beautification than with the present messy sprawl for whose existence business must accept a major blame but which no individual firm acting alone can easily do anything about without some sacrifice of funds and perhaps internal effectiveness.

WHY THE OPPOSITION?

But if all these measures on which business has repeatedly lost in its contest with legislators and the public have been so clearly in the busi-ness interest, it is curious that business has so consistently opposed them. Why has business not taken the long view of where its own interests lie —or even the short view, as in the case of trust busting?

I believe the American business executive is proud of the fact that he runs his business on facts, not sentiment. He does what needs and can be done. He constantly sheds obsolete practices, produces new organizational charts, scraps inefficient plants, moves to new cities, and generally hesitates not at all to fire old colleagues who no longer carry their own weight. Indeed, he is always looking ahead for new ideas, new opportunities, new ways of doing things. Gone is the old greeting, "How's business?" For some time it has been "What's new?" It is new-ness that he works with and welcomes.

Yet with all his calculating pragmatism, all his unsentimental zeal to junk what is old and decaying, and all his visible eagerness to find and adopt new things for his business he seems to be enormously contra-dictory when it comes to new ideas about social reform and the relations between business and government.

There are, I believe, four possible explanations for business' obvious opposition to new things in the social and "guidelines" area that have so often turned out to be so good for business. An examination of these reasons will, I believe, help clear the air and perhaps set the stage for a more positive business posture respecting some of the major issues of our times. Here are the four possible explanations:

FEAR OF HIGHER TAXES

Fear that new social programs (such as the Poverty Program) will produce new taxes to pay for what is proposed explains some opposition. To the businessman, higher taxes mean higher costs. Yet since these facilitating taxes will presumably hit all firms equally, no firm would presumably suffer a relative disadvantage. Rational behavior would therefore suggest a considerable moderation of opposition if taxes were the only reason for that opposition.

Fear of a "bigger" Washington

Here is where non-rational considerations are more visible. In the Truman days much opposition to expanding state activity was based on what may be called the "slippery road psychosis." It will be recalled that this was a time of vigorous ideological and economic competition between East and West. France and Italy were torn with communist-inspired strikes. England was nationalizing steel and inland shipping. Russia was taking over in the iron curtain countries. Understandably, communism and socialism were feared not only as institutions but as ideas. In this atmosphere of fear, threat, and dislocation, things that proved distasteful at home were often and stridently labelled as socialistic or communistic. Hence Mr. Truman's proposed Compulsory National Health Insurance program was quickly labelled as "socialized medicine." Jackson Pollock's wildly non-representational paintings became "socialistic art."

Few people seriously suggested these as being of themselves purely socialistic ventures. Rather they were viewed as the intrusive beginning of socialistic ideas and practices. Once started, it was suggested, there was no way to turn back. We would be faced with the implacable certainty of going down this *Road to Serfdom,* as Frederick von Hyack called it in his bestseller of those times. To start on this so-called socialistic road via National Health Insurance or any other activity that broadened Washington's base was viewed as starting on a slippery, one-way, descending road to inevitable socialism.

Today, this deterministic notion of how the world works is no longer as strong as it once was, but it has always been strong in one fashion or another, the most extreme form being the ringing declaration that "That government which governs least, governs best." Big government continues to be perceived as bad government. The uncertain and unpredictable consequences of power lurk firmly in our minds.

So business, which perceives itself as having most at stake, has always tended to oppose the expansion of government, even when such expansion was in business' best interests, because of the uncertainty of where this would lead. Since the advent of socialism in the Soviet Union, socialism has been promoted as the teleological consequence of an expanding government. As a consequence, the fearful uncertainty about the outcome of specific new social or control ventures was replaced by an even more fearful certainty—the certainty of socialism. Hence, this argument would say, business opposed state-sponsored goodness because goodness automatically leads to badness.

Associated interests of business

A third possible reason for business' opposition to the expansion of government might be called the "associated interest" theory. This theory says simply that when some forms of proposed government expansion are clearly threatening to the unrestricted freedom of certain businesses, all other businesses come naturally to their defense. The Food and Drug Act is a good example. When the food and drug industries were clearly threatened with regulation, the machine tool industry was easily persuaded to denounce such legislation. It felt an associated interest, or a commonalty of interest, with other businesses threatened by the government when truth in packaging is proposed and viewed as cramping the food processors, the insurance industry is easily persuaded to come to its defense. When it comes to looking at what Washington does or proposes, most businessmen, regardless of industry, view themselves as being in the same boat. Washington is "them." Everybody else is transformed into a cohesive "us."

The discomforts of change

The fourth, and I believe, most persuasive explanation for business' chronic opposition to Washington, even when the proposals are visibly necessary, sensible, and wanted by the public, is that business simply abhors change.

That may sound odd in view of the fact that change is the most palpable of all facts that business deals with. Indeed, business is a great and constant creator of change, a constant reactor to change, and, generally speaking, a master at dealing with it.

Yet it is crucial to note that the changes which business habitually deals with are a very special and limited kind of change. These are the day-to-day changes in business' accustomed "internal environment"—changes in customer and competitive behavior. These are the routine and expected changes thrown up almost automatically by the competitive world which business is organized to deal with.

It is precisely because this sort of change is such a constant condition of the business world that businessmen so constantly fear and oppose a different kind of change—man-made change emanating from Washington. Business opposes this kind of change in the *external* environment as automatically as it accepts and deals with the routine competitive changes in its *internal* environment. It opposes man-made changes in the external environment not because it is opposed or unaccustomed to change, but precisely because it is familiar with and constantly bombarded by it as a matter of routine. It already has its hands full. Hence its opposition to man-made external change is not an ideological opposition to government; it is merely the way businessmen try more effectively to manage their businesses and their time. The more the external environment can be kept from changing, the more time is available for effectively dealing with the constant changes already happening in the internal environment.

Hence, opposition to Old Age and Survivors Insurance in the 1930's, Medicare in the 1960's and trust-busting in the 1890's can be viewed not as opposition to progress, not as a failure of businessmen to see their own interests clearly, but as an example of how serious dedication to doing a specific job can greatly distort a man's values and preference outside of the strict confines of his regular job.

Viewed this way, the executive's chronic opposition to regulation, welfare programs, and causes which he has so predictably failed to stem has not necessarily been ideologically founded. He is not necessarily ideologically opposed to new and different things. Indeed, he has been anything but ideological. His posture has been, and is by this explanation, consistently pragmatic. He has merely opposed man-made changes in the external environment because they would tend to compound the difficult uncertainties and changes he must already deal with so constantly in his internal environment. In being negative he is only fighting for survival—not for his business in the sense of its being attacked by Washington, but survival of himself as a manager of his time and affairs.

In short business has been negative not because businessmen are opposed to change but precisely because they are so constantly involved in and whipsawed by change. They have been negative to proposed changes in the external environment because this is their natural reaction as administrators of high-risk organizations. They have been negative not because they have been indifferent or hostile to the needs of humanity in general, but because they simply have expressed their own specific human needs to reduce uncertainty and change in the external environment of their businesses.

Viewing their behavior as the simple normal responses of responsible men trying pragmatically to reduce environmental uncertainties and changes suggests the absence of any ideological animation in their views and actions.

IDEOLOGY OR PRAGMATISM

Whether this explanation is so depends in part on how one defines ideology. Ideology can be deliberate or merely implied. A deliberate ideology can be a consciously, though not necessarily a carefully developed philosophy. Or it can be a derived or inherited dogma, handed down from family or associates and unconsciously ingested like polluted air or the everyday standards of civility we learn on our mother's knee.

An implied ideology, on the other hand, is one in which we infer a man's ideology from his behavior and his words, rather than the man himself thinking in consciously ideological terms. It is this last posture which, I believe, describes most businessmen. They act in a manner we generally call conservative. They often make strongly conservative statements. They may even pronounce themselves as avowed conservatives. Generally this is little more than unwilling cant. They really have no theory worth the name, no viable philosophy capable of description, no encompassing commitment capable of serious scrutiny. They may declare themselves as "a political conservative and economic liberal." But ask for an explanation and you generally get incoherence or sterile platitudes. Ask for how this confession of ideological posture works in specific situations, and you generally get confused contradictions. (I might add that this is not unique of businessmen. Labor union officials and farmers stutter just as badly.)

All this comes down to a very simple fact: what so often looks to the critics and students of businessmen's posture in public affairs as a conservative ideology is nothing of the sort. It is simply a pragmatic conservative posture. The fact that it is consistent, predictable, and often rather vigorously proclaimed does not alter the fact that it is a simple and primitive pragmatism.

WHY THE FAILURE OF PRAGMATISM?

It will be said that if the measures business has always opposed have actually been in the long-term interest of business to support, then a reasonably careful pragmatist would have seen this and therefore supported what he in fact opposed. If that were so, then the only explanation of his continued opposition must be that it has indeed been ideologically motivated. He opposes things that are in his own best interests because they violate his ideological commitment.

The answer is that in a good many areas businessmen are very poor pragmatists. When it comes to regulation of business, government expansion, social welfare measures, and other matters in the external environment, they are poorly equipped to see what is happening and whether what is happening is either good or bad for them. When they step out of their own *metier* they, like most people, are generally incompetent—a fact which does not prevent them from being opinionated about affairs outside their *metier*.

Thus, even in areas remote from their normal affairs, they do not hesitate to speak, and generally to speak with unabashed self-confidence. Thus we see vigorous attacks on non-objective art, on psychoanalysis, on rioting students at Berkeley, on General De Gaulle, on African nationalists, on contra-tonal music, on civil rights marchers—in fact on anything and anybody who is making change, who challenges old and familiar ways.

It is an unhappy fact that the more successful the large corporation executive in his occupation as professional manager, the less likely that he is very well equipped to evaluate the consequences of his own business of proposed man-made changes in the external environment. Yet the higher up he is in the organization the more he is called upon to take stands and make pronouncements about the proposals.

THE STRUGGLE FOR PERSONAL SUCCESS

The reason he is so poorly equipped is that in learning for, say, 30 years to master the task for managing the internal environment he has generally cut himself off from studying and trying to understand the external affairs that he had had no time to study or understand. Indeed, he has no real inclination for such study. If he had, he would not have devoted himself so sedulously to the company's problems and hence not have risen to the top.

It is no surprise therefore that he is a poor pragmatist when it comes to the externals. He simply lacks the equipment. His struggle for success inside the company has incapacitated him for understanding the externals sufficiently for him to make good decisions about them in the interest of his own company. As a result, when it comes to proposed man-made changes of the externals he responds to his familiar internal needs to reduce change and uncertainty. Hence he opposes the external changes being proposed. So he gets tagged, as most American industry is tagged, as being a chronic opposer of what the majority believes is good for society, as being systematically and ideologically opposed to what the public has over the years clearly felt was good for society.

There is very good evidence that the long process of rising to the corporate top generally blinds a man from appreciating the benefits of man-made external changes, and makes him out as a chronic opposer of the public's wider wishes. The best evidence, perhaps, is to look at the posture of high level big business leaders who have reached the top by ways other than the usual slow and arduous 30-year, promotion-by-promotion path.

Take only the cases of particularly well-known public figures from business:

All of the Rockefeller brothers are, by most standards, politically liberal and receptive to (indeed, creators of) powerful man-made changes in the external environment. All of them run (or, in the case of Nelson Rockefeller, have run) large business enterprises, but none of them clawed his way arduously to the top. They were born there. (Interestingly, they are also great art fanciers, and Nelson Rockefeller particularly of non-objective art.)

Norton Simon, another art fancier and patron, while with a reasonable legacy, forged by himself the diversified empire he now leads. From the beginning he was a boss in business, never really a subordinate.

Charles Percy, the new Senator from Illinois, was singled out as the protege of his benefactor at Bell & Howell when he was still in college and was pulled into its presidency before he was 30. He went through no arduous, long-time or narrow conditioning to reach the top.

Henry Ford II suddenly inherited the presidency of Ford Motor Company when he was almost fresh out of Yale and his father, Edsel, died unexpectedly. Interestingly, in his early years, before the implacable requirements of running a business had enforced his life as much as they did through the ensuing years, he held much more "liberal" views than he does even today.

Arnold Maremont, the socially and politically active liberal head of Chicago's Maremont Industries, essentially inherited the business which he built.

The same is true of other so-called business liberals: Joseph Block of Inland Steel, who sided with President Kennedy on the famous steel industry price-increase controversy; Edgar Kaiser, under whose leadership Kaiser developed the famous comprehensive medical center plan for its workers and their families and who pioneered in large firms the idea of profit sharing for hourly employees; Thomas Watson, Jr., Chairman of IBM, who has so frequently departed from the usual big-business posture regarding man-made changes in the external environment; the Reynolds brothers of the Reynolds Aluminum Company; and Gardner Cowles of Cowles Communications.

All of these men are considered by their business colleagues as politically liberals. All are visibly receptive to a greater measure of government dabbling in the environment than the average big business leader. And, of course, none of these men worked his way up to the managerial top. They all inherited the top. The younger a man when he reaches the top, or when his accession to the top is not dependent on a generation of dedicated apprenticeship, the more likely that he will better see the company's interests in supporting man-made changes in the external environment. He will not have gone through a disciplining and narrowing process that tends to distort his vision and deprive him of the ability to see some important things that may be good for his company even though they involve an expansion of the government. He will be more flexible, more tolerant of diversity, more understanding of the necessity and virtue of man-made change.

THE CHARACTER OF THE INDUSTRY

The character of the industry in which an executive operates also affects his attitude toward man-made changes. While bankers are usually thought to be especially conservative politically, this is not true of certain segments of the banking business. It is no accident that the top officers of large banks with a long history of intense international business involvement are often viewed by their more insular colleagues in domestic banking and in other businesses as excessively liberal on domestic issues. Constant contact with different cultures and different institutions in foreign lands quickly makes them see that to do effective business abroad requires flexibility of viewpoints and tolerance for the way of different institutions and cultures. They are inescapably forced into accepting the variable character of the environment. They constantly see how in other lands business can live very well indeed with a great variety of governments and public controls. These experiences force upon them a more understanding and tolerant view of the legitimacy of unaccustomed externals. The resulting attitudes spill over into their ways of thinking about domestic affairs at home. Contrary to their colleagues in more insular business, they have learned to deal with and adapt to man-made changes. They are not automatically frightened into opposing changes because they have had to understand and work with external changes for years abroad. For them, these external changes are actually part of their *internal* facts of life, as easily and objectively evaluatable as the more narrowly defined internal realities of less widely exposed businessmen.

One reason American Jews and Catholics in business are, by and large, less hostile (or more hospitable) to man-made external changes is simply that the minority antecedent conditions of their lives has automatically made them more aware of the world around them. To be made consciously aware of one's environment generally means to, in some way, seek more information, and more understanding. And with information about and understanding of the environment has come a more hospitable attitude toward suggestions for its man-made improvement, without paranoid fear of automatic injury to their businesses.

It is almost impossible to exaggerate the importance of good information in assessing the factors which condition a man's attitudes toward the world around him. One of the most distressing facts about so many highly intelligent business leaders I know—men whom I respect and admire—is how poorly informed they are about matters on which they have strong views. A weekly "inside-dope" newsletter from Washington, speeches by like-minded sycophants at association meetings and luncheon clubs, and the business press are generally very inadequate for a man's continued education about the realities of our world. Yet the high-level executive makes decisions each day about the future shape and direction of his world based on information so flimsy and often so inaccurate that if the same inadequate standards were used by his subordinates in connection with such lesser decisions as the layout of a newly proposed production line or a new pension plan he would not hesitate to fire them on the spot.

All this is, of course, somewhat of a grand simplification of the dynamics of our world and of how men's minds and actions are shaped. But to simplify does not mean to miss the basic point or to fail to catch the central reasons for its existence. It means only that the point and its reasons are highlighted in order to amplify the character ". . . the character as an artist amplifies a picture by modifying . . ." by modifying perspective and intensifying or moderating colors.

I have said that business' chronic negativism is firmly rooted in the admirable fact that the businessmen are merely trying to do the best job they can and keep to a minimum the uncertainties with which they must deal. Their negativism is not ideological, it is a consequence of keeping their nose to the operating grindstone. It is only the businessmen who have had the luxury of not having to claw their way to the top or keep so close to the grindstone who have more generous views about external man-made changes.

THE DANGERS OF NEGATIVISM

But while the work-oriented causes for this negativism may be admired, it may also be feared. Since business negativism has always turned out as a lost cause, this posture suggests something threatening. It suggests a dangerously explosive and politically destructive posture. If the people who consist of the external environment and who command the majority of votes always seem to favor things that business always or predictably opposes, one of these days these people will begin actively to oppose business.

While we may understand and appreciate the cause of business' opposition to man-made changes in the external environment, this is no reason to applaud that opposition. Indeed, we don't applaud companies whose excessive preoccupation with their production and financial problems makes them insensitive to their customers. We say they have got to stop looking into the mirror and start looking out the window. We say they are product oriented because they are preoccupied with internal problems such as high fixed costs and huge investments in plants with limited flexibility. We say that unless they get market oriented and do what the market demands, they will meet the awful fate of the dodo and the dinosaur. The organism that is so preoccupied with itself that it will not adjust to the requisites of its external environment will be consumed by that environment.

Hence a management can, with admirable professional zeal, get so preoccupied with its internal problems, get so narrowly product oriented, that, in its worst form, it will render itself impotent in the market place. It will be producing excellent buggywhips for a market that no longer exists.

That, at least, is the marketing view of things. This same view says that the chronic opposition of business to proposed man-made changes in the external environment, no matter how commendably professional the reasons, is also a form of narrow product orientation that can produce for the entire business society the same sort of competitive impotence in the political market. It can be suicidal.

As business becomes more complex and demanding internally, it will provide even less time than now for its maturing top executives to develop the skills and viewpoints to know more easily and generously what the political market's needs and values really are, what is really good for the whole society. As business complexities require increasing attention to the internal environment, there is likely to be an even greater gap between the public's aspirations and the business community's appreciation of the intensity and perhaps even good sense of these aspirations. As the gap expands, so will the hostility. It is a dismal prospect.

FORCES CHANGING THE POSTURE OF BUSINESS

Can anything be done to close the gap? The fashionable answer is to suggest educational retooling of mature executives. This, I believe, will help very little. They may retool in technical internal matters. But their ideas about externals will very likely by this time be too firmly molded. What is needed is proper tooling from the beginning, and constant tooling when young men mature and grow in an organization.

But while things are dismal they are not hopeless. There are forces at work within business that suggest some hope. The increasing internationalization of business will increasingly expose more executives to the variable nature of the external world, to the necessity for understanding and accommodation, to the legitimacy and feasibility of diversity, to the broad view of the corporate self-interest. If these men are exposed to the international scene early and constantly enough, the fallout value to American business' posture at home will be inestimable.

A second meliorating force at home is the increasing use of more systematic consumer information in internal operations. This reflects the need to see the world from the consumer's viewpoint, not the producer's.

Business long ago abandoned the idea that "they can have any color as long as it's black."

But only recently has it probed consumer motivations and value systems. Today this is largely confined for use in product development and advertising. But it is likely that it will spill over into regulatory and public policy issues. (Indeed, some of this is already being done for business by Opinion Research Corporation at Princeton.) As business does more of this monitoring of the consumer and his environment, and as it does it more effectively and routinely, businessmen will be faced with implacable facts of the real world, not the filtered facts of impressionistic surveys made at their country clubs. They will face a reality which they will see cannot be fought as naïvely and wastefully as they now often fight it. They will change—as they have for example in the last few years on the civil rights issue.

Indeed, the civil rights turmoil is the third fact of our existence that makes the future encouraging. The economic pressures produced by Negro militancy, combined with the exploding Negro population, has forced business not only to open its doors to Negroes, but its minds to the social aspect of their external environment. When a large national firm's plant in Los Angeles was virtually destroyed during the Watts riots, the president told a small gathering of industry executives:

Suddenly I saw we could close our eyes to this issue no longer. I went out and saw the ghetto, not because I'd never been there, but because circumstances forced me really to look at what so often I'd only seen. It was appalling. If we don't straighten this matter out, we'll be in an awful mess. We're going to get on board of this civil rights thing—and seriously. I'll be first to admit that we've been blind to the Negro problem in our company because I've been blind. Well, that's over. We're going to do our part.

For this executive a powerful transformation has obviously begun. Never again will he be blinded by the pressing requisites of the internals. Because of Watts he will begin to see things he has never before seen. And as a consequence he will get sympathetically on board of lots more public issues than civil rights. Never again will he be "product oriented."

Finally, the fifth and perhaps most powerful force tending to change the business posture on major public issues is that the widening use of long range planning has, like the computer, forced business explicitly to state its assumptions regarding the future. This has forced, in the more sophisticated uses of long range planning, a searching inquiry about future conditions in the external environment. One national consulting firm even offers a search service in precisely this area.

Hence notions about the future will increasingly be subjected to careful scrutiny, often requiring documentation to substantiate the probabilities of certain events. This substantiation will require research and facts—and these will be chastening. No amount of personal preference will be able to assuage the reality which economic and sociological calculation will clarify and point up.

But the important consequence of long range planning will come in another fashion. Long range planning is not so much an attempt to predict the future as to deal with it. Prediction, by emphasizing the operational and strategic consequences of the uncertainty it is designed to reduce, makes the executive more willing to face that future. And if I am correct that it is his abhorrence of more uncertainty which accounts for the executive's historic opposition to proposed man-made changes in the external environment, then more systematic (if not necessarily better) prediction of the probability, direction and scope of such changes will moderate his opposition. Once this moderation sets in, I believe he is likely also to be less paranoid, more understanding, and more congenial and responsive to the broader aspirations of the voters who are also his customers.

It is then, and only then, that business will be as fully on board and in the mainstream of American aspirations as can reasonably be expected. Everybody will benefit, and business perhaps more than anybody.

C. The setting and acceptance of standards

Changes in his environment are leading the marketing man, and other businessmen, to become increasingly concerned about ethics, says J. Howard Westing. At the same time, businessmen are faced with a decay in traditional standards of ethics such as those grounded in religious teachings. Facing this decay and the inadequacy of relativism, Westing argues for the establishment of normative standards based on respect for truth, for persons, for property and for human institutions.

8. SOME THOUGHTS ON THE NATURE OF ETHICS IN MARKETING*

J. Howard Westing

Business is having trouble with its ethics today. But, then, business has always had trouble with its ethics. As far as one may care to go back into history he will find intellectuals castigating businessmen for their

---

*From *Changing Marketing Systems,* American Marketing Association, December, 1967, pp. 161–63.

bad ethics. It appears that, for the most part, the criticism went unheard, or unheeded. It is true that during much of human history businessmen lived on the very fringe of "good" society and that this semi-ostracism may well have resulted in part from the bad ethics imputed to business-men. During most of this time the businessman, while he may have de-plored his social alienation, did not seem to care enough to pay the price for social respectability.

Today, at least in the sense of caring, the situation seems to have changed. This is not to say that the businessman today is willing to pay a *high* price for moral respectability, but he is sufficiently concerned to want to know the price. The concern of the businessman is evident in a variety of ways: in the increasing flow of brochures and pamphlets published by companies on the social responsibilities of business; by the willingness to question whether business may have goals other than profit maximization; by the concern being exhibited over racial equality, slum clearance, and pollution control; and, most of all, by an amazing eagerness to discuss the subject of morality and ethics. I well recall about ten years ago organizing a seminar for executives on business ethics and being told by our business advisors that executives not only would not come, but would resent the implications implicit in a session on ethics. On that occasion we toned down the title somewhat and got an adequate, but disappointing, turnout. More recently we have held a number of undisguised seminars on ethics and have had an enthusiastic response, both in numbers and participation. I believe that anyone who has had the temerity to talk on this subject will bear me out in the statement that if one is willing to discuss this "hairy" subject he will soon have more opportunities than he cares to accept.

If it is true that there has been a notable change in the attitude of businessmen toward ethics, how does one explain it? Let me offer this hypothesis. The executive today is no more nor less concerned about ethics than was his counterpart a century ago. The man has not changed, but his environment has. In a subsistence economy, ethics get short shrift. This is not only true over time, but it is equally true geographi-cally at a point in time. I think it can be said that there is a direct relation between per capita income and the ethical standards of a country—and, incidentally, this variation in standards poses one of the knottiest ethical problems possible for a company engaged in trade with developing countries. But, to get back to the point, when one is destitute he is less likely to indulge his ethical impulses than when he is comfortable or satiated. Since, in the United States today, we are materially more comfortable than we have ever been before, our con-cerns naturally tend to turn from further satisfaction of our physical needs to the satisfaction of needs in higher categories of the need hierarchy —and ethics fall into one of those categories. If this line of reasoning is correct, I think it leads to the conclusion that, in the future, businessmen are likely to become still more concerned with ethical consideration. And, as professors of business subjects, we should be anticipating this concern or once again we may find ourselves rationalizing business practice rather than moulding it.

A tremendous amount of time and effort can be spent on the argument over whether ethics in business are worse than in such fields as law, medicine, politics, or education. Personally, I think a good case can be made for the likelihood that, at a given time, the levels of ethics in all major occupational groups of a society are very nearly the same. With no social barriers and few economic barriers to the entry into the various occupational fields it is unlikely that they would attract people with widely varying ethical standards. One could, of course, argue that the professions attract those with a high sense of humanitarianism and worldly renunciation, and such people might have higher ethical ideals. However, this position is somewhat hard to defend if one notes the level and trend of income prevailing in the professional fields and the rush to the highly specialized fields where income is likely to be maximized and the service element minimized. It seems more likely to me that any differences which exist result, not from intrinsic differences in the moral standards of individuals or groups, but from the fact that moral temptations and pressures may be greater in some fields than others. Quite obviously, if one is attempting to assess the moral stamina of two individuals, he must either measure their performance under similar conditions or make allowances for the differences in the environments where they are tested. Perhaps it is the failure to make such allowances that causes the businessman to come off badly when ethical comparisons are made between him and members of other occupational groups. If the corroding effects of the "love of money" are recognized —as they have been throughout history—it must be admitted that the businessman is subject to more frequent and more extreme ethical temptations than most other men. Thus, he may not be ethically weaker, just more sorely tried.

The above issue is an interesting one and, I believe, one that deserves more thought than it has received. However, in one sense it is irrelevant, and in another sense it might even be harmful. It would seem to me to be positively harmful if it led any substantial number of businessmen to conclude that complacency was warranted. Society today, as well as the businessman himself, is uneasy about the state of ethics in business. Under these conditions, complacency may cost the businessman a further loss of his rapidly vanishing freedom. This, of course, is a pragmatic rather than a philosophical argument. The issue of whether the ethics of the businessman are better or worse than those of others is irrelevant because it involves a measurement against the wrong standard. There will be argument on this point, but I maintain that the issue should not be whether the ethics of the businessman are *relatively* as good as those of others but whether they are *absolutely* good enough to sustain the good life in a highly complex society.

This point goes to the very heart of the issue of ethics, and unless it can be resolved, I doubt that there is much chance of any real progress of the ethics front. The absolute position identifies, and at times almost equates, ethics with religion. This has been the traditional position, and it was a viable position so long as religion held real or nominal authority over a majority of the people. It seems to me there was a time, within my memory, when most people—non-church members as well as members—acknowledged the *rightness* of a code of ethics based upon the second table of the Decalogue. Many may not have complied with the code in practice, but an admission of its rightness at least gave society a point of reference—a north star—for guidance.

Today, in his quest for scientific verification of everything, man has to a large extent discarded normative standards such as the ethical component of the Decalogue. In most areas even scientific man does not discard conventional wisdom until he has found it wrong and has discovered something better to replace it. In the field of ethics, unfortunately, modern man has been too impatient for this. Ethical principles were so clearly not based on empirical research that he discarded them without having even begun a search for anything to replace them. Someone might argue that relativism or situational ethics has replaced the more formalized code, but I would contend that as a replacement relativism is an illusion. In an economic order, in which the central motivating principle is based on selfish advancement, ethical performance can only decline unless there is some countervailing force to offset the drive to better one's self at the cost of others.

One could easily move from the position that if the traditional standards are not working and relativism will not work we are in a perilous, and perhaps hopeless, position. I suspect that not a few people may be close to this point without having bothered to take their bearings and define their position. May we not, however, be able to reason our way to an intermediate position—one that establishes ethics as a normative standard without making it a part of religion?

To do this one must make the assumption that our world is an orderly world—not only the physical environment but the social environment as well. More specifically, the assumption about the social environment of man must be that living together in society is possible over the long term only if we recognize and comply with inherent social laws which are as inviolable as the physical laws of the universe. Just as we can defy, but not break, physical laws, we can defy, but not break, social laws. This does not seem to me to be an unreasonable assumption. Could not our rising concern over ethics be an implicit recognition of the fact that our increasingly intimate social relationships demand that we regulate our associations by better ethical norms?

If one wonders why we have made so much progress in discovering the physical laws of our universe and so little in finding the ethical laws, he might note that physical cause and effect relationships are mostly short term whereas social cause and effect relationships may not come to light in less than generations or centuries. We do know that societies rise and fall but we have never done much more than speculate idly about the reasons. Admittedly, the difficulty of discovering such ethical verities will be difficult, but with man in possession of something approximating ultimate power the penalty for not discovering these hidden relationships may well be extinction. If the issue is this stark we certainly ought to get on with the job.

Let us look at the matter for a moment from the point of view of the religionists, of which group I consider myself to be a member. We have always tended to be a bit hazy and uncertain about the *other* worldly and the *this* worldly aspects of religion. When one considers that traditional religion traces its antecedents back to a time when society was ruled as a theocracy, it can be seen that the man-to-God and man-to-man relationships would not be clearly distinguished. We have tended to carry this full set of religious rules over into a society that is now sharply divided into spiritual and secular segments. The second table of the Decalogue is in substance a prescription for how man must live with man in ethical terms if communal life is to succeed. In this connection it is interesting to note that, while all major religions differ significantly in their man-to-God prescriptions, they all agree quite well in their ethical prescriptions. As a matter of fact, in this universality of ethical norms we might find a promising approach to the development of a set of secular ethical standards. If we would disregard the question of how these norms came into being, translate them into modern phraseology, and begin to check them against human history we might well have a start toward our difficult goal. Essentially, in terms of broad principles, the universal religious code of ethics demands respect for truth, respect for persons, respect for human institutions, and respect for property. These principles would seem to be sufficiently non-controversial so that they could be accepted as secular norms.

Now, how does one get from this high plain of lofty principles, to the more mundane level of operational ethics? It seems to me that one must make the transition in a series of steps.

First of all, there is the law, which is or ought to be the lowest common denominator of ethical practice. I do not by any means subscribe to the facile but faulty maxim that says, "If it's legal, it's ethical."

To say this, I think, exhibits a misunderstanding of both law and ethics. Law codifies only that part of ethics which society feels so strongly about that it is willing to support it with physical force. The common misunderstanding also frequently gets us into the dilemma of passing laws that are unenforceable because society does not feel certain enough about them to apply the force which is implicit in law. So, the man who thinks he is ethical because he is not knowingly violating civil laws is, in fact, only practicing ethics at its lowest level. Furthermore, if no one did any *better* than that, society could degenerate morally, but could never regenerate.

Probably in the field of business the next level of ethical performance is measured by company policy. Of course, not all company policy has an ethical dimension, but when it does deal with it, policy must transcend the ethical level of law. If it were lower than the law, the policy would be illegal, if it were equal to the law it would be pointless, so it must transcend the law. It might be observed that we enforce ethical principles at this level, not with physical force, but with economic force. We fire, demote, reduce pay, etc. These are powerful sanctions and this avenue represents an approach that has not been explored very far. With the present tendency of companies to assume social responsibilities there could be substantial achievements in the ethical realm that would probably benefit business as well as society.

There are ethical problems that cannot be reached through company policy and are not appropriate for law. These concern matters in which an industry's competitive environment exerts a depressing effect on ethical conduct and the competitive situation does not allow the individual companies to practice the ethics they would like. The only way we have found to deal with such issues is through industry codes of ethics and they have had a spotty, and not very inspiring, history. Part of the trouble here has been that industries have so frequently tended to confuse bad ethics with hard competition. Many groups have tried to write hard competition out of their industries through the vehicle of ethical codes and have found that it did not work for long. Then they have concluded that codes of ethics will not work. I believe, that with better understanding of what they are supposed to do, industry codes deserve another chance and stronger support. It might be noted that the force behind ethical codes is strictly a social kind of sanction. Such sanctions may not have much raw power, but in a prosperous economy with people striving to satisfy acceptance goals, the force is not inconsiderable.

Finally, we arrive at the epitome of ethics, where a man is face-to-face with an ethical issue and must decide it in a way that will satisfy his personal standards. This is the touchstone of ethics in a free society. In the end the other levels of ethics all derive their substance from the performance of each individual as he wrestles with ethical issues. If he does not have adequate standards and is not willing to pay an economic price to satisfy his standards our economic society is inevitably going to suffer from degenerating ethics.

As I see it, then, our task is two-fold: to define ethics in a way that will gain intellectual acceptance for it, and to induce its practice by the business community. The business educator is of critical importance to both.

D. Some causes of unethical behavior

In a brief statement, Thomas M. Garrett argues that incompetence, cowardice, and myopia underlie problems of business ethics as well as problems related to legality and profitability.

9. ETHICS, LEGALITY AND PROFITABILITY*

Thomas M. Garrett, S. J.

Ethics, legality, and profitability all suffer from three fundamental weaknesses: incompetence, cowardice, and myopia. In the world of business one tends to breed the other. Incompetence tempts men to hide their mistakes by trickery and dishonesty. Other men, afraid that the trickster will take away their business, follow suit. Both forget that the short-run profit will disappear when their incompetence comes to light and their dishonesty leads to a loss of business. It is necessary, then, to attack the problem of incompetence before we can improve either the ethics, the legality or the profitability of marketing.

We can illustrate this problem by looking at the case of the advertising salesman who promises too much because he does not understand the functions or limits of advertising, and the capacity of his own agency. In an effort to produce, both the salesman and the agency may be tempted to use bribery in an effort to get results and "kickbacks" in an attempt to make a profit. In the long run, the salesman will be fired, and the company, if it does not lose business will certainly lose face. The final result is that profits fall off. The force of cowardice is well illustrated by the ancient and dishonorable battle cry "cheat or starve."

During the Payola Investigations many record companies replied to the FTC charges by stating that if they did not bribe disk jockeys their

---

*From *Marketing Precision and Executive Action,* June, 1962, pp. 29–30.

competitors would get all the business. As a matter of fact, we know that the record industry fell into a pattern of competition in which trickery was substituted for value. Once this pattern was established only the bravest and biggest of men had the courage to oppose it. It is important to note that cowardice can breed this sort of impossible situation.

The shortsighted and myopic approach to business is probably most characteristic of the firm which is poorly financed and feels that it must make a quick killing or go into bankruptcy. These firms feel that "ethics are a luxury." Hypnotized by this situation and this slogan, they forget that repeat sales depend on public confidence and that temporary success may be the very thing which destroys long-range profits.

In addition to the three fundamental weaknesses I have mentioned, there is a fourth which seems to be American. I refer to the attitude which makes men believe that the evil other men do is not their concern. In its most extreme form, this attitude causes men to stand by and watch hoodlums attack an elderly person. In business the same attitude leads to a practical tolerance of even widespread dishonesty. I say "practical tolerance" because the very people who act like spectators are often the most noisy in denouncing these same evils.

As a result of this attitude, many businessmen do not organize in such a way as to make effective self-policing a reality. They allow the scoundrels to continue unimpeded. As a result, the public tars all businessmen with the same brush. The honest, like-it-or-not, must wear the same black eye as the dishonest.

I am aware of the fact that the anti-trust legislation does not always encourage effective self-policing. However, it may be that we need to rethink this question. No change in legislation, however, will do any good unless we are ready to change our basic outlook.

When all is said and done we must realize that there will always be some unethical practices in the business world. This is a result not only of the fundamental attitudes I have mentioned above, but, in many cases, of the very nature of the product being sold. Nevertheless, I believe that by encouraging certain positive attitudes we can go far towards changing the total situation. In the first place, we must convince people that real service will produce a profit. For example, in most product fields, advertising which gives useful consumer information is more effective, and therefore, more profitable than mere shouting. Such advertising is profitable precisely because it renders a real service.

In the second place, we must stress the mutual interdependence of all businessmen so that they will be ready and willing to take aggressive and effective action against those who are harming not only the public but the world of business.

E. Filling the gap between law and morals

In a report of the American Marketing Association Committee on Ethical Standards and Professional Practices, Wroe Alderson discusses the relationship of socioeconomic class, ideologies and personal ideals to "the acceptance of the general principles we call ethics." He also notes the important role of sanctions, especially ecological sanctions, in our evolving concept of what constitutes socially responsible behavior by marketing people.

10. ETHICS, IDEOLOGIES AND SANCTIONS*

Wroe Alderson

The Committee on Ethical Standards and Professional Practices of the American Marketing Association has undertaken a broad study of ethical problems arising in connection with marketing and advertising. The interests of the Association far transcend the adoption of a code of standards to govern the conduct of research and consulting organizations. The Association is concerned with the role of marketing in modern society, the prevailing ethical standards of American business, and the unique responsibility which the marketing aspect of business assumes in undertaking to modify cultural values. Marketing may be described as applied economics insofar as it is concerned with meeting established demand, but it would be much more accurate to call it applied anthropology when the impact on values in our culture is taken into account.

The Association's objective, through its Committee on Ethical Standards and Professional Practices, is nothing less than to review the foundations of ethics as they pertain to everyone engaged in marketing activities, whether salesmen, advertisers, professional marketing researchers or business leaders. This memo will lay out a broad framework for the consideration of ethics in marketing and then propose a research program and the means for carrying out this research.

RULES GOVERNING HUMAN BEHAVIOR

Our discussion should start with a recognition that rules governing human behavior are of several types and that ethics deal with only

---

*Report of the Committee on Ethical Standards and Professional Practices, American Marketing Association, December, 1964, pp. 1–20.

one form of control which a group imposes on its members. The field might be divided broadly into three parts—namely, law, manners and morals, and ethics. These categories are distinguished by different ways of generating the rules which the members of a society are expected to observe.

Under the law, rules are generated out of legislative research and debate. Under our form of government the enactment of the law generally means that the majority of citizens have concluded that this standard should be enforced on everyone. In the field of manners and morals the only penalties are those of social disapproval and the only rewards are those of gaining respect or recognition from one's fellows.

The requirements with respect to manners reflect the esthetic standards for social behavior in a particular social group or community. A group may disapprove of a member who makes himself obnoxious in any way so that it is not pleasant to be in his company. However, the purely esthetic requirements of good manners shade over into problems of morals if the obnoxious individual continues to impose himself on the group in spite of their obvious disapproval.

Problems of morals as such involve standards of right and wrong rather than purely esthetic considerations. The term "morals" is generally used as if it implied something less than what is intended when we use the term "ethics." The distinction would appear to lie in whether a definite and unvarying rule can be applied or whether the individual is faced with a more complex decision as to his conduct. There would probably be general agreement that we are still in the field of morals if a definite and specific rule exists which individuals would generally be expected to obey.

The field of ethics is concerned more particularly with cases where the individual is guided only by very general principles of action rather than specific rules. Thus, the individual may be said to face an ethical problem at the point where the rules run out or where there is a conflict between specific rules requiring the application of general principles. Many decisions involving questions of morality are made more or less automatically because the individual accepts a well established rule and there is no ambiguity about its application in the particular instance.

Most mature people in business or the professions do not lie or steal, and businessmen in particular are generally concerned about keeping their word once it is given. Thus, most people in marketing research, for example, would follow a simple set of standards most of the time and only falter when there were complications in the situation which caused some confusion as to what should be done. This distinction between morals and ethics will be observed throughout this discussion and we will generally be concerned with ethics proper rather than with questions of law or morals.

ETHICS

There has been a vast amount of discussion on the subject of ethics at various levels, from that of every-day conversation to that of professional philosophical analysis. It is one of the most difficult topics for philosophical discussion, involving such profound questions as the relation between facts and values. There will be no attempt here to engage in deep philosophical analysis but rather to provide an overview which may prove useful for considering the ethical problems which arise in marketing. With respect to philosophical discussions of ethics and the more general problems of values, a brief bibliography is appended.

The view suggested here is strongly influenced by cultural anthropology and social psychology. It might be called idealistic relativism, although some might consider this a contradiction in terms. Such a view would hold that ethical standards are relative to particular cultures, positions in society, or historical epochs but that there is convergence over time towards some set of ideal principles for determining right and wrong. It is an undeniable fact, even if we restrict our view to Western culture, that many thousands of people have died for their ethical and religious beliefs at the hands of others who held quite different beliefs. The most notorious example was the religious wars of the 17th century, but these conflicts did not mark the first time nor the last time that this has happened.

Philosophical writers who seek the basis for justifying a single set of standards argue that when two people accept conflicting ethical principles they cannot both be right. They fail to point out that both sides can be wrong as judged by some ultimate ideal principle for making ethical decisions.

Idealistic relativism would begin with a descriptive approach to the kind of ethical principles which masses of people actually entertain. We will confine ourselves to some of the principal views which are important in the United States today, ignoring almost entirely the strange contrasts which can be observed in comparing one culture with another.

The first general type of ethics is the equalitarian ethics which has deep roots in the American tradition. The Declaration of Independence asserts that all men are created equal. This implies that all men are in some sense entitled to equal treatment or to the enjoyment of equal opportunity. The writer has been a member of discussion groups in which a cross-section of businessmen found this principle of equality very difficult to swallow. The principle must have been more generally acceptable in Colonial days when many people were in direct touch with the frontier and were forced to rely on their own resources, including their own abilities to settle disputes.

After the American colonies won their independence, the French Revolution proceeded under the banner of liberty, equality and fraternity. It was a great leveling movement which reasserted the worth of the individual in radical form. It can be assumed that working class people today generally accept the equalitarian ethics and it is certain that they usually adopt forms of religious worship which tend to reinforce their equalitarian standards.

The second and perhaps dominant ethical view in the United States may be called the ethics of emulation. This point of view comes naturally to what *The Saturday Evening Post* used to call "people on the way up." It is a highly competitive viewpoint natural to people who are struggling for social position and economic independence, but it is a well regulated version of competition. It is the viewpoint of ambitious and energetic people who want to get ahead but who associate the acquisition of specialized skills with getting ahead. This, of course, is what is often called "middle-class ethics." The term "middle-class ethics" is in no sense derogatory, and surveys have shown that the great majority of American people regard themselves as members of the middle class.

The competitive spirit of this view of ethics carries over into the training of the young, with every parent anxious to secure some competitive edge for his offspring in making a career. This view toward the training of children tends to contrast sharply with that held by people lower in the social scale who tend to embrace the equalitarian ethics. The equalitarian father asserts that one man is as good as another and he would prefer that his son become a good solid workman and not become estranged from his family by engaging in the struggle to go ahead.

It was the ethics of emulation, of course, which Max Weber had in mind in his great book, *The Protestant Ethic and the Rise of Capitalism*. It is quite clear that the ethics of emulation has a special relationship to business enterprise and provides the foundation for most of the codes of business and professional ethics.

The ethics of leadership is the ethics which is characteristically associated with people who have already arrived at the top. In its most advanced form, the ethics of leadership applies to the heads of very large organizations, but it can permeate far more deeply into the general population. That is to say, nearly every adult has had some experience in making decisions on behalf of other people even though it is only his own family, his lodge, or his club or church committee.

The ethics of leadership is concerned with the relationship between power and responsibility. At its best, the ethics of leadership takes into account the aspirations of all members of an organization and in major decisions undertakes to select alternatives in the light of the benefits which can be generated for all concerned. Leaders differ, of course, as to the level of their own aspirations and the level which they are prepared to impose or try to evoke among others that belong to the organization. Such a leader of a large organization tends to identify his destiny with that of the organization he heads and to be forced inevitably to the development of creative plans rather than simple decisions as the basis for maximizing benefits for the organization. It is the ethics of leadership which Chester Barnard had in mind when he said that "one function of the leader is to project a morality which his organization can live by."

The penalty of leadership, on the other hand, is to live under a condition of ethical tension and ambiguity because of the many diverse claims made upon the leader by employees, stockholders, customers, suppliers, his community and his nation. It would be invidious to select individual business leaders for mention. Among political leaders of the past, some who represent the fullest personal identification with the welfare of their nations were Abraham Lincoln, Frederick the Great, William the Silent of the Netherlands, and King Henry Navarre of France. (It happens that three of these four were assassinated, while Frederick was a bent and weary old man at fifty. The writer does not believe that these are a representative sample in this respect.)

PROFESSIONAL ETHICS

Codes of professional ethics which might be created for various functions under the broad classification of marketing would doubtless contain elements of all three of the general ethical views which have been mentioned. Most fundamentally, perhaps, a code of ethics reflects the ethics of emulation and, in a sense, attempts to regulate competition. Codes of ethics sometimes tread on hazardous legal ground because of the attempt to enforce active competition in general under the anti-trust laws.

Codes of ethics are more likely to have legal approval if the rules concentrate on standards of quality of goods or services and do not venture into the area of price. Many individual businessmen are thinking primarily of price-cutting when they speak of unethical practices in their fields. Obviously a code of fair practice could become an instrument of monopoly if the law would permit. The so-called codes of fair practice under the National Recovery Act demonstrated the preoccupation of businessmen with prices during the period when legal immunity was granted. Even when these NRA codes did not mention minimum price schedules, they were often concerned with the way in which price should be calculated.

On the other side of the effort to regulate competition—namely, the maintenance of quality—there is a basic economic marketing concept in evidence. That is the notion that competitors should not be allowed to "spoil the market," delivering inferior goods and services and hence destroying consumer confidence in the product. Even when codes are limited to quality maintenance, however, there are anti-trust questions which may arise.

A code might be used, for example, to restrict activities such as market research to a limited group like members of the American Marketing Association. Such a code would be suspect if any form of threat or coercion was utilized to enforce the code. There is also the sound marketing principle that the notion of quality undergoes changes in the steady adaptation of the market to needs of consumers. Thus, it would be hard to enforce a rule that surveys should be based entirely on personal interviews when studies have shown that under certain circumstances mail questionnaires yield superior results.

But while professional codes of ethics might primarily reflect the ethics of emulation, there is room for other considerations. Codes should be equalitarian in the sense of recognizing the principle of equal opportunity. While it is true, for example, that experienced market research organizations should be able to provide better services, there should always be an open opportunity for new research organizations to enter the field. There are some interesting ethical problems as to the kind of "puffing" which might be tolerated in a newcomer and frowned upon in established agencies. Should the new agency promise to do only what it knows it can do with its present staff or should it be allowed to bid on jobs where it does not actually command the necessary resources but is confident that it can mobilize them? This is only one example of the ways in which a business or professional code should give consideration to the problem of entry into a field. No matter how well established an organization is today, there was always an initial effort when it was just getting started.

Similarly, the ethics of leadership is deeply involved in professional codes, and the group involved has a right to expect especially high standards of performance from its leaders. We have had some examples of the depressing effect on public morale of apparent missteps by the executives of outstanding companies.

The determination to be a leader implies that an individual has confidence that he has special qualifications to lead and these qualifications must embrace ethical sensitivity as well as technical skills. A leader often takes justifiable pride in his leadership, but he should be too proud to cheat or to compete in an underhanded way. There is probably a vestige of the aristocratic idea of noblesse oblige in most leaders in large affairs. This is an almost instinctive feeling that he who has large gifts should expect more of himself. Jesus had something to say about this in the Parable of the Talents. So far as codes of professional ethics are concerned, leaders in the field should have a broader perspective, and out of their experience should have come to approach more closely the ideal principles of ethics toward which all cultures and classes can be said to be converging.

IDEOLOGIES

Whatever personal ideas an individual may have, he may also subscribe to an ideology. An ideology might be defined as the individual's conception of the kind of a system under which he would like to live. The notion of ideology is obviously closely related to ideals and, in turn, to ethics. Reinhold Niebuhr once wrote a book called *Moral Man and Immoral Society*. Certainly the individual's attempt to apply ethical principles and his conception of the kind of society in which he is living or would like to live react strongly upon one another. Ideology, therefore, becomes an additional dimension of relativism in the significant conflicts of our times.

Specifically, there are very different ways of looking at a national economy and the role of Government as between citizens of the United States, for example, and those of the Soviet Union. Starting from these very different ideologies, Americans or Russians can appear to come to opposite conclusions about what is right or wrong. In Russia the notion of increasing the private sphere of activity would probably be regarded as a radical or revolutionary notion. In the United States it is the individual who favors the expansion of the public or government sphere who is likely to be called a Red.

Many of our forefathers were regarded as radicals when they fought to enlarge the private sphere of activity under the absolutist regimes of 17th and 18th century Europe. These views culminated in the writings of British and French economists and political pamphleteers who would be regarded as being on the conservative side today because they favored private rather than public action. Restricting our view to the contemporary scene in the United States, there are undoubtedly important differences in ideology and some of these ideologies are intimately connected with what we call market orientation or a marketing viewpoint.

A conservative ideology would be one which reflected a preference for private action over public action wherever a clear-cut choice is offered. In the United States conservative opinion would tend to limit public functions to maintaining law and order, providing for the external defense of the country and collecting taxes to pay for these functions. In general, there is an underlying distrust of Government and its expansionary tendencies.

A liberal ideology would be one which reflected a preference for public action over private action wherever a function could be performed in one way or the other. Liberal opinion tends to see a progressive need for government action in many cases previously handled by private agencies. The TVA was a good example of the liberal thrust into a new area of government operation. Liberals tend to have an underlying distrust of private enterprise and particularly of big business.

A third viewpoint might be called functionalism and this is the view with which the writer has been identified in marketing theory. A functionalist, operating at the level which has been suggested, might display a preference for having a function performed by either a public agency or a private agency, according to his judgment as to which type of agency can perform the function most effectively. In the area of decision between private and public agencies, the writer leans toward a conservative version of functionalism. This would suggest a reliance on market process insofar as possible, but coupled with an awareness of a whole series of market imperfections. Lord Keynes became famous through calling attention to a basic imperfection in the investment market. But even the most competitive markets may require institutional machinery to make them function smoothly. The wheat and cotton exchanges are good examples.

Marketing specialists, however conservative they might be in their general economic and political views, become aware of a host of imperfections in nearly every type of market. Their professional job is to remedy these imperfections insofar as this can be done through private means. In a given type of market, however, a marketing specialist may become convinced that the only possibility of remedying an imperfection of the market so that goods can move is through the enactment of the law. Furthermore, marketing specialists may become convinced that some particular product or service can best be supplied by government so that they favor public performance of a particular activity despite a general reluctance to expand the public sector.

The functionalist viewpoint might tend to favor public activity wherever individual requirements tended to be identical and where there were urgent needs which were difficult to finance through private agencies. Similarly, functionalism would tend to favor the assignment of a function to the private sector and to depend on market processes where there was a great diversity in individual requirements. In this respect one might say that the heterogeneous market provides the ultimate stronghold for the manifestation of the marketing concept and the defense of a free market economy.

Ideologies as well as personal ideals determine the acceptance of the general principles we call ethics. The writer has asserted that economics is the second most culture bound of all academic disciplines because it takes the existing type of economy as its point of departure. The most culture bound discipline of all is marketing because marketing specialists tend to place such a high value on the untrammeled operations of the market. There is all the more need for a marketing specialist to place any assertions about right and wrong in a broad human perspective.

SANCTIONS

For each type of rule governing human behavior, there is a corresponding type of sanction which may be invoked in enforcing it. Sanctions are rewards and penalties which are presumed to be effective in inducing acceptance of the rule of behavior and conformity with it.

With respect to the law, there are penalties for breaking a criminal statute or damages which may be awarded to a plaintiff in a civil suit. Over the years there has been much discussion as to whether the effectiveness of a legal deterrent increased directly with the amount of the punishment. There is room for doubt concerning this correlation, growing out of the history of law in Great Britain and other countries. At one time there was capital punishment for 200 crimes under English law but, so far as we know, with no noticeable effect on the crime rate.

What is probably most effective with respect to the majority of business and professional people is a general fear or uneasiness about breaking the law regardless of whether the penalty is light or heavy. Certainly the amount of consideration given to the anti-trust laws by businessmen would indicate that the deterrent effect is far greater than that reflected by the number of anti-trust convictions.

There are some interesting ethical issues with respect to the observance of anti-trust or economic statutes generally. In many of these areas the businessman first acts and the courts then decide whether he has violated the law. Should a businessman refuse to take action unless he is absolutely sure that his action is in accordance with the law? In many areas this would mean that he never took action at all because not even the courts will know whether the law has been violated until the case goes to litigation.

Some business executives complain that they have over-conservative legal counsel who stultify action and others say that their only salvation has been the use of legal counsel to tell them what they can do rather than what they cannot do. A recent winner of the Parlin Award said that he had joined the family business in 1917 and that anti-trust prosecution or some Federal administrative action had been going on in every year since that time.

Under the headings of Manners and Morals the sanctions supporting the rules consist largely of the approval or disapproval of relevant groups. In business this can mean members of the same industry, consumers of a company's products, or the general public which may be interested in labor policy or aspects of a company's public relations.

Sometimes social approval is expressed in a positive way through awards and distinctions. There are literally thousands of such awards bestowed annually, ranging all the way from the Nobel Prize to certificates of excellence for performance in various fields. The existence of such awards may exert considerable influence in some fields. Most awards, however, are made for a lifetime of activity while others recognize specific achievements. The award which is made to a man because of his established eminence in a field is quite different in its effect from awards given to encourage the relatively unknown person. In making an award to an established figure, an organization is often seeking to honor itself as much as the recipient of the award. This is a consideration which might be taken into account in reviewing some of the award programs which have been sponsored by the American Marketing Association or its chapters.

ORGANIZATIONAL AND ECOLOGICAL SANCTIONS

There are two kinds of sanctions which are of special importance because they bear primarily on individuals occupying leadership positions. The first of these might be called organizational sanctions. The responsibilities of leadership impose constraints on the individual, limiting his freedom of action. There are situations in which the individual in a responsible position is glad when a legal sanction is imposed because it enables him to take action which his conscience tells him is overdue. When the writer was in the consulting business the possibility of employing a Negro economist was on his conscience for some time. For one reason or another this action did not take place until the state of Pennsylvania passed a Fair Employment Practices Act. It then seemed relatively easy to take this step and to point to the new law as the sanction for this action.

There are many occasions on which considerations of organizational balance and structural soundness provide the executive with sanctions he can point to in justifying the limitations within which the organization must work. An overriding consideration in the management of an organization is securing the basis of its survival in its industry. A very severe sanction inclines the leader to try to maintain the health of the organization because internal disorders can develop with alarming rapidity if there is not a sound internal adjustment.

Finally, there is the concept of ecological sanctions which is concerned with adjustment to the external environment. Looking outward, the executive must be concerned with the habitability of the environment or habitat. The word habitability is meant to convey the concept of the capacity of the environment to support life. Thus, as he surveys the inside of the organization, the leader will be concerned with conditions that insure survival and externally he will be concerned with habitability since a decline in habitability will eventually threaten survival. Ecological sanctions in the long run set severe and fully determined limits on the outlook for habitability and hence for survival.

There are two ecological sanctions which are the most severe of all. One is the threat of atomic warfare and the other the possible consequences of the population explosion. The marketing function is very much involved with both of these ecological sanctions. On the one hand, defense marketers continue to cooperate in the accumulation of nuclear arms. On the other hand, marketers in more peaceful fields continue to make plans as if there would be an unending exponential growth in the number of individuals and families available to buy food, clothing and shelter.

Perhaps we throw up our hands and say that we are too deeply involved to do anything about either of these major threats. On the other hand, there are many occasions which tend to spoil the environment which we could do something about if we were aroused to undertake it. The willful or thoughtless destruction of forests and streams, the mining out or farming out of many areas without any thought for generating new industries to sustain stranded populations, the noxious fumes, traffic hazards and unsanitary conditions that assail the senses in our cities are among the conditions which reduce the satisfactions of living and may eventually threaten survival itself.

More and more the marketing profession will have to be concerned with the kind of goods and services we offer for sale as well as with standards of behavior in selling them. The marketing profession undertakes to change cultural values and hence cannot escape criticism and the bestowal of praise or blame for favorable or unfavorable changes in these values.

There is reason to hope that business and professional leadership is becoming steadily more conscious of ecological sanctions. Ecological sanctions can have the same impact as other sanctions on standards of human behavior. Sanctions can enter directly into the decision taken by an executive because in his own judgment it would be harmful to his organization to violate the sanction. Sanctions can also help the executive in bringing an organization around to his way of thinking when its members become aware of the nature of these sanctions. Organizational and ecological sanctions help to fill the gap between law and morals, on the one side, and ethics proper, on the other, by lending support to the dictates of conscience.

The view which has been called idealistic relativism holds with most cultural anthropologists that there are differences in the way people make up their minds about decisions concerning right and wrong which cannot be ignored. It is fruitless for the philosopher to argue that they would make up their minds in exactly the same way, intelligence, ethical sensitivity and all other things being equal, because of the unique experiences of the individual within his cultural setting.

On the other hand, the writer has been influenced by the philosopher, Edgar Singer, and the viewpoint he called instrumental idealism. An ideal is something you can approach by ever closer stages but never reach. The ultimate ideal would be for every responsible individual to apply exactly the same principles in resolving ethical dilemmas. Surely there is some empirical evidence that this trend is manifested in history. Each epoch finds that it has better technologies and greater control over nature than the last one. Each decade discovers that it must do better because it can do better.

Our version of a brighter future embraces the elements of equal opportunity, the dynamics of competition and the special sanctions which bear upon the responsible leader. But to explain the leader in ethical conduct we must make the further assumption that he hungers and thirsts after righteousness. Such a drive offers a direct parallel with what Singer calls the aims of science—namely, "the progressive reduction of error."

F. The anatomy of ethical decisions

Robert Bartels proposes a series of matrices to assist in exploring and understanding how ethical standards in business are derived in a marketing economy and how ethical decisions are made. Three of the matrices concern the influence on business ethics of humanistic social expectations, noneconomic institutions, and economic role expectations. The fourth concerns the manner in which ethical decisions are based upon moral decisions "impelled by social sanction but modified by economic exigency."

11. A MODEL FOR ETHICS IN MARKETING*

Robert Bartels

Interest expressed in business ethics has not always been identified as a concern for ethics alone. Thus, demands for standards of ethics have grown up in defense of various rights—of labor, of competitors, of the community.

Journal of Marketing, Vol. 31 (January, 1967), pp. 20–26.

Emerging social consciousness in defense of rights was indicated in legislation such as the Sherman Anti-trust Act and the Pure Food and Drug Act. Direct concern for business ethics appeared strongly during the 1920's. The business literature of that period contains many titles dealing with ethics per se, such as "Adventures on the Borderlands of Ethics," "The Ancient Greeks and the Evolution of Standards in Business," "Book of Business Standards," "The Ethics of Business," and "Christian Ideals in Industry."

Each recurrence of interest in ethics has raised the question: Have business practices become *less ethical,* or has business consciousness become *more ethically sensitive?*

Whichever it may be at this time, several aspects of the present interest are symptomatic of our times. First, tests of ethics are applied to problems of our day: to price-fixing and to price-cutting, to deceptive labeling and to advertising, to coercive trade practices, and to conflicts of interest in a pluralistic society. Second, concern is shown for ethics in both operational and administrative marketing problems. Third, responsibility for ethics in marketing is attributed increasingly to individuals on the higher management levels.

A review of what is currently said about business or marketing ethics reveals it to have several distinguishing characteristics.

Emphasis has been given to subjective factors, action, and the performer's viewpoint, more than to objective factors, interaction, and the relationships between individuals. In other words, emphasis has been given to lists of actions regarded as ethical or unethical, rather than to the determinants which place an action on the list.

Specific rather than general concepts of ethics usually have been expressed. The ethics of management-customer relations has not been integrated with the ethics of management-employee relations. The standards of one company have not been conceptually integrated with those of other companies, except perhaps through agreements.

The absolute rather than the relative character of ethics has been emphasized. Once determined, the universality of ethical standards has been assumed. Exceptions have been dealt with as deviations from a general principle, rather than as the conflict of actions stemming from two perhaps valid principles.

Conflicts of this sort have increased as the growing volume of international business has multiplied the frequency of cross-cultural marketing situations.

Inasmuch, therefore, as marketing ethics is part of general ethics in business, there is merit in an attempt to construct a model for ethics in marketing. A model in this sense is a logical framework in terms of which two basic questions might be asked and answered: *How are ethical standards set? How are ethical decisions made?*

ELEMENTS OF A MODEL

A model represents an attempt to explain the nature and behavior of some phenomenon, to show causes and effects in related variables. If a sufficiently credible theory of behavior can be built, it may serve as a basis for behavior in specific situations. Preliminary to model-building, however, some basic premises must be laid down. The following assumptions, therefore, are made:

1. It is assumed that "ethics" means a standard by which *business action may be judged "right" or "wrong."*

Where judgment is involved, there is always a standard. However, standards differ, and so actions regarded "right" by one standard may be in conflict with and judged unethical from the standpoint of another standard. Then an understanding of the standard in terms of which action is made may be more useful than a mere appraisal of the action itself.

The ethics of another society, or of our own society at an earlier time, may differ from what we regard to be "right" today. If so, inasmuch as we cannot always change other people but must deal with them as they are, we can at least *understand* the reasons for their actions and view ethical conflict objectively, in terms of its bases.

2. It is assumed that ethics is a standard for judging the rightness not of action per se, but of *action of one person relative to another.*

Ethics is a basis for judgment in personal interaction. It pertains to the fulfilment or violation of *expectations.* Simply to make an untrue statement about a product is in itself not unethical, nor to make a shoddy product—that may be bad management, but it is not necessarily unethical.

Neither is it unethical to make the false statement to a person who does not expect to be told the truth—that may be the level of trade practice.

However, if a customer *expects* to receive truthful information and a product of specified quality, and if he does not, and if his expectation is a general expectation sanctioned by society, failure of the other party to fulfill these expectations is an unethical act. Furthermore, if a particular customer expects little or does not know what he is entitled to expect, and if society makes this determination for him, such a failure is also unethical. Ethics is a concern for *people,* not just for acts or things.

3. It is assumed that *business is primarily a social process,* within which it is an economic process, and that, within the latter, marketing is a specialized process involving role relationships and interactions.

Marketing is something that people do *as people,* not merely as buyers and sellers, nor even just as economic men. Marketing is a process engaging whole men, social entities, who have commitments both within and without the marketing process, and whose marketing behavior reflects their total institutional involvement.

To grasp the full import of the social standard of ethics in marketing, one must recognize the orientation of marketing in society. Marketing is a function of the economy, which is but one of seven identified major social institutions: the family, the church, the school, the economy, the government, the military, and leisure. Each fulfills certain needs of mankind, the economy providing for the material or consumption needs of people, acquiring and creating products, distributing them, and regulating consumption processes.

As a social institution consists of relationships among participants in roles essential to the performance of the needed function, each institution has myriad sets of expectations and obligations among these participants. Thus, in each institution are evolved *ethics* peculiar to the relationships and activities involved. In turn, the norms of behavior in each or all institutions are the product of the general cultural characteristics of the society, which differ among societies, producing dissimilar standards, codes, and patterns of behavior among men in their role relationships.

As marketing is part of the economic process, participants in this process occupy distinct role positions; and their interactions constitute the personal aspect of marketing—the part of marketing in which ethical considerations arise. Ten role positions are identifiable—four may be thought of as inside the technical organization of the business enterprise; four are outside private participants; and two are outside public sectors of the marketing economy:

1. Managers	6. Intermediate
2. Employees	customers
3. Owners	7. Resources
4. Other	8. Competitors
financiers	9. Government
5. Consumers	10. Community

4. It is assumed that the *expectations* of the participants in the respective marketing roles are known.

The fact is that many of the marketing role expectations are known, but that they are subject to change as society evolves. Actually, the number of roles engaged in the marketing process has increased over the years, and their expectations have become more clearly articulated.

In this connection, consider the monolithic and quite autonomous character of the business enterprise from the time of the Industrial Revolution throughout most of the 19th century. The owner-manager was typically one individual, representing a single interest. Management-government relationships were minimized by the philosophy of laissez-faire; management-consumer relationships, by the philosophy of caveat emptor; management-employee relationships, by the dominance of entrepreneurial interests; and management-competitor relationships, by the philosophy of rugged individualism.

Gradually, throughout the 19th century and thereafter, the expectations of economic participants other than managers became more clearly formulated and sanctioned by society in general. Employees were among the first to achieve recognition of their demands for reasonable working hours, humane treatment, and safe working conditions. These demands were voiced through the countervailing institution of the labor union.

Expectations of competitors gave rise to trade regulation; and when competitors themselves were not sufficiently vocal, the government, on behalf of the society's general interest in the economy, represented the interests of competitors. The Sherman Act and the Federal Trade Commission Act and their amendments followed.

Expectations of the public in the role of consumers were expressed, feebly at first in enactments prohibiting sale of harmful and adulterated products, later in the "Consumer Movement," and more recently in the entrepreneurial philosophy known as The Marketing Concept.

5. It is assumed that *ethics is a matter of social sanction,* not of mere technical appraisal.

Not every expectation has the social sanction which makes it a matter of ethical significance. Many expectations are purely technical, expressing the expectation of technical competence, conformity to job requirements, etc.

If a sales manager sets a high quota for a salesman, that expectation may have no ethical implications. Whether the salesman fails or succeeds in meeting the quota may be of no ethical importance. However, if the sales manager puts such pressure on the salesman to meet a quota that the salesman must resort to reprehensible practices to accomplish this, or must neglect personal obligations and health, then ethical implications of the sales manager's expectations appear.

Likewise, to be expected to make a profit, even a large profit, for owners is not an ethical expectation; but if it is at the expense of other managerial obligations, the ethical considerations are involved.

The following concepts have now been incorporated into the model:

1. *Ethics as a standard of rightness in behavior.*
2. *Social interaction as the realm in which ethical judgment is made.*
3. *Noneconomic and economic institution influences upon personal behavior through role participation.*
4. *Role expectations constituting ethical obligations through social sanction.*
5. *Social sanction, rather than technical requirement, as the basis of ethical judgment.*

MODEL MATRICES

The model by which the above elements are related, as a means of explaining how ethical standards are determined and how decisions are made in compliance with ethical standards, consists of a series of matrices relating sets of variables.

Three pertain to the influence upon ethical standards of cultural values, noneconomic role expectations, and expectations of roles involved in the economic processes. A fourth matrix provides an explanation of the manner in which decisions are made in compliance with ethical standards.

CULTURE INFLUENCES

Matrix #1 in Table 1 illustrates the influence of the cultural characteristics of society upon all of its major institutions. In it are related, along the horizontal axis, the distinguishing culture characteristics of a society and, along the vertical axis, the major institutions of the society.

TABLE 1
Matrix #1
CULTURE CHARACTERISTIC CLASSIFIED BY SOCIAL INSTITUTIONS

Social Institutions	Culture Characteristics					
	A	B	C	D	E	F
1. Family						
2. Church						
3. School						
4. Economy						
5. Government						
6. Military						
7. Leisure						

This suggests the influence of such basic cultural factors as law, respect for individuality, nature of power and authority, rights of property, concept of deity, relation of the individual to the state, national identity and loyalty, values, customs, and mores, state of the arts, etc., upon each of the institutions.

Thus are found in the characteristics of our own society sanctions for the following ethical expectations, among others: that personal integrity should not be destroyed or compromised; that checks and balances are essential to general welfare in a pluralistic society; that the state is subordinate to persons; that preservation of competition is laudable; that freedom of initiative is essential; and that economic entrepreneurship is rewarded by profit.

From these generalizations, marketing actions may be judged unethical on the basis of fundamental humanistic social expectations. Competitors derive from this logic their expectations of fair play in competition. Consumers derive their expectations of honest representation. Employees derive their expectations of humane treatment.

Contrasting cultures of different societies produce different expectations and become expressed in the dissimilar ethical standards of those societies.

NONECONOMIC FACTORS

A second aspect of the model is shown in Matrix #2 in Table 2, where the noneconomic influences upon economic behavior are suggested.

TABLE 2

Matrix #2

NONECONOMIC INFLUENCE UPON ECONOMIC BEHAVIOR

Economic Roles of Participants	*Noneconomic Social Institutions*					
	Family	*Church*	*School*	*Government*	*Military*	*Leisure*
1. Manager						
2. Employees						
3. Owners						
4. Other financiers						
5. Consumers						
6. Intermediate customers						
7. Resources						
8. Competitors						
9. Government						
10. Community						

The influence of culture characteristics upon business ethics is felt through their effects upon behavior in both the economic and noneconomic activities. General concepts of rightness imbue an individual with ethical standards which, if consistent, he applies in all of his role relationships. Attitudes nurtured in family relationships influence behavior in business relationships, as between manager and employee. Religious concepts of brotherhood, individualism, and the dignity of man influence management relations with customers, competitors, and resources.

Matrix #2 represents the possibility that standards developed in each of the six noneconomic institutional relationships determine ethical stan-

dards for behavior in each of the ten economic roles and influence behavior among these economic role participants. In this matrix, six noneconomic institutions are shown along the horizontal axis and ten roles
of economic participation along the vertical axis. At each of the 60 resulting coordinate points is suggested the influence upon economic behavior of that participant's activities and relationships outside the economy.

For example, family organization and solidarity in some cultures result
in exclusion or discrimination against nonrelatives employed in business.
In church-dominated societies, numerous prescriptions are set forth for
consumption. Under socialistic governments, competitive interaction is
highly restricted. Thus may be observed some of the influences upon
managerial decisions that lie outside the realm of purely economic motivation. In other words, in matters of business ethics men do not act entirely as "economic men" but as social beings.

ROLE EXPECTATIONS

In the two matrices previously shown, the influence of general cultural
factors and of noneconomic expectation is shown. In addition to that,
ethical standards are created by the expectations which arise *within* the
behavior patterns of the economy itself—among the ten types of economic
participants.

This is suggested in Matrix #3 in Table 3, in which are related along
both horizontal and vertical axes ten economic role positions. Sets of

TABLE 3

Matrix #3

SETS OF ECONOMIC RELATIONSHIPS THROUGH WHICH EXPECTATIONS AFFECT BEHAVIOR

Economic Participants	Economic Participants									
	1	2	3	4	5	6	7	8	9	10
1										
2										
3										
4										
5										
6										
7										
8										
9										
10										

interactions are suggested by the 90 possible inter-role relationships. Thus, in the marketing process areas of ethical judgment arise in the relations of managers to consumers (often identified as seller-buyer relations); of managers to intermediate customers (identified as channel relations); and of managers to competitors and to others indicated.

In trade relations arise expectations quite apart from those induced by other social institutions and by cultural factors, and which also have direct bearing upon the formation of ethical standards.

For example, consider the question of whether a vendor, by failing to "stand behind" the quality of his products, is guilty of an unethical act. Cultural expectations of integrity, disclosure, and honesty are involved. Moreover, circumstances of a mass-market economy produce expectations that individual events be governed by policy, that personal relations be handled impersonally, and that incidental risks be assumed by the party who stands to lose least.

In addition to this, particularly in a buyers' market, vendors publicize their willingness to guarantee performance, to make refunds, and to assure satisfaction. Although these are obligations assumed by consent, they are so general in some trades that buyers may take them for granted. Thus, by experience, announced policy, and application of general social expectations, one may infer a sufficiently clear standard of behavior to assume that the ethics of responsibility in trade relations is definite.

Because of the diversity of trade policies and practices, the certainty of such an ethical standard is not so assured as the illustration suggests, or as one might hope.

Nevertheless, among the marketing participants there are highly specialized expectations that evolve, which have the character of ethical standards: expectations of the integrity and protection of distributive channels, of protection of customers against detrimental product and price changes, and of freedom to innovate and to compete.

However, there are debatable areas of interests and interactions where ethical behavior is less defined, and where courts and other authorities may have to interpret more fundamental values of the society relating to the economic process. Such areas today are found in resale price maintenance, tax exemption of cooperative enterprises, time-price differentials in consumer sales-financing, and practices that have evoked controversy over truth-in-lending and truth-in-packaging.

IN SUMMARY

An attempt has been made to identify and to illustrate the manner in which ethical standards are formulated in a marketing economy. They derive from both general and technical expectations sanctioned by society, either in general or the society of small groups. With an understanding of economic and noneconomic influences upon decision and behavior, it is presumed that "rightness" in interpersonal action may be determined.

Knowledge of the problems of ethics, however, does not provide the solution to ethical problems. This poses a second requirement of a model for ethics, namely, a guide to action, presuming that the standards of action are known.

COMPLEXITY OF ETHICAL DECISIONS

Assuming that standards of ethics are determinable, managers faced with problems requiring ethical decisions and actions have no simple, single course of action.

First, not everyone is aware of or subscribes to a universal code of ethics. Therefore, decisions often necessitate superimposition of one's own standard, compromise of it, or surrender of it. These actions are not without some conflict and adjustment within one's frame of reference.

Second, in a pluralistic society not one but many expectations must be met. Therefore, resolution of what is right to do produces a balance of obligations and satisfactions. Ideally, full satisfaction of the expectations of all parties would constitute the most ethical behavior. This is impossible, for expectations are often contradictory and sometimes exceed social sanction. Therefore skill and judgment must be used to guide one in determining the point at which his own integrity can best be maintained.

Third, because marketing obligations are of both a noneconomic and economic nature, fulfilment of social expectations cannot be divorced from the economic limitations within which business decisions must be made. Thus, the complexity of determining what in a society are the standards of ethical behavior is compounded by the multiplicity of factors affecting application of the standard.

THRESHOLD OF ETHICAL SENSITIVITY

Of prime importance in application of an ethical standard to relations among economic participants is a manager's threshold of ethical sensitivity, that is, his level of interaction at which he finds within himself satisfaction in his actions toward others.

Although these levels may be identified variously, a useful classification is suggested by the stages through which the bases or standards of ethics have evolved during the past century.

SELF-INTEREST

Perhaps the lowest level of sensitivity to ethical obligation is that on which little, if any, consideration is given to the expectations of others.

This is the basis upon which it is popularly believed that most businessmen operate, seeking profit for themselves to the exclusion of others' interests. Such a description was more true of the 19th century business manager than of today's. No obligations to competitors, customers, employees, dealers, government, or the community was acknowledged. "Laissez-faire," "caveat emptor," and "the public be damned" were expressions of the ethics of self-interest.

This is not to say that then *no ethics existed;* after all, the standards of that day that permitted such behavior were sanctioned by society *of that day.* Individual self-interest and collective collusion characterized the "ethics of collusion," in which owner-manager interests were predominant and profit was an end in itself, rather than a measure of economic capacity to fulfill many ethical obligations.

LEGAL ETHICS

As the social conscience rose, rejection of the "ethics of collusion" took form in legislation compelling or prohibiting certain types of business behavior.

Thus emerged a threshold of sensitivity which might be called the "ethics of compulsion." The Sherman Anti-Trust Act was an important waymark in the formulation of legal standards—legal ethics. It illustrated the manner in which society, expressing its cultural and noneconomic values, forces or compels obligations upon business participants. With such legal formulations, there is no justification for a lower standard of action. However, laws are often a minimal standard, sometimes representing compromise in their enactment and subject to judicial review and interpretation. There are, therefore, higher bases upon which decisions may be made.

VOLUNTARY CODES

In contrast to the forms of compulsion typified by the Sherman Act, there appeared during early years of this century a movement of voluntary formulation of codes of ethics by businessmen.

Trade groups were the medium in which this commonly occurred, although individual firms sometimes stated their own ethical tenets. As these were voluntary, they represented an "ethics of compliance," that is, compliance with acknowledged obligations to various other parties in the economic process. They often presented standards where no laws applied, or elevated the legal minimum with a willingness for fuller discharge of responsibilities.

Such standards, however, being purely voluntary and societal, were also relative, arbitrary, and revocable. They represented the accepted standard of the social group, whether that group was society in general or the small group of the business community.

CONVICTION

Still another basis of ethical decision is that of illumined personal convictions.

One could not say that the self-interest of the 19th century was very illumined. Neither did the laws and codes of later years always evoke spontaneous compliance. However, personal convictions concerning one's duties and obligations to others in society, as they participate in the marketing processes, probably furnish the greatest encouragement for an evolving body of ethics.

Such ethics usually arise from an integrated sense of social and personal values, and from respect for law, honesty, fairness, and the like. They often bring religious concepts to bear upon business-relationship problems, interpreting men's obligation to men from the basis of men's relation to God. Concepts of divine sonship, brotherhood, stewardship, forgiveness, mercy, and the like are applied to business relationships.

Thus, an "ethics of conviction"—even of spiritual conviction—is evolved. In recent years acknowledgment of the relevance of religious convictions to business behavior has increased.

In Matrix #4 in Table 4 are shown the relationships in which managers act, and the bases upon which their decisions as to what is ethical action rest. One basis is not always equally useful, and the decision-maker will move from one to another, depending upon the situation.

When in doubt concerning the adequacy of a decision, gravitation is toward higher levels of social expectation and conviction.

TABLE 4

Matrix #4

DECISION BASES IN MANAGEMENT ROLE RELATIONSHIPS

Bases of Decision	Management Relations with Roles								
	#2	#3	#4	#5	#6	#7	#8	#9	#10
Qualitative factors:									
Self-interest									
Law									
Social standard									
Conviction									
Balance of Multiple claims									
Quantitative economic limitations									

BALANCE OF CLAIMS

With conscious awareness of all expectations and of the extent of his corresponding obligations, one may be forced to modify behavior in any one relationship because of the interrelationship of many claims.

Priority of some claims over others for satisfaction may be decided on the basis of such principles as rotation of claims, superiority of owner-interests in a capitalistic economy, superiority of market-interests in a market economy, national interests, legal requirements, or the demands of power blocs. Most ethical decisions do require a balancing of numerous claims.

ECONOMIC CIRCUMSTANCES

A final basis of decision is the extent to which economic circumstances permit doing what one may feel he is ethically obligated to do.

In a private economy, one is forced to act within economic limitations. If there is no profit for a period, the expectation of owners may be denied. If working capital is low, creditors may be required to wait for payment. If costs increase, changes may be made in the product and service normally expected by the customer.

In other words, *ethical decision under private capitalism is a moral decision impelled by social sanction but modified by economic exigency.*

IMPLICATIONS

An attempt has been made in this article to examine the anatomy of marketing decisions having ethical implications.

One is concerned, first, with the manner in which "rightness" of action is determined in a given society. Standards derive from the culture, from various institutional processes and structures, and from the expectations nurtured among the economic participants. With determinable standards, one next must select a course of particular action. He is guided by the level of his ethical sensitivity, by the strength of complementary and contrasting claims, and finally in some instances by economic capacity to act.

Employment of a model for ethics such as that proposed will sharpen one's grasp of the factors involved; but until that can be achieved, he will go a long way in his ethical marketing decisions if he possesses the basic qualities of unselfishness, honesty, fairness, and sincerity.

Part III

THE BATTLEGROUND: AREAS OF CONFRONTATION

The earlier readings, which have focused on the role of marketing in society and on the philosophical base of marketing, have suggested the subject matter for Part III, the areas of confrontation in the marketplace. Many of the tasks of marketing are performed in conflict situations. Though generally buyers are as satisfied as sellers in millions of daily transactions, there remains the arena in which seller confronts buyer and seller confronts seller, and in times of short supply where the buyer confronts buyer. The selected areas of conflict presented in Part III include advertising, demand creation, consumerism, and marketing research.

A. Advertising

The first two readings focus on the problems of advertising. Jules Backman examines the main criticisms of advertising made by economists. He then emphasizes the role of advertising, its informational value and its value as an efficient tool of marketing. Relationships to competition, costs, economic growth, and the degree of affluence of a society are also reviewed.

The second author, Colston E. Warne, sets forth some criticism of advertising and states that we must look at the actual effects in the marketplace if we are to judge advertising. He suggests that there exists an "unwitting recklessness" about advertising and proposes a "Consumer Manifesto" which is worthy of examination. The reader will find it interesting to probe Warne's suggestion that it is possible to shift from *caveat emptor* to *caveat venditor*.

12. IS ADVERTISING WASTEFUL?*

Jules Backman

With some exceptions, economists generally have criticised advertising as economically wasteful. All the criticisms are not so extreme as one widely used economics text which states:

> Overall, it is difficult for anyone to gain more than temporarily from large advertising outlays in an economy in which counteradvertising is general. The overall effect of advertising, on which we spent $14 billion [actually $15 billion —JB] in 1965, is to devote these productive resources (men, ink, billboards, and so forth) to producing advertising rather than to producing other goods and services.[1]

Most critics do not go this far in condemning advertising. However, they do emphasize that advertising may be wasteful in several ways: by adding unnecessarily to costs, by an inefficient use of resources, by promoting excessive competition, and by causing consumers to buy items they do not need. This article brings together the scattered criticisms of advertising and answers to them and thus presents an overview of the debate in this area. The nature of these criticisms and the significance of waste in a competitive economy are first reviewed. Attention is then given to the vital informational role played by advertising, particularly in an expanding economy. Advertising is only one alternative in the marketing mix, and hence its contribution must be considered among alternatives rather than in absolute terms.

VARIATIONS ON A THEME

The criticism that advertising involves economic waste takes several forms.

COMPETITION IN ADVERTISING

The attack usually is centered on competition in advertising which some critics state flatly is wasteful.[2] Others have been concerned about the relative cost of advertising as a percentage of sales. Sometimes an

---

*Journal of Marketing, Vol. 32 (January, 1968), pp. 2–8.

[1] George Leland Bach, *Economics* (5th ed.; Englewood Cliffs, N.J.: Prentice-Hall, Inc., 1966), p. 437. See also Kenneth Boulding, "Economic Analysis," *Microeconomics*, Vol. 1 (4th ed.; New York: Harper & Row, 1966), p. 513.

[2] Nicholas H. Kaldor, "The Economic Aspects of Advertising," *The Review of Economic Studies*, Vol. 18 (1950-51), p. 6.

arbitrary percentage, such as 5%, is selected as the dividing line between "high" and more "reasonable" levels of expenditure.[3]

Such cutoff points are meaningless, since the proper relative expenditures for advertising are a function of the product's characteristics. It is not an accident that relative advertising costs are highest for low-priced items which are available from many retail outlets and subject to frequent repeat purchases (for example, cosmetics, soaps, soft drinks, gum and candies, drugs, cigarettes, beer, etc.).

Particularly criticized are emotional appeals, persuasion, and "tug of war" advertising where it is claimed the main effect is to shift sales among firms rather than to increase total volume of the industry. For example, Richard Caves states: "At the point where advertising departs from its function of informing and seeks to persuade or deceive us, it tends to become a waste of resources."[4]

In a competitive economy competitors must seek to persuade customers to buy their wares. We do not live in a world where a company stocks its warehouse and waits until customers beat a path to its doors to buy its products. If this is all that a business firm did, we would have economic waste in terms of products produced but not bought as well as in the failure to produce many items for which a market can be created. In the latter case, the waste would take the form of idle labor and unused resources.

Inefficient use of resources

Economists have criticized advertising most vigorously as involving an inefficient use of resources. This criticism has been directed particularly against advertising where the main effect allegedly is a "shuffling of existing total demand" among the companies in an industry. Under these conditions, it is stated, advertising merely adds to total costs and in time results in higher prices. There undoubtedly is a shifting of demand among firms due to many factors including advertising. But this is what we should expect in a competitive economy. Moreover, there are many products for which total demand is increased (for example, television sets, radio sets, cars, toilet articles) for multiple use in the same home. In the sharply expanding economy of the past quarter of a century there are relatively few industries in which total demand has remained unchanged.

It must also be kept in mind that the resources devoted to competitive advertising usually are considered to be wasteful "in a full-employ-

---

[3]Joe S. Bain, *Industrial Organization* (New York: John Wiley & Sons, Inc., 1959), pp. 390–91. See also *Report of a Commission of Enquiry Into Advertising* (London: The Labour Party, 1966), p. 42. The Reith Report defined "substantially advertised products" at 5% or more.

[4]Richard Caves, *American Industry: Structure, Conduct, Performance* (Englewood Cliffs, N.J.: Prentice-Hall, Inc., 1964), p. 102.

ment economy" because they may be utilized more efficiently in other ways. Thus, the extent of "waste" involved also appears to depend upon whether the economy is operating below capacity. This point is considered in a later section.

ADDS TO COSTS

Sometimes, it is stated that if advertising succeeds in expanding total demand for a product, the result is a shift of demand from other products, the producers of which will be forced to advertise to attempt to recover their position. The net result of such "counter-advertising" is to add to costs and to prices.

But all increases in demand do not necessarily represent a diversion from other products. Thus, an expanded demand for new products is accompanied by an increase in income and in purchasing power flowing from their production. Moreover, during a period of expanding economic activity, as is noted later, the successful advertising may affect the rate of increase for different products rather than result in an absolute diversion of volume.

CREATES UNDESIRABLE WANTS

Another variation is the claim that advertising is wasteful because it ". . . creates useless or undesirable wants at the expense of things for which there is greater social need. When advertising makes consumers want and buy automobiles with tail fins, tobacco, and movie-star swimming pools, there is less money (fewer resources) available to improve public hospitals, build better schools, or combat juvenile delinquency."[5] It is claimed that many of these types of products are useless and antisocial. Criticism of advertising is nothing new. In the late 1920's Stuart Chase claimed: "Advertising creates no new dollars. In fact, by removing workers from productive employment, it tends to depress output, and thus lessen the number of real dollars."[6]

These are value judgments reached by the critics on the basis of subjective "standards" which they set up. "What is one man's meat is another man's poison," as the old saying goes. The real question is who is to decide what is good for the consumer and what should be purchase?

In a free economy, there is a wide diversity of opinion as to what combinations of goods and services should be made available and be consumed. Obviously, tastes vary widely and most persons do not want to be told what is best for them. In any cross section of the population of the country there will be a wide disagreement as to what constitutes

---

[5]"Advertising and Charlie Brown," *Business Review*, Federal Reserve Bank of Philadelphia (June, 1962), p. 10.

[6]Stuart Chase, *The Tragedy of Waste* (New York: Macmillan Company, 1928), p. 112.

the ideal components of a desirable level of living. Each one of us must decide what purchases will yield the greatest satisfactions. We may be misled on occasion by popular fads, advertising, or even advice of our friends. But these decisions in the final analysis are made by the buyers and not by the advertisers, as the latter have found out so often to their regret.

COMPETITION AND "WASTE"

The critics of advertising are really attacking the competitive process. Competition involves considerable duplication and "waste." The illustrations range from the several gasoline stations at an important intersection to the multiplication of research facilities, the excess industrial capacity which develops during periods of expansion, and the accumulations of excessive inventories.

There is widespread recognition that inefficiencies may develop in advertising as in other phases of business.[7] Mistakes are made in determining how much should be spent for advertising—but these mistakes can result in spending too little as well as too much.

We cannot judge the efficiency of our competitive society—including the various instrumentalities, such as advertising—by looking at the negative aspects alone. It is true that competition involves waste. But it also yields a flood of new products, improved quality, better service, and pressures on prices. In the United States, it has facilitated enormous economic growth with the accompanying high standards of living. The advantages of competition have been so overwhelmingly greater than the wastes inherent in it that we have established as one of our prime national goals, through the anti-trust laws, the continuance of a viable competitive economy.

INFORMATIONAL ROLE OF ADVERTISING

Advertising plays a major informational role in our economy because (1) products are available in such wide varieties, (2) new products are offered in such great numbers, and (3) existing products must be called to the attention of new customers who are added to the market as a result of expansion in incomes, the population explosion, and changes in tastes.

The most heavily advertised products are widely used items that are consumed by major segments of the population. This does not mean

---

[7]Committee on Advertising, *Principles of Advertising* (New York: Pitman Publishing Corp., 1963), p. 34; and Neil H. Borden, "The Role of Advertising in the Various Stages of Corporate and Economic Growth," Peter D. Bennett (ed.), *Marketing and Economic Development* (Chicago: American Marketing Association, 1965), p. 493.

that everyone buys every product or buys them to the extent that he can. Some of these products are substitutes for other products. For example, it will be readily recognized that cereals provide only one of many alternatives among breakfast foods. In some instances, heavily advertised products compete with each other like, for example, soft drinks and beer. In other instances, additional consumers can use the products so that the size of the total market can be increased (for example, toilet preparations).

Potential markets also expand as incomes rise and as consumers are able to purchase products they previously could not afford. As the population increases, large numbers of new potential customers are added each year. Continuous large-scale advertising provides reminders to old customers and provides information to obtain some part of the patronage of new customers. The potential market is so huge that large scale advertising is an economical way to obtain good results.

In addition, the identity of buyers changes under some circumstances and new potential buyers must be given information concerning the available alternatives. It has also been pointed out that some of these products are ". . . subject to fads and style changes" and that ". . . consumers become restive with existing brands and are prepared to try new varieties." Illustrations include cereals, soaps, clothing, and motion pictures.[8]

The consumer has a wide variety of brands from which to choose. Product improvements usually breed competitive product improvements; the advertising of these improvements may result in an increase in total advertising for the class of products.

When any company in an industry embarks on an intensified advertising campaign, its competitors must step up their advertising or other sales efforts to avoid the possible loss of market position. This is a key characteristic of competition.

On the other hand, if any company decides to economize on its advertising budget, its exposure is reduced and its share of market may decline if its competitors fail to follow the same policy. Thus, for some grocery products it has been reported that ". . . competition within a sector may have established a certain pattern with regard to the extent of advertising, and any company dropping below this level faces possible substantial loss of market share.[9]

These results flow particularly if the industry is oligopolistic, that is, has relatively few producers who are sensitive to and responsive to actions of competitors. However, as the dramatic changes in market shares during the past decade so amply demonstrate, this does not mean

[8]Lester G. Telser, "How Much Does It Pay Whom To Advertise?", *American Economic Review, Papers and Proceedings,* December, 1960, pp. 203–4.

[9]National Commission on Food Marketing, *Grocery Manufacturing,* Technical Study No. 6 (Washington, D.C.: June, 1966), p. 14.

that the companies in such oligopolistic industries will retain relatively constant shares of the market.[10]

The informational role of advertising has been succinctly summarized by Professor George J. Stigler:

. . . Under competition, the main tasks of a seller are to inform potential buyers of his existence, his line of goods, and his prices. Since both sellers and buyers change over time (due to birth, death, migration), since people forget information once acquired, and since new products appear, the existence of sellers must be continually advertised . . .

This informational function of advertising must be emphasized because of a popular and erroneous belief that advertising consists chiefly of nonrational (emotional and repetitive) appeals.[11]

Elsewhere, Professor Stigler has pointed out that ". . . information is a valuable resource," that advertising is "the obvious method of identifying buyers and sellers" which "reduces drastically the cost of search," and that "It is clearly an immensely powerful instrument for the elimination of ignorance. . . ."[12]

Often this information is required to create interest in and demand for a product. Thus, it has been reported:

. . . to a significant degree General Foods and the U.S. food market created each other. Before a new product appears, customers are rarely conscious of wanting it. There was no spontaneous demand for ready-to-eat cereals; frozen foods required a sustained marketing effort stretching over many years; instant coffee had been around for decades, supplying a market that did not amount to a tenth of its present level. General Foods' corporate skill consists largely in knowing enough about American tastes to foresee what products will be accepted.[13]

Similarly, J. K. Galbraith, who has been very critical of advertising, has recognized that:

A new consumer product must be introduced with a suitable advertising campaign to arouse an interest in it. The path for an expansion of output must be paved by a suitable expansion in the advertising budget. Outlays for the manufacturing of a product are not more important in the strategy of modern business enterprise than outlays for the manufacturing of demand for the product.[14]

---

[10]Jules Backman, *Advertising and Competition* (New York: New York University Press, 1967), chap. 3 and 4.

[11]George J. Stigler, *The Theory of Price*, (3d ed., New York: Macmillan Company, 1966), p. 200.

[12]George J. Stigler, "The Economics of Information," *The Journal of Political Economy*, June, 1961, pp. 213, 216, 220. See also S. A. Ozga, "Imperfect Markets Through Lack of Knowledge," *Quarterly Journal of Economics*, February, 1960, pp. 29, 33–34, and Wroe Alderson, *Dynamic Market Behavior* (Homewood, Ill.: Richard D. Irwin, Inc., 1965), pp. 128–31.

[13]"General Foods Is Five Billion Particulars," *Fortune*, March, 1964, p. 117.

[14]J. K. Galbraith, *The Affluent Society* (Boston: Houghton Mifflin Company, 1958), p. 156.

We live in an economy that has little resemblance to the ideal of perfect competition postulated by economists. However, one of the postulates of this ideal economy is perfect knowledge. Advertising contributes to such knowledge. Thus, in such an idealized economy, even though advertising may be wasteful it would still have a role to play. But in the world of reality, with all its imperfections, advertising is much more important. Advertising is an integral and vital part of our growing economy and contributes to the launching of the new products so essential to economic growth.

How much is informational?

In 1966, total expenditures for media advertising aggregated $13.3 billion.[15] It is impossible to determine exactly how much of this amount was strictly informational. However, the following facts are of interest.

Classified advertising was $1.3 billion.
Other local newspaper advertising, largely retail, was $2.6 billion.
Business paper advertising was $712 million.
Local radio and TV advertising was $1.1 billion.
Spot radio and spot TV advertising was $1.2 billion.
National advertising on network TV, network radio, magazines and
    newspapers was $3.7 billion.
Direct mail was $2.5 billion.

Classified advertising and local advertising are overwhelmingly informational in nature. Certainly some part of national advertising also performs this function. These figures suggest that substantially less than half of total advertising is of the type that the critics are attacking as wasteful;[16] the exact amount cannot be pinpointed. Moreover, it must be kept in mind that a significant part of national advertising is for the promotion of new products for which the informational role is vital.

From another point of view, even if there is waste, the social cost is considerably less than suggested by these data. Thus, in 1966 about $10 billion was spent on advertising in newspapers, magazines, radio, and television; another $746 million was spent on farm and business publications. Without these expenditures, these sources of news and entertainment would have had to obtain substantial sums from other sources. It has been estimated that ". . . advertising paid for over 60% of the cost of periodicals, for over 70% of the cost of newspapers, and for 100% of the cost of commercial radio and TV broadcasting."[17] Thus,

[15]This total excludes a miscellaneous category of $3.3 billion.
[16]For the United Kingdom, the "disputed proportion" of advertising expenditures has been estimated at about 30% of the total. Walter Taplin, *Advertising, A New Approach* (Boston: Little, Brown & Co., 1963), p. 126.
[17]Fritz Machlup, *The Production and Distribution of Knowledge in the United States* (Princeton, N.J.: Princeton University Press, 1962), p. 265.

advertising results in a form of subsidization for all media of communication. Without it, these media would have to charge higher subscription rates or be subsidized by the government or some combination of both.

ADVERTISING AND EXPANDING MARKETS

Economic growth has become a major objective of national economic policy in recent years. Rising productivity, increasing population, improving education, rates of saving, and decisions concerning new investments are the ingredients of economic growth. In addition, there must be a favorable political climate including tax policies and monetary policies designed to release the forces conducive to growth.

Advertising contributes to economic growth and in turn levels of living by complementing the efforts to create new and improved products through expenditures for research and development. One observer has described the process as follows:

. . . advertising, by acquainting the consumer with the values of new products, widens the market for these products, pushes forward their acceptance by the consumer, and encourages the investment and entrepreneurship necessary for innovation. Advertising, in short, holds out the promise of a greater and speedier return than would occur without such methods, thus stimulating investment, growth, and diversity.[18]

Among the most intensive advertisers have been toilet preparations (14.7% of sales), cleaning and polishing preparations (12.6%), and drugs (9.4%). The markets for these products have been expanding at a faster rate than all consumer spending.

Between 1947 and 1966, personal consumption expenditures for these products increased as follows:[19]

	1947	1955	1966
	(millions of dollars)		
Toilet articles and preparations	1,217	1,915	4,690
Cleaning, polishing and household supplies	1,523	2,480	4,487
Drug preparations and sundries	1,313	2,362	5,062

[18]David M. Blank, "Some Comments on the Role of Advertising in the American Economy—A Plea for Revaluation," L. George Smith (ed.), *Reflections on Progress in Marketing* (Chicago: American Marketing Association, 1964), p. 151.

[19]*The National Income and Product Accounts of the United States, 1929–1965, Statistical Tables* (Washington, D.C.: U.S. Department of Commerce, August, 1966), pp. 44–49; and *Survey of Current Business*, July, 1967, pp. 23–24.

As a share of total personal consumption expenditures, the increases from 1947 to 1966 were as follows:

Toilet articles and preparations from 0.76% to 1.01%
Cleaning, polishing and household supplies from 0.94% to 0.97%
Drug preparations and sundries from 0.82% to 1.09%

These increases in relative importance are based upon dollar totals. However, the retail prices of these products rose less than the consumer price index during the postwar years.

Between 1947 and 1966, the price increases were as follows:

Total consumer price index 45.4%
Toilet preparations 14.6
Soaps and detergents 2.6
Drugs and prescriptions 22.8

Thus, the increase in relative importance of these highly advertised products has been even greater in real terms than in dollars.

Between 1947 and 1966, the increase in *real* personal consumption expenditures has been:

Toilet articles and preparations from 0.68% to 1.12%
Cleaning, polishing and household supplies from 0.87% to 1.05%
Drug preparations and sundries from 0.82% to 1.24%

Clearly, advertising appears to have contributed to an expansion in the demand for these products and to the growth of our economy with the accompanying expansion in job opportunities and in economic well-being. There may have been some waste in this process—although all of such expenditures cannot be characterized as wasteful—but it appears to have been offset in full or in part by these other benefits.

The charge of large-scale waste in advertising appears to reflect in part a yearning for an economy with standardized, homogeneous products which are primarily functional in nature. An illustration would be a refrigerator that is designed solely to be technically efficient for the storage of food. However, customers are also interested in the decor of their kitchens, in convenience and speed in the manufacture of ice cubes, in shelves that rotate, and in special storage for butter. These are additions to functional usefulness which "an affluent society" can afford but which a subsistence economy cannot.

ADVERTISING IN A HIGH LEVEL ECONOMY

The concept of waste must be related to the level achieved by an economy. Professor John W. Lowe has observed that "Perhaps a good deal of the 'wastefulness' assigned to advertising springs from the fact that a large part of the world's population cannot consider satisfying *psychological wants* when most of their efforts must be devoted to *needs.*"[20] (Italics added.)

In a subsistence economy, scarcity is so significant that advertising might be wasteful, particularly where it diverts resources from meeting the basic necessities of life. Such an economy usually is a "full employment economy" in the sense that everyone is working. But the total yield of a full employment subsistence economy is very low, as is evident throughout Asia, Africa, and South America.

Professor Galbraith has noted that "The opportunity for product differentiation . . . is almost uniquely the result of opulence . . . the tendency for commercial rivalries . . . to be channeled into advertising and salesmanship would disappear in a poor community."[21]

In the high level American economy, there usually are surpluses rather than scarcity. The use of resources for advertising to differentiate products, therefore, is not necessarily a diversion from other uses. Rather, it frequently represents the use of resources that might otherwise be idle both in the short run and the long run and thus may obviate the waste that such idleness represents.

THE MARKETING MIX

The concept of waste cannot ignore the question—waste as compared with what alternative? Advertising cannot be considered in a vacuum. It must be considered as one of the marketing alternatives available. Generally it is not a question of advertising or nothing, but rather of advertising or some other type of sales effort.

It is a mistake to evaluate the relative cost of advertising apart from other marketing costs. It is only one tool in the marketing arsenal which also includes direct selling, packaging, servicing, product planning, pricing, etc. Expenditures for advertising often are substituted for other types of selling effort. This substitution has been readily apparent in the history of the discount house. These houses have featured well-advertised brands which were presold and, hence, virtually eliminated the need for floor stocks and reduced the need for space and many salesmen.

Advertising is undertaken where it is the most effective and most economical way to appeal to customers. It is a relatively low cost method of communicating with all potential customers and this explains its widespread adoption by many companies. To the extent that less efficient

---

[20] John W. Lowe, "An Economist Defends Advertising," *Journal of Marketing,* Vol. 27 (July, 1963), p. 18.

[21] John K. Galbraith, *American Capitalism: The Concept of Countervailing Power* (Boston: Houghton Mifflin Company, 1952), pp. 106–7.

marketing methods must be substituted for advertising, we would really have economic waste.

SUMMARY AND CONCLUSIONS

There is wide agreement that the informational role of advertising makes a significant contribution to the effective operation of our economy. There is also agreement that inefficiency in the use of advertising is wasteful, as are other types of inefficiencies that are part and parcel of a market-determined economy. The gray area is so-called competitive advertising, largely national, which is the main target of those who insist advertising is wasteful. Although precise data are not available, the estimates cited earlier indicate that the charge of competitive waste applies to substantially less than half of all advertising expenditures.

Competition unavoidably involves considerable duplication and waste. If the accent is placed on the negative, a distorted picture is obtained. On balance, the advantages of competition have been much greater than the wastes.

Advertising has contributed to an expanding market for new and better products. Many of these new products would not have been brought to market unless firms were free to develop mass markets through large-scale advertising. There may be some waste in this process, but it has been more than offset by other benefits.

Where burgeoning advertising expenditures are accompanied by expanding industry sales, there will tend to be a decline in total unit costs instead of increase, and prices may remain unchanged or decline. In such situations, it seems clear that advertising, while adding to total costs, will result in lower total *unit* costs, the more significant figure. This gain will be offset to some extent if the increase in volume represents a diversion from other companies or industries with an accompanying rise in unit costs. Of course, such change is inherent in a dynamic competitive economy.

Advertising expenditures have risen as the economy has expanded. At such times, the absolute increase in sales resulting from higher advertising expenditures need not be accompanied by a loss in sales in other industries. This is particularly true if a new product has been developed and its sales are expanding. In that event, new jobs probably will be created and help to support a higher level of economic activity generally.

The claim that resources devoted to advertising would be utilized more efficiently for other purposes ignores the fact that generally we have a surplus economy. All of the resources used for advertising are not diverted from other alternatives. Rather, it is probable that much of the resources involved would be idle or would be used less efficiently.

Even more important would be the failure to provide the jobs which expanding markets create.

Finally, advertising does not take place in a vacuum. It is one of several marketing alternatives. The abandonment of advertising could not represent a net saving to a company or to the economy. Instead, such a development would require a shift to alternative marketing techniques, some of which would be less efficient than advertising since companies do not deliberately adopt the least effective marketing approach. On balance, advertising is an invaluable competitive tool.

13. ADVERTISING—A CRITIC'S VIEW*

Colston E. Warne

In the face of repeated attacks from educators, Congressional committees, and journalists, the advertising fraternity has veered between a posture of a misunderstood and aggrieved innocent and that of a repentant sinner.

In response, some of its leaders have launched fervent appeals for basic reform. Others have mounted intensive campaigns to refute critics and to demonstrate the essential purity of the guild. From the earliest days of organized advertising associations, extreme candor has featured discussions in the advertising press. Such utterances as, "Our house is not clean," "We need a rededication to truth," "Let's kick out the scoundrels who are besmirching our profession," will be heartily applauded at advertising conventions.

And equally applauded will be able spokesmen like Professor Britt, who attempts to exorcise advertising's challengers by applying an aura of righteousness and essentiality to the industry.[1]

ADVERTISING'S UNFAVORABLE IMAGE

At the present time, we are witnessing a re-rededication to truth in advertising and to the "unsoiled sale." This is accompanied by public relations campaigns to correct the unfavorable image of the industry. Yet exposé books continue; Congressional hearings bring out dubious practices in ever-widening fields of sales persuasion; and as the consumer continues his nightly television fare of pseudo-scientific comparisons with Brand X, a crisis of confidence besets the whole industry. Significantly,

Journal of Marketing, October, 1962, pp. 10–14.
[1] Steuart Henderson Britt, *The Spenders* (New York: McGraw-Hill Book Co., 1960).

after recent exposés, it has become far less possible for the leading advertising agencies to proclaim that the trouble stems from a small and notorious fringe of marginal operators. H. Lloyd Taylor, Division Advertising Manager of duPont, said at an advertising meeting in Dallas:[2]

Ad people themselves are to blame for the fact that "the yoke of public ridicule has moved from Wall Street to Madison Avenue". . .

How many of us here can say that he's never been a party to deceptive advertising; that he has never, at the very least, allowed advertising of one kind or another to go by him that encouraged favorable but untrue inferences about his product?

And who among us has not been so mesmerized by the lyricism of a piece of copy, or the beauty of a layout, or the poetic tintinabulations of a musical commercial, that he has ignored the consumer's rightful desire to be told quickly and clearly—without a lot of meaningless guff—how the product will benefit him?

Payola of one kind or another seems to have become the accepted modus operandi in a good deal of merchandising effort. And advertising itself has taken on aspects of a form of payola in its cooperative advertising and advertising allowance programs. It is certainly no secret within the industry that these "bribes" to retailers for shelf space and special in-the-store attention in the form of advertising allowances are on the increase. In the old days, it used to be spiffs and PM's—push money paid directly by the brand advertiser to the retail clerk for each sale of a given brand. This principle of spiffs and PM's has now spread throughout distribution in the form of the advertising allowance. Or to put it another way, in the name of advertising, the presumed objectivity of the sales clerk with respect to competing brands within a given store has been corrupted. Thus the final sale, the last opportunity for products to stand one against another in open competition, has been subjected to a truly subliminal manipulation.

EFFECTS OF ADVERTISING

In fairness, we are not concerned here with the intentions of advertisers. The careful critics of advertising have to be concerned, first and foremost, not with what the advertisers believe they are doing, but with what the actual effects of these activities are on the marketplace. To be sure, a single generalization can scarcely encompass the total effect of the various aspects of this $12 to $13 billion industry which includes within itself the employment of partisan persuasion to diverse ends. What must concern the observer today, however, are some of the broad-scale or "mountain-range" effects. Many of these effects of adver-

---

[2]*Advertising Age*, Vol. 32 (November 27, 1961), p. 2.

tising which disturb serious commentators have to be viewed in the context of the burden that historical and technological development has placed on this industry.

None of us must overlook the fact that the rapidly evolving industrial revolution which transferred our population from the farm to metropolitan areas in a short 30 years created a social vacuum in product knowledge. Man does not live by bread alone, but certainly man does live and must live with the goods he uses to sustain his existence. Furthermore, daily and countless exchanges of goods and services and the manner in which we deal with each other when we make these transactions contribute a compelling impact on the nonmaterial aspect of our lives. The ethics of a culture, as Toynbee has suggested, can be and are often expressed most poignantly at the point of exchange of goods and labor in the accent placed on prevalent values in the marketplace.

SIGNIFICANCE OF ADVERTISING

During the past 50 years, while modern technology has been not only drawing modern man away from the farm but flooding his life with new and complicated products, the social problem of acquiring the knowledge needed to adjust to the selection and use of these products fell, without either planning or forethought, on the shoulders of an infant advertising industry just growing out of its "space-peddling" stage.

Through no fault of its own, advertising was unaware of the implications in the task that almost by accident was handed over to it. Nor was the advertising industry alone in its lack of awareness. After all, it was not until the 1920's that social commentators began to sense the threat of a misallocation of resources that was implicit in turning over the function of providing product information to the partisan efforts of competing brand advertisers.

Indeed, only in the 1920's did the consumer movement, or consumer consciousness, first begin to develop vigorously. Even today neither our sociologists nor our economists have paid much attention to the broader significance of advertising. In the days of 1929 excesses, when *Liberty Magazine* carried in one issue as many as 19 different testimonials from Mabel Normand, the general reaction was a naïve one—how could anybody believe that Mabel Normand honestly meant her praise for 19 different brands of goods? No one foresaw then that the appeal to irrationality in the choice of goods was far more serious than the vulgar aspects of testimonial advertising.

We have gone far since that day. Practitioners of advertising have eaten the fruit of a new tree of knowledge. Many today openly proclaim their objective to be appeals to the irrational or the irrelevant. Even those who have paid out the highest fees to motivational researchers, though, have not actually intended thereby to destroy the theoretical basis of a free enterprise system. These very same advertisers who hold that sales appeals must be irrational point in the next breath to those sales as "votes for advertised goods"—as public acclaim of their efforts. They cannot have it both ways. If sales must be achieved through irrational means, then those sales are the empty votes of a disenfranchised electorate and merely represent consumer manipulation to producer-dictated ends. In the absence of rationality in purchase, consumer sovereignty becomes a meaningless concept. And here the critics of advertising must point out that any weakening or destroying of the effective exercise of consumer sovereignty is a serious attack on this vital balance wheel in our economy.

BIGGEST CONSUMER

We stand today as the giant consumer among nations. And the advertising industry with an unwitting recklessness has immodestly boasted of its role as the chief creator of our immense capacity to devour goods and services. Unlike most of advertising's defenders, however, it would not be fair to lay *all* the blame for the mounting waste of our natural resources on Madison Avenue's fashionably draped Brooks Brothers' shoulders. However, insofar as advertising does succeed in destroying rational choice of goods by appealing to irrational motives, it is contributing to the time when we may find ourselves a have-not nation with respect to important resources; and advertising is also substituting tinsel for substance in our living standard. Thus, perhaps the first and most serious question that the critics of advertising are now raising about the manner in which this industry currently functions is its conscious or unconscious assault against the exercise of a meaningful consumer sovereignty.

NECESSARY EXTRAVAGANCES?

The claims have been made that a waste of resources in the form of unstable goods, built-in obsolescence, meaningless product differentiation, a wasteful distributive system, speeded-up replacements, not to mention the costs directly linked to advertising appeals, are necessary extravagances to keep the economy afloat.

If these claims be true, if it is indeed necessary that we must maintain a vast business-sponsored WPA, a gigantic make-work movement in order to keep our economic system functioning, then the time has come for us to face this most lamentable fact and to call it by its real name—a make-work program.

It is difficult to believe that American ingenuity has been so strained that only through this kind of mounting outlay of men and resources can we manage to keep ourselves functioning economically. But if we *do* have to shore ourselves up with a make-work program, then there are other areas of activity (low-cost housing, for example) where the task would be more productive and less wasteful. Historically, we seem to apply the advertising make-work stimulus in inflationary times and taper it off in recessions.

NATIONAL ADVERTISING OUTLAY

Aside from this promotion of waste through attempts to destroy consumer sovereignty, perhaps the second most disturbing feature of advertising as it functions today lies in the area of the monopoly power it has placed in the hands of the most substantial spenders (that is, investors in advertising). The national advertising outlay is not evenly divided among contenders for custom. It bulks with a very heavy weight at the top. It appears difficult, if not impossible, today to launch a new brand of food or drug without the outlay of as much as $10 million. If this is true, then what we face is a fantastic tax upon freedom of market entry.

In addition to this restriction of access to the market that advertising exercises, there is also that other monopoly aspect of its functioning—namely, through irrational sales appeal, advertising attempts to grant any given brand advertiser an aura of incomparable quality for his product. Thus, it is not one toothpaste or another, but love versus fear; and not one cigarette or another, but tars and nicotine versus taste. Here is where the much-sought-after brand loyalty enters the picture. It is one of the great claims of the advertising practitioner that he can conjure up one degree or another of brand loyalty by the magic of images.

Obviously, to the extent that partisan advertising alone creates brand loyalty, it creates a noncompetitive market situation. It is little wonder that in recent years we have seen a flight from price competition into promotional rivalry and that along with that flight have come fewer ounces in the package, a lowering of product quality control, an increase in promotional costs, and a rapidly stepped-up wave of mergers in the consumer goods field. Not only the small company but the middle-sized company stands a decreasing chance to survive in a period when market survival depends upon the magnitude of promotional outlays rather than upon efficient production reflected in lower prices. By providing in our society few significant sources of product information beyond those in the hands of partisan persuaders, we have not only made it ever more difficult for the consumer to be able to exercise rational choice, but we have also constricted opportunities for entrepreneurship.

CURES

There is, however, an avenue by which we may be able to rid ourselves of what appears to be a growing hardening of the arteries in this section of our economic system. That way is grade labeling and the development of product standards.

There is probably no idea more abhorrent to most of organized advertising. In areas where we have had objective grades established for goods, advertising has not ceased to function. It has tended to be a different kind of advertising, with more emphasis on price than glamor; but it has certainly functioned as a market factor in the distribution of such goods as eggs, turkeys, milk, and ice cream, to name a few of the very few product areas where some objective standards of quality have been established and enforced.

To be sure, established objective grades for quality tend to open up the market to the smaller firms. Grade A on the frozen turkey gives the small processor a place in the supermarket counter immediately next to the big brander and often an opportunity to win the sale through a lower price. The small contender, once he has an entry to the market, can sometimes make his mark with his prices.

BIGNESS OF COMPANIES?

In those areas of production where advertising plays a dominant role —food, drugs, cosmetics, tobacco, and liquor—there is little in the literature of economics to lend credence to the belief that the largest concerns are the most efficient. In meat packing, for example, it appears that bigness is an acutely crippling weight on efficient functioning. As to automobiles even (judging from the hearings before the Senate Committee on Monopoly), the biggest producers do not report the lowest costs.

The advertising industry counts too heavily on lack of sophistication when it offers as one of its justifications for its existence the statement that advertising is responsible for mass production. Mass demand cannot be said to have been the egg to the production chicken. The overfed and too-long nurtured immodesty of advertising is most evident in this industry argument. Mass production did not flow from a copywriter's pen. It is, rather, a total cultural achievement. Its technology has come from our common heritage in the development of science. Its fortunate development in the United States centrally stemmed from our wealth of natural resources; from our possession of one of the widest free trade areas in the world; and from our development of economics of scale. Advertising has today carried production concentration far beyond the point dictated by the requirements of these economics of scale, and has had a blighting effect upon traditional competition.

FICTITIOUS PRICES?

In recent years, moreover, fictitious prices have become illicit marketing sirens, not only of fringe companies but of major concerns. Through the advertising of exorbitant preticketing levels and subsequent price cuts, the consumer has been asked to believe that an article is made to sell at a higher sum in order to induce him to buy it at a fraction of that price. This sort of advertising practice represents the unfortunate transfer of the ethics of a going-out-of-business sale to the center of the marketplace.

DECEPTIVE PACKAGING?

Still another practice which has recently heaped condemnation upon advertising has been deceptive packaging—a practice which has also amply demonstrated that the package is itself a most effective advertising medium. Consumers are deeply disturbed over the attempt of companies to avoid rational price comparison by "jiggling" the size and weight of branded goods, with a bold assist from specialists in package design. The overweaning aim has been not to serve the consumer but to develop display values which will insure "sales vitality."

Still another indictment should be added. There is such a thing as saturation in advertising.

Granted that this informational agency, properly employed as an accurate and descriptive educational mechanism, has a real and substantial place in our culture, this does not delegate it to subject human consciousness to the shriekings of an Oriental bazaar. Even Grand Canyon would be spoiled if a thousand hawkers were permitted to proclaim the superlative virtues of each outlook spot. Too much is too much, particularly when embellished at times by miracles not yet discovered even by scientists.

A CONSUMER MANIFESTO

Herein lies the need for a *consumer manifesto* which would include as a minimum the acceptance of the following basic elements:

1. The new communication media—radio and television—were not created for advertising. The airwaves are owned by the consuming public; and the costs of radio and television, whether indirectly assessed through advertising or directly through the cost of electricity and tele-

vision acquisition and maintenance, are consumer costs. Advertisers are there incidentally as nonpaying guests in the home and are not to be obnoxious, long-winded, stupid, or inane. Program content is rightfully not the creature of the advertiser, dedicated by his dictates to cater to the lowest common denominator of mass taste.

2. The countryside belongs to the consumer, not to the advertiser. There is no inherent right to create incessant affronts to the human eye every hundred yards along a highway—a procession of billboard slums.

3. Newspapers and periodicals have their central responsibility to their readers, not to their advertisers. This responsibility is compromised whenever dubious standards of advertising acceptance prevail or where choice is warped by planted stories designed to sell, not to inform.

4. Legislative and self-regulatory efforts to impose truth in advertising and to ban false and misleading advertising, although possessed of great merit, have thus far proven notoriously ineffective. They need to be improved. No prohibitions on false advertising, however drastic, can suffice to compel advertising to play its essential role in our culture. Truth in advertising is not a residue left after the elimination of falsehood. Advertising has ever been prone to discover new techniques of subtle deception wherever prohibitions have been imposed. What is today needed is the application of a supplementary approach.

5. Specifically, a policy is proposed of *caveat venditor*—let the seller beware—a policy to be enforced by our social and legal institutions. An advertisement should be a warranty to the purchaser of the price and quality of an article. Thus, the burden of proof as to an advertising claim will lie squarely upon the seller of a branded good. A claim should be accurate and complete as to all essential details, and should constitute a full disclosure of both the merits and demerits of the good in its intended use. Advertising should not be poised on the slippery edge of irrelevance, misrepresentation, or deception. The obsolescent and socially destructive idea of *caveat emptor* should be appropriately buried as a relic of the days of simple markets and well-understood commodities.

This suggestion that the seller be held legally bound by his statements (including the clear implications that these may give to the ordinary consumer) is by no means a revolutionary one. It has been already incorporated into a number of court opinions and is beginning to find a place in economic and judicial attitudes. It should now be fully integrated into the legal structure. Full disclosure in one form or another has already emerged in declarations of ingredients in foods and drugs; hazardous substances have to have full warnings on their labels. Moreover, the drift of court opinion has been toward the acceptance of the principle that in placing a product upon the market, the manufacturer assumes a responsibility to the consumer which goes far beyond the mandate of *caveat emptor*.

TRUTH IN ADVERTISING

There are probably no consumers who are not willing, even eager, to be told with accuracy and candor about new or truly improved products, or for that matter to have their memories jogged about the merits of existing products. The consumer has no quarrel with advertising as such. His basic quarrel is simply that this medium has been misused. As a whole, it has not been designed to inform, but has been powered for a lesser objective—the promotion of brands. And being so powered, it has less often led to consumer enlightenment than to consumer bewilderment.

It is all very well for advertising partisans to plead that only one out of five Americans is disgusted with its actual performance and that in the main the nation is well content with the toothy blondes who greet them with beckoning hands filled with the fruits of our culture. Correct it may be that the majority of the consumer "electorate" basks contentedly in the advertising sun. But the revolt against advertising has come from opinion leaders, and the rise of American educational levels may well extend the area of alienation.

Must life be made meaningful solely by the efforts of specialists in stimulation who, in quest of self-profit, seek to coax or cajole? Has not the most important force—that of self-initiation—been omitted?

The critic of advertising does not wish to establish a standardized consumer after his own image. A discerning critic wishes more deliberative choice, more autonomous human beings who operate in an environment which, with truthful information sources, fosters freedom of choice and free competition of ideas in the marketplace—not the preconditioned "standard package" of acceptable goods of the advertiser.

It is advertising that is concentrating its techniques upon the manipulation of human personality into profitable molds. To be sure, it is no hidden persuader. It is instead a private agency of human conditioning of not inconsiderable power, designed generally to create an image of sterile optimism, an obsession with material things . . . with change . . . with motion . . . and with superficial appearance. Its failure to date has not been so much in craftsmanship as in its refusal to recognize that accurate advertising is a phase of educational experience and should maintain the standards of education. It should be fact-faithful, presenting the imperfections as well as the advantages; it should have perspective; it should be tentative and as unbiased as possible. Artificial product differentiations and romantic fantasies may for a time capture unthinking consumer loyalty; but these techniques are no substitute for unadulterated truth.

B. Products and prices

Advertising is frequently criticized because it improperly stimulates wants and because it stimulates undesirable wants. In the following article, Jean Boddewyn examines the matter of "wicked wants" and refers to Galbraith's writings to make his point. Boddewyn clarifies the meanings of wants and needs, and in so doing raises some of the basic issues underlying the conflict areas in marketing.

14. GALBRAITH'S WICKED WANTS*

Jean Boddewyn

A sizable portion of *The Affluent Society* by John Kenneth Galbraith deals with the "paramount position of production" in American society.[1] According to the author, goods are not always produced for the obvious reason that they are needed: the provision of employment and income, the concern for national security, and "vested interests in output"—all explain the prevailing preoccupation with production apart from the very goods it delivers. The conventional case for production does not stop there either.

A commonly accepted theory of consumer demand justifies the production of *any* good or service on the grounds that it satisfies pre-existing needs simply because—like in the famous remark about Mount Everest—"they are there." The theory goes on to say that there is no limit to these wants and that their urgency does not diminish appreciably as more of them are satisfied.

Confessing the difficulty of settling the case for or against the satiation of wants, Galbraith focuses his attack on their origin: are these wants original with the consumer? His answer is negative: as society becomes more affluent, wants are increasingly dependent on the process by which they are satisfied (the "Dependence Effect").[2] As such, the demand for many goods does not arise in spontaneous need but is fueled by the efforts of advertisers and salesmen ("Madison Avenue") who bring into being wants that previously did not exist.[3] Such contrived needs are not particularly pressing:

Journal of Marketing, October, 1961, pp. 14–18.

[1] John Kenneth Galbraith, *The Affluent Society* (Boston: Houghton Mifflin Company, 1958).

[2] This theme is treated in chapter 8 of *American Capitalism* (2nd. ed rev.; Boston: Houghton Mifflin Company, 1956), and in chapters 10 and 11 of *The Affluent Society*.

[3] Same reference as footnote 1.

The fact that wants can be synthesized by advertising, catalyzed by sales-manship, and shaped by the discreet manipulations of the persuaders shows that they are not very urgent. A man who is hungry need never be told of his need for food. If he is inspired by his appetite, he is immune to the influence of Messrs. Batten, Barton, Durstine and Osborn. The latter are effective only with those who are so far removed from physical want that they do not already know what they want. In this state alone men are open to persuasion.[4]

Galbraith sets great store by this conclusion because of its implication for a philosophy of welfare. If wants are created artificially, it can no longer be assumed that welfare is greater at a higher level of production than at a lower one. The higher level of production has merely a higher level of want creation, and it grows out of the process of production itself.

So, one would expect to find in *The Affluent Society* a rather elaborate exposition of the nature of wants. But the evidence advanced by Gal-braith is rather scanty; in a grand manner, he rests his case on the remark that few serious scholars will deny that wants are, in fact, the fruit of production.[5]

Lest the man who thinks for himself remain unconvinced, Galbraith goes on to quote Keynes and Dusenberry on emulation and prestige, but in a rather perfunctory manner. Thus left with the choice of weapons, it seems appropriate to embark upon an inter-disciplinary study of the nature of wants and needs.

HOMO HISTORICUS

Galbraith aphorizes that "it is not necessary to advertise food to hungry people, fuel to cold people or houses to the homeless."[6] Yet it took close to two hundred years (approximately 1550–1750) to introduce in Europe and North America, a nourishing and easily cultivated vegetable —*the potato*. At the time, the assessment of the tuber by experts was generally favorable. Besides, recurrent famines and soils unsuited for other crops pointed to the potato as an obvious remedy; but its adoption met with considerable opposition.[7]

On our shores, the potato was served as an exotic rarity at a Harvard installation in 1707, but it was not brought into cultivation in New England until the arrival of Presbyterian immigrants from Ireland in 1718. As late as 1740, it was still a practice with masters to stipulate with some apprentices that they would not have to eat potatoes. The prejudice was pretty general against the tubers that they were unhealthy

---

[4]*Ibid.*, p. 158.
[5]*Ibid.*, p. 154.
[6]*American Capitalism, op. cit.*, p. 97.
[7]Redcliffe N. Salaman, *The History and Social Influence of the Potato* (Cambridge, England: The University Press, 1949), p. 51; and William E. Safford, *The Potato of Romance and Reality,* Smithsonian Report for 1925 (Washington, D.C.: U.S. Government Printing Office, 1926), p. 524.

and shortened man's life. It was only when some people of the better sort chose to eat them as a palatable dish that the mass of the population followed suit.

In France, it took the highly picturesque efforts of Antoine-Augustin Parmentier ("The Father of the Potato") to introduce *Solanum Tubero-sum* in the diet of the French. Long after agriculturists, government officials and even clergymen had failed to convince the people, Parmentier obtained the patronage of Louis XVI and planted potatoes in fifty-four acres of notoriously arid and sandy soil in the vicinity of Paris. When, in the summer of 1785, the tubers were blooming, he picked a great bouquet of potato blossoms and hastily drove to Versailles to present them to the monarch. After a short hesitation, Louis XVI kindly accepted the offering, picked a potato flower, and put it in his button-hole. Queen Marie-Antoinette wore it in her hair that same evening. Thus properly sponsored, Parmentier posted guards around the potato field in order to arouse the curiosity and envy of the Parisians. At night, however, the soldiers were purposely relieved of sentry duty. Soon Parmentier was told that some of his potatoes had been stolen. He was delighted to learn it and saw in this theft the proof of his success: "If people steal potatoes," he said, "they must have lost their prejudice against them!"[8]

Only in Ireland was the potato adopted quickly—and this only in the face of a serious social upheaval. After the failure of the revolt against England at the beginning of the 17th century, the diet of the people had become so restricted and its supply in this period of turmoil so precarious that sheer necessity broke down rural prejudices which it might otherwise have taken generations to overcome. The complete collapse of public security together with the disruption of normal peasant life opened the door to a food which, though peculiar in its cultural requirements, strange in appearance and taste, offered the people a sporting chance of warding off the famine and pestilence which hammered at their door.[9] Potatoes soon became the main food of the Irish. Two hundred and fifty years later, the Irish Potato Famine sent the Fitzgerald and Kennedy families to the United States—eventually to have one of their descendants advised and represented by none other than John Kenneth Galbraith.

It seems ironic that Galbraith should envision that in a poor land the whole force, male and female, of J. Walter Thompson, Du Pont Cellophane, and the marketing research firm of Mr. Elmo Roper would without question be at work producing potatoes and other such "neces-

---

[8]Pierre Larousse, *Grand Dictionnaire Universel du XIX Siècle* (Paris: Maison Larousse, 1874), Vol. 12, p. 308; *La Grande Encyclopédie* (Paris: Société Anonyme de la Grande Encyclopédie, 1886–1902), Vol. 27, p. 190.

[9]Salaman, same reference as footnote 7, p. 220.

sities."[10] It seems, instead, that their services would have been welcomed by Parmentier *et al.*

HOMO SOCIALIS

A discussion of the nature of wants and needs often represents a futile exercise in taxonomy. Yet Galbraith's *marginalist* view of wants as being piled up on top of each other—with the "basic" ones at the bottom and layers of less and less urgent ones on top of them—must be challenged.

To paraphrase Galbraith's statements, few serious social scientists will deny that needs and wants are, in fact, split along lines other than his "basic-artificial" dichotomy. Instead, *all of man's specific needs are artificial to the extent that they are largely determined for him and not by him.*

As J. A. C. Brown has put it: "That man possesses certain needs is a biological fact; how he satisfies them is a social or cultural fact."[11] In other words, there are psychic and somatic needs such as survival, approval, hunger, thirst, and sex—whatever their exact nature and number. All other needs are demands for what can satisfy these elementary besoins. And these needs are specified by one's culture, and are inculcated through such socio-psychological processes as child-raising, schooling, associating with one's peers . . . or advertising.

Of course, a hungry man need never be told of his elementary need for food. He learns from his society, however, that only particular food items *ought* to satisfy his hunger. The history of the potato is quite revealing on this count, and parallel stories could be told regarding the introduction of pickled eels, rattlesnake jam, or the more prosaic oleo-margarine—not to mention tomatoes!

For the social scientist, then, there is no such thing as "plain" bread, sidemeat, or oatmeal—at least not in the sense meant by Galbraith. Even the hospitals, schools, roads, and cleared slums advocated by him constitute *artificial needs;* and they reflect contemporary American cultural preferences for health, education, speed, and comfort. Like all novelties, they have to be fitted somehow into the current pattern of consumption; and this requires both appraisal and publicity.

On this count, however, it is often argued that no "Madison Avenue hoopla" is needed to introduce new products. This should be done instead—so the argument goes—through the educational activities of private and public consumer bodies, using informative advertising of a sane and reasonable variety.

The trouble with this proposition is that it is far too rational for its

---

[10]*American Capitalism,* same reference as footnote 2, p. 97.

[11]J. A. C. Brown, *The Social Psychology of Industry* (Harmondsworth: Penguin Books Ltd., 1954), p. 47.

own good. It rests on an idealistic definition of reasonableness; and it considers education as a simple matter of proof and demonstration according to the rules of logic and on the basis of "factual" evidence.

Yet this is the type of argument that people intuitively distrust—be it for lack of intellectual agility or congenital suspicion of cold facts. *People would rather believe people than facts*—social scientists have made this point time after time.

New ideas—and a new product is basically a new idea of how to satisfy needs—are mostly *transmitted through personal influence.* As such, leaders at all levels of society are the real targets of advertising; and Parmentier's success rested on that realization. Katz and Lazarsfeld have reached similar conclusions in their studies of mass communications.[12] Whyte made the same point in an article describing the acceptance of the then new air-conditioner in a Philadelphia suburb: the clustering of the new appliances in certain blocks of an otherwise homogeneous neighborhood discounted the influence of factors such as income or advertising.[13]

Britt has confirmed these views about rationality and "word-of-mouth" advertising in *The Spenders.*[14]

HOMO IN-OECONOMICUS

Together with other economists Galbraith considers the growth—absolute and relative—of advertising expenditures as *prima facie* evidence of the wasteful and irrational practices commonly associated with monopolistic competition.

Alderson has seriously challenged this view; he maintains, instead, that monopolistic competition may well result in *fewer* differentiated products:

> It is assumed that the decision to make a product differing from those of other producers originates with the supplier and usually for the purpose of avoiding direct competitive comparisons with other products. The fact is overlooked that historically diversity is already present in the market at the time a producer decides to concentrate on one of the variations which appears to be demanded by the consumer.[15]

Hence, differentiation through advertising may be less wasteful than supplying the diversity of consumer tastes on a custom basis. Besides,

---

[12]Elihu Katz and Paul L. Lazarsfeld, *Personal Influence; The Part Played by People in the Flow of Mass Communications* (Glencoe, Ill.: The Free Press, 1955).

[13]William H. Whyte, Jr., "The Web of Word-of-Mouth," *Fortune,* November, 1954, pp. 140–43 and 204–12.

[14]Steuart Henderson Britt, *The Spenders* (New York: McGraw-Hill Book Co., 1960).

[15]Wroe Alderson, "Large Scale Enterprise in Modern Competition," *Cost and Profit Outlook,* February, 1952, p. 1.

Chamberlin of "monopolistic competition" fame brushes aside the distinction between "rational" and "irrational" preferences—the latter supposedly concocted by "Madison Avenue":

> On the one hand, it may be said that if Palmolive were abolished, people might be no "worse off" after they had got used to using Lux and Lifebuoy instead. But on the other hand, it is equally true that if baseball were abolished and bull fights subsituted, people might be equally well or better satisfied after they were adjusted to the change, in which case their preferences for baseball should be classified as irrational. . . . There is a case, of course, for improving knowledge in all these matters, but no reason to think that improved knowledge would leave us with fewer or weaker preferences. . . . The alternative is not necessarily to assume that all preferences are rational, but only that they are on the same footing . . . .[16]

What is also overlooked is that advertising—a form of *impersonal* selling—is often a substitute for more costly forms of *personal* selling. Forgetting for the sake of the argument the social and aesthetic satisfactions involved in the process, it may well be that the crying of wares and the haggling over goods practiced in more primitive societies are relatively more onerous time-wise and cost-wise than the advertising expenditures of our days.

Alderson adds that economists make a false dichotomy between production costs and selling costs. Here again reigns a *marginalist view* of selling costs as something superimposed on production costs. Actually, both types of costs are complementary. What matters—to limit ourselves again to purely monetary terms—is the *total delivered cost* of an item, and not whether 10, 40, or 90% of that delivered cost represents selling costs.

As a matter of fact, Galbraith prefers to dismiss the argument about advertising on the grounds that "Madison Avenue" is the result of opulence, something we can afford, rather than the cause or condition of it. This opinion can hardly pass for a refutation of more orthodox views.

HOMO ETHICUS

Such propensity for paradox and disdain for proof mirror Galbraith's predilection for non-economic issues. Obvious delight at wagging a doctoral finger at Wicked Society reveals him as a moralist in economist's clothing.[17]

Ethical considerations are, of course, not out of place in an economic study. Convictions—implicit or explicit—regarding personal or societal ends certainly inform all economic analyses to a degree. Studies of wants

---

[16]Edward H. Chamberlin, "Product Heterogeneity and Public Policy," *American Economic Review*, Vol. 40 (May, 1950), pp. 88–89.

[17]Same reference as footnote 1, p. 147.

are not wanting in this respect if only because there is more than one way to look at besoins:

A *demand* is a want for which the consumer is prepared to pay a price; a *want* is any thing or service the consumer desires or seeks; and a *need* is any thing or service the consumer ought to have to keep alive and healthy or to keep efficient or simple because somebody (not necessarily himself) thinks he ought to have it. *Thus while demand is an economic conception, want is psychological, and need, partly at least, ethical.*[18] (Italics mine.)

John Kenneth Galbraith would agree; where other economists pose as morally neutral, he flaunts his code of ethics rather patently. Unlike Keynes who could smile on human foibles provided they contributed to employment and income, Galbraith (like Queen Victoria) is "not amused," GNP notwithstanding. Whereas Keynes thought that public works were good for the *economy*, one gathers from reading Galbraith that they are mostly good for the *soul*.

The economic concepts of marginalism and rationality, however, hardly seem appropriate for such a virtuous preoccupation with our wicked, wicked wants!

C. Consumer discontent

The next three articles deal with the broad area of consumerism. Congress has become increasingly consumer conscious and indeed, the 1968 Congress was labeled by some as the "Consumer Congress." The problems of the consumer are examined by Richard H. Holton from the standpoint of "imperfections in the state of information in consumer markets." He suggests conditions of information, which if met, result in consumer satisfaction.

Betty Furness, who was President Johnson's Special Assistant for Consumer Affairs, explains the role of government in consumer matters. She recognizes the need to accept responsibility in the marketplace, responsibility on the part of both government and business. In this connection, the reader will want to consider her thesis that government should be a "stimulator."

Louis L. Stern is concerned with the problems of protecting the consumer. He examines the reasons for the increased concern and questions if rising income and additional new products are responsible. "What rights do consumers have?" he asks. He concludes his article by suggesting a posture of "full disclosure" on the part of the marketer.

---

[18]P. Florence Sargant, *The Logic of British and American Industry* (Chapel Hill: The University of North Carolina Press, 1953), p. 98.

The three articles should provide the basis for a stimulating dialogue on consumer-government-marketing relationships. Certainly one of the pressing issues today is that of consumerism.

15. GOVERNMENT–CONSUMER INTEREST:
CONFLICTS AND PROSPECTS
(THE UNIVERSITY POINT OF VIEW)*

Richard H. Holton

One of the paradoxes in the area of business-government relations at present is that while income per capita is at an all-time high and still rising, we are nevertheless encountering a substantial new wave of interest in consumer problems. Significant consumer legislation has recently been passed, more is under consideration, and still more may be waiting in the wings. Apparently a rising standard of living will not serve to paper over some imperfections in consumer markets which must be bothering the public in general, or at least Congress in particular.

In the public discussions of these consumer problems it seems odd that the work done by those economists and market researchers who have studied consumer demand is of such limited value in considering the issues involved or in understanding the need for improvement. Economists' studies of consumer demand have focussed primarily on consumption functions, both in the aggregate and for particular products. Market researchers have understandably concentrated on the economic and behavioral factors determining the demand for particular products, especially on those factors which are relevant for decisions by the marketing manager. By and large, it is only because of an accidental by-product here and there that this work has shed any light on the public policy issues in the discussion of consumer legislation.

I would submit that our understanding of the issues involved and our ability to anticipate new problem areas on the consumer front are enhanced if we look on the problem as being primarily a matter of imperfections in the state of information in consumer markets, and of costs of improving on the state of information. These imperfections in information vary greatly among individual consumers, and (for any individual consumer) there is great variation among the many kinds of goods and services on the market. Thus in this case as in others, it is a mistake to talk about "the" consumer or "the" purchasing decision in any generalized way.

---
*From *Changing Marketing Systems,* American Marketing Association, December, 1967, pp. 15–17.

In one model of consumer markets, we can assume consumers have full and perfect knowledge of all the alternative means of disposing of their income, including saving it. With that assumption of full and perfect knowledge, consumer expenditures (to drop any concern about savings for the moment) would be allocated among the available goods and services in some particular way. If we drop the assumption of perfect knowledge, the consumer must then spend some time and effort if not money in improving his state of information about the prices and characteristics of the alternative goods and services available on the market. We can assume that if, in this case with imperfect state of information, the consumer spends his money in a different pattern than he would if information were complete and perfect, in a sense his welfare is still maximized. It is maximized because he must have made the decision to buy the things he did rather than to seek out more information. It was his judgment, then, that the marginal cost of additional search would have been greater than the increase in satisfaction deriving from a more informed allocation of his expenditures among the available goods and services.[1]

The pattern of discussion of consumer issues these days seems to suggest that the consumer feels that the market for consumer goods, insofar as he individually is concerned, is imperfect if he buys goods and services which he would not have bought had he "known better," i.e., if the state of information had been better. Consumers no doubt recognize that they cannot be expert buyers of everything, so they do not expect to have full and perfect information. But can we not say that consumers are probably most unhappy in those instances where there is the grossest distortion of their buying behavior because of incomplete and imperfect information?

The consumer's information about the prices and quality of the alternative goods and services he might buy comes from at least the following sources: (1) his own experience, (2) word-of-mouth from friends and acquaintances, (3) advertisements, (4) retail clerks, (5) labels and other point of purchase sources, (6) consumer publications such as *Consumer Reports*, (7) formal classes in school, especially high school home economics courses, and (8) certain government publications. Each of these sources is inadequate in one respect or another and we need not take time to inventory these. I would like to focus particularly, however, on one's own experience with a product or class of products as a means of providing information for the purchasing decision.

Typically the individual who is interested in fending off any additional consumer legislation argues that the consumer is protected quite adequately already by competition itself. If consumers find the product of any particular seller unsatisfactory, that seller cannot survive in the

---

[1] See George J. Stigler, "The Economics of Information," *Journal of Political Economy*, Vol. LXIX (June, 1961), pp. 213–25.

market place. As we all know, the rhetoric on this matter is often very colorful indeed. Rarely is it pointed out, however, that the kind of competitive system referred to assumes that consumers learn rather quickly which brands or which firms they prefer. In fact, however, much depends on the rapidity of this learning process.

To be more specific, the consumer may have gained quite satisfactory information from his own experience in the case of those items which he buys frequently, whose quality and performance characteristics are apparent either before he buys or after he has used the item once, and which exhibit a rate of technological change which is slow relative to the frequency of purchase.[2] Several of the items normally found in the supermarket might meet all three conditions for a particular consumer. But at the other end of the spectrum are a substantial number of goods and services which fail to meet one or more of these criteria. Automobile tires are a clear case in point. Here the frequency of purchase is low, the quality is not apparent (at least not in any very satisfactory way) even after the tire has been used and discarded, and the rate of technological change is fast relative to the frequency of purchase. But other items of this sort could be cited: automobiles themselves, appliances, some clothing items, casualty insurance, life insurance, medical care, appliance and automobile repair, and home maintenance services all come to mind. Funeral services can also be mentioned as an especially interesting case; I leave it to your own imagination to determine whether we can say that the quality of the service is apparent either before or after purchase and whether the rate of technological change is slow or fast relative to frequency of purchase. I trust we can all agree, however, that the frequency of purchase for the individual consumer is low.

In those cases where the three conditions are met, the process of learning can be rapid and quite complete. When the conditions are not met, the learning process may never be "complete" in any very satisfactory sense. The rate of technological change can so alter the body of information to be acquired by the prospective buyer that past information already learned will be obsolete.

The rebuttal to the above line of reasoning is in part that the consumer has access to the other sources of information as a means of improving the buying decision; he does not have to rely exclusively on his own experience with the item in question. If the consumer engages in sufficient search and research, he can acquire the information needed to make a wise choice in the market.

One of the problems is, however, that the consumer typically buys such a large number of individual items over the course of a year, let us

---

[2]See Joe S. Bain, *Industrial Organization* (New York: John Wiley & Sons, Inc., 1959), p. 214, for comments on the role of consumer information in product differentiation.

say, that he simply does not have time to become an expert buyer of everything. He faces an allocation problem, namely in the allocation of his own time. He must decide how to divide his time between the buying search and the many other ways in which he might spend his time. Within the time he allots for buying search, he must decide how to allocate time among the alternative goods and services. He might be able to become an expert consumer of a few things, but for many goods and services he will be quite amateurish, and understandably so.

The seller, meanwhile, is usually much more a specialist, either in one product or more commonly in a relatively narrow range of products. Furthermore, the seller's volume of any one line is likely to be great enough to support some time and talent devoted to shaping the consumer's choice. This leads to a kind of imbalance, so to speak, in the market for consumer goods: the part-time, amateur buyer faces a full-time, professional seller. This is a slightly exaggerated way to put it, but the image is reasonably accurate. It is little wonder, then, that the consumer often feels that he is at something of a disadvantage in dealing with the seller.

The low income consumer is often in a particularly weak position in the market place; for him, the imperfection of the sort we are concerned with here is likely to be especially great.[3] Because of his low income, the rate at which he is exposed to particular purchasing decisions is correspondingly low, so the learning process would be slower because of this fact alone. But in addition, he is less well educated and therefore less well equipped to seek out information in the first place or to understand it well if he were to find it. If he lives in a Watts, he may find that the retailers to which he has easy access geographically do not include those with the lowest prices. This lack of information, coupled with either a reluctance or an inability to articulate his questions about a product, makes him easy prey to the expert door-to-door salesman. Perhaps the brand loyalty of low income people, and their preference for major brands, reflect the lack of information and/or an ability to cope with that information. The major brand label is in effect a proxy for information.

If we see the so-called "consumer problem" as being especially difficult in those instances where frequency of purchase is low, performance characteristics are not apparent, and technological change is rapid, and if we recognize that the consumer must allocate his time in the search process, I would submit that we can understand a bit better a number of the developments in consumer affairs over the past few years. Tire standards have been developed; all three conditions permitting rapid and satisfactory learning by the consumer have been absent in the tire market

---

[3]See David Caplovitz, *The Poor Pay More: Consumer Practices of Low Income Families* (New York: Free Press of Glencoe, 1963).

without the standards. Truth-in-packaging was a matter of concern perhaps not because the supermarket items most affected were not high frequency items, with characteristics apparent and subject to slow technological change but rather because the consumer needed help in coping with the volume of information available to him in the supermarket. With several thousand items on the shelves in the modern supermarket, there is obviously a huge amount of information available on the labels. Those opposing truth-in-packaging as unnecessary because the consumer already was being provided with ample information missed this essential point. And those people pressing for truth-in-packaging on the grounds that the consumer needed more information likewise missed the point. Given the consumer's problem of allocating his time, what was needed was not so much more information as such but more information presented in a manner facilitating price and quality comparisons. The same statement might apply to the truth-in-lending debate.[4]

Automobile insurance and even life insurance is now coming in for considerable attention on the consumer front. Again, the learning process for the individual consumer is rather slow for reasons which are fairly apparent. Medical care and pharmaceuticals have also been drawing criticism. Jessica Mitford's book on the high cost of dying brought to light the imperfections in the market for funeral services. Recently, too, the ICC has investigated the movers of household goods; here again the individual consumer learns very slowly, largely because of low frequency of purchase of this particular service. The news releases of the Federal Trade Commission give ample testimony to the problems encountered in home maintenance markets; firms specializing in aluminum siding and aluminum storm doors and the like seem to appear with distressing frequency on the FTC docket—again, a low frequency purchase.

One possible explanation of the increased interest in consumer affairs might be that the problem of consumer information is probably getting worse rather than better over time, largely because the American consumer is increasingly well off. His rising income may mean that he can afford the luxury of not shopping carefully.[5] If this is so, the nature of competitive discipline in the market place might be shifting to emphasize expertise in advertising and merchandising, since people might now be less inclined to make careful price and quality comparisons. This shift is only conjectural, but it would seem to have a certain logic. One hears

---

[4]For a fuller discussion of the conflicting views of consumer markets, see Raymond A. Bauer and Stephen A. Greyser, "The Dialogue That Never Happens," *Harvard Business Review*, November-December, 1967, p. 2 ff.

[5]My colleague, Louis P. Bucklin, reports in a recent working paper, however, that well-to-do housewives are likely to visit more, rather than fewer, food stores than housewives from the lower income groups. This finding might or might not be inconsistent with the hypothesis that over time consumers have come to be less careful shoppers.

that the rate of technological change is increasing: if so, the consumer's knowledge once acquired becomes obsolete more quickly than in the past. Furthermore, an increasing portion of the technological change in consumer goods may be below the threshold of perception. Thus the consumer increasingly must rely not on his own perception of performance, but on what others, notably the advertisers, tell him about the performance of the item. If there is anything to this notion, we should reconsider the common complaint about automobiles and consumer durables in general, namely that "they don't make 'em the way they usta." Maybe that should be turned around to say that consumers don't buy the way they used to; when incomes were lower perhaps the price and quality shopping was more carefully done and perhaps the quality of the product was more apparent to the consumer at the time of purchase because the product was technologically simpler.

The business community is well advised to give more attention to the question of consumer discontent. We have no accurate measure of the extent and nature of consumer dissatisfaction. The number of complaints which consumers register with retailers and manufacturers is low as a percentage of total retail transactions. But how much do we all grumble about one kind of purchase or another without registering a complaint? This consumer grumbling may be the seedbed of discontent which brings forth an enthusiastic reception for the writings of a Vance Packard or a Ralph Nader, regardless of the validity of the points such authors make. We might well reflect further on the proposition that if there is an antibusiness attitude in the country, it might be based in substantial part on latent consumer dissatisfaction in the market place.

16. RESPONSIBILITY IN MARKETING*

Betty Furness

It is a pleasure to participate in this interplay of ideas on the government's role in marketing.

I have been talking a great deal lately with representatives of the marketing profession. Today, I have the opportunity to catch them at their source.

You are some of the people who taught marketers what they know about marketing. I have a prize opportunity to sell the sellers on consumer service.

Such a selling job is very much a part of the government's role in marketing.

*From a speech given at the American Marketing Association Conference, Washington, D.C., December, 1967. Reprinted in *Changing Marketing Systems*, American Marketing Association, December, 1967, pp. 25–27.

It has been said—and I believe rightly—that after a private difficulty becomes a public problem, it generally takes the government ten years to do something about it.

An important part of my job is to try to get industry to solve the problem itself during the ten years.

And believe me, the ten years is running out on a great many problems.

The President last year proposed the biggest consumer legislative program of any American Administration. He proposed twelve consumer bills and the 90th Congress enacted four of them in the first session.

You know that several of these bills—both those passed in the first session and those we hope to see passed in the second—deal directly or indirectly with marketing.

The meat inspection bill concerns you and probably will make the work of meat marketers easier.

The Truth-in-Lending bill will concern you as will the disclosure acts dealing with real estate sales, pension plans, welfare plans, and mutual funds.

Truth-in-Funds, Truth-in-Plans, Truth-in-Lands, Truth-in-Lending.

Truth, after all, is your product. You are responsible for transferring the product from the maker to the buyer and if it gets bruised in the process that'll be your responsibility, too.

Now, I'm not trying to imply that Diogenes is out looking for an honest marketer. He wouldn't need a lantern for that and I'm sure he would be quite comfortable with this group here.

But we do know, we all know, that deceptive products have been marketed well and good products have been marketed deceptively. It will happen again. It will continue happening, as a matter of fact, until the business involved banishes the practice, the consumer catches on, or the government steps in.

I do believe that the product, more often than the marketer himself, sets the pace of deceptive selling.

If the marketer has a good product, he has no need to conceal its faults.

If he has a bad one and is determined to sell it, he has no choice.

The responsibilities of the entire industry then fall on the marketer. If the rest of the assembly line had done its job and produced a good product, the marketer could sell his wares for what they are.

I'm here to tell you, gentlemen, that the government would rather have the assembly line pass just the product, not the buck. I should think we will be able to reach some accord on that matter.

I say this, because I believe the role of the government in marketing should be a walk-on at best. We act only when it is necessary and we don't want it to be necessary.

Unfortunately, that hope is not always realized and the government's responsibility to protect the citizenry must be met.

We must protect the citizenry against unfair business practices of any kind, deceptions of every sort. And we should not forget that business itself is counted in the citizenry. The deceptive products of one manufacturer must not be used as a cudgel against another.

But we want business to police its own affairs if it possibly can or conceivably will, both because we think that's the best way of doing it and because the government does have other things to do.

And so we would like the government's role in marketing to be more of a stimulant than a depressant.

So I'm here today:

To remind you that marketing has both a business interest and a social responsibility in consumer service.

I am here to urge you to be more diligent in passing the concept of responsibility and that awareness of the business interests on to the marketing profession. They are essential tools of the trade, I think.

The American consumer is becoming more and more articulate about his displeasure with the American marketplace.

He is causing the marketer trouble if he wants to, and he hasn't reached the end yet.

When he finds out he's not getting what he thinks he's getting, he may turn on the marketer or turn to the government.

When he finds out he isn't getting what he deserves, he can develop a good case of tart and tingling spite.

When he found out about the quantity of impure meat sold in this country every year, he became angry and articulate enough to change the situation. He will do that again if he is not adequately or honestly served.

Meat inspection bills, you remember, have been going up and down Capitol Hill for years with very little hope of passage.

The expectations of many of Washington's learned observers was that 1967 was a year like all years; there would be no meat legislation.

And, then, the consumer aroused by the press let Congress know what he wanted. The Congress, in its wisdom, took his ire seriously and we got the most progressive meat law since 1907.

That, gentlemen, can happen again and the government will have to act. It applies to other products as well as meat.

The consumer is not going to settle for confusion. When he expects one thing and gets another, it's just possible he will sit down and write his congressman.

If enough of his fellow consumers follow suit, we will have more legislation.

Don't you think it would be better for the seller to be sure he's selling what he says he is than for the government to furnish that assurance? I think so.

I think the marketing profession has a very basic responsibility here, both to the consumer and to the marketplace itself.

I think the consumer should be told by his marketer what's actually in the box he buys.

It may be revolutionary to suggest that the manufacturer or the marketer give the consumer the basic facts about the design-life of a product. But I believe it's his due.

Why shouldn't the housewife know that there are "X" number of hours of service in her washing machine or that the life expectancy of a toaster falls short of a golden wedding anniversary?

He should be told what the design-life of a product is.

He should be told what the warranty or guaranty on that product really means. Does it cover the design-life of the product, or merely a small part of it?

This, I think, is a very important matter to consider.

The manufacturer knows, and the marketer knows, what the design life of their product is. Shouldn't the consumer also know?

Wouldn't that make him a more satisfied and regular customer?

Doesn't he have a right to know?

The President considers the right to know one of the four basic consumer rights and to a very great degree, the consumer must depend upon the marketer to fulfill that right.

The right to know must include the whole broad area of consumer education.

By consumer education, I do not mean home economics alone; though that's a valuable part of it.

I mean a whole curriculum in and out of school. Not just cooking and sewing or household hints. Not just supermarket shopping habits. Not just training of housewives.

I'm talking about teaching all consumers—men, women and youths alike—what they need to know about the American marketplace and its products, whether diapers or dollars.

The consumer must know not only what he's buying and how long it will last, he should be taught how to use it and use it effectively.

He should be taught how to buy wisely for it is to the benefit of business as well as the consumer.

The marketing profession created the galloping American economy. Through your creativity, your able research, your skillful mastery of the American system of communication, you stimulated this country into the greatest economy in history.

I know you can turn all those skills toward telling the consumer what he should know about the marketplace you built.

Do you not have a social responsibility to do that?

Consumer education is a two-track system.

Business must first be educated toward the consumer and then the consumer toward the product.

I think we are now getting underway along both of these tracks.

I am pleased to see that the AMA is taking such an interest in this. It is predicted that at least 40 of your 50 chapters "will have programs in the general areas of social responsibility and public involvement" this year.

That's good because you are the experts in this field. You are the people who teach the marketers and provide them with the research that keeps them going.

Your influence on the marketplace is great and your pride of profession is no doubt the same.

I urge you to take that pride and that influence to prevent the American consumer from being consumed. I urge you to direct your attention particularly toward the consumer who is poor.

The 32.7 million American consumers at the bottom of the income scale are seldom interviewed by market researchers. Yet they buy food and clothing and many other things.

This market deserves closer attention for business and humanitarian reasons.

Industry, educational institutions and the government are making a cooperative attack on the crippling causes of poverty.

They are providing training and job opportunities for the unemployed in poverty areas. They are encouraging the development and improvement of small neighborhood businesses.

The poor will buy more of everything in the future if we can help them rise above the poverty line. But now is the time to get the facts about this non-affluent market.

What do the economically deprived buy?

What do they need and want?

We know too little about what is *really* needed in our urban ghettos and rural shanty towns.

Across-the-board research in these areas could uncover new avenues of opportunity for both consumers and business.

This calls for new and specialized techniques. Questionnaires and methods of communication developed by middle-class people for middle-class consumers won't work for poor consumers.

Many of you are college and university marketing professors. Can't more of this kind of research be fitted into business school programs for undergraduates? For candidates for higher degrees?

Actually, we need continuing research in *every* area of the American consumer market. We need to keep up with the attitudes and opinions of 200 million consumers—some who are poor, some rich, some young, others old.

Business is never static. Neither are consumers.

Business must know its consumers and must serve them.

Since the marketer is the man between business and the consumer it must be through him that they know each other.

I come here, then, to act out the government's role as stimulator:

Urging better understanding of the consumer.

Urging better service to the consumer.

Urging more communication with the consumer.

I think these must be the roles of us all.

17. CONSUMER PROTECTION VIA INCREASED INFORMATION*

Louis L. Stern

What about consumer protection?

The great concern of businessmen about recent demands for consumer protection is indicated by the establishment of: (1) a consumer-information service by the National Association of Manufacturers, known as Techniques in Product Selection (TIPS); and (2) a program of cooperation between the Association of Better Business Bureaus and federal departments and agencies that affect consumer-business relationships.

Although the NAM and ABBB programs may be public-relations efforts to modify demands for consumer protection, nevertheless their creation reflects businessmen's concern that, "Unless business moves to organize some communication apparatus, it will soon be confronted with a benevolent, bureaucratic structure that will take over such functions."[1]

Nor is such concern unfounded. Consider recent proposals to establish an Office or Department of Consumers, and for the federal government to engage in "Consumers Union" types of product evaluation and reporting. Is it madness to speculate that the precedents set by the Drug Amendments of 1962 (1962) and the "fair labeling and packaging" bill might lead to proposals for a "fair advertising" law?

Probably no other Congress ever faced as many consumer-protection proposals as the 89th. Even the U.S. Supreme Court showed an interest in consumer protection, as evidenced by its handling of the *Rapid Shave* case.[2]

*From *Journal of Marketing*, Vol. 31 (April, 1967), pp. 48–52.

[1] "GF's Cleaves Calls for Food Industry Consumer Information Unit," *Advertising Age*, Vol. 36 (April 19, 1965), p. 16.

[2] *Colgate Palmolive Co.* v. *FTC*, 85 S. Ct. 1035.

Other signs of increasing government interest in consumer protection include:

1. Completion by Congress, the Food and Drug Administration, the National Commission on Food Marketing, and the Consumer Advisory Council of voluminous reports relating to consumer protection.

2. Establishment of a special division within the U.S. Department of Agriculture to handle the Department's labeling programs.

3. Establishment by the Office of Economic Opportunity of an experimental program of consumer education.

4. Within the Federal Trade Commission, setting up of a new office of federal-state cooperation; new studies of consumer-goods marketing practices; and new trade-regulation guides and rules pertaining to the marketing of consumer goods.

But perhaps the best indication of the great amount of government interest in consumer protection is the statement of Charles Sweeny, Chief of the FTC's Bureau of Deceptive Practices: "The present Commission is more deeply determined to combat consumer deception than any Commission I have known in my 30 years of service."[3]

Why is there so much interest in consumer protection?

One reason is that rising incomes and a cornucopia of new products have multiplied the number, value, and variety of consumers' market transactions. Therefore, there are far more opportunities for consumer deception than ever before. Furthermore, the mounting variety of consumer products is increasing the competitiveness of our economic system. In turn, this may be leading to a deterioration of business ethics, thus giving rise to added interest in consumer protection.

Yet it is not at all clear that deception in the marketplace has, in fact, increased. What is clear is that the history of the United States is a record of accumulated social and technological efforts to protect the individual from adversity of every sort. The drive for consumer protection may be viewed as simply a continuation of those efforts.

THE NEED FOR PRODUCT INFORMATION

Do consumers have a right to be informed, as distinct from a right not to be deceived?

Our economic system is based on the belief that free and intelligent decisions in the marketplace, rather than by government fiat, will produce the most efficient allocation of resources toward the achievement of private and social goals. To exercise free and intelligent choices in the marketplace, consumers must have access to terms of sale and product information.

---

[3]"Druggist May Be Liable for Brand Copy in His Ads," *Advertising Age*, Vol. 36 (June 7, 1965), pp. 1 and 135, at p. 1.

However, it is likely that the loss of personal relationships in the marketplace has reduced both the availability and the reliability of product information.

A second factor contributing to the problem is the rising level of technology. New materials, new operating principles, new functions, new designs, and new packaging have increased the difficulty of choosing one product or brand over another. The growing number of synthetic textiles and textile mixtures with varying prices and performance characteristics amply illustrates this situation.

Because of their usually greater complexity, durable products may reflect more advances in technology than nondurable products. Hence, the problem of adequacy and comprehension of product-performance information may be compounded in the case of durable goods. Furthermore, consumers are less capable of personally evaluating durable products because the long life and varied conditions under which these products are used cloud post-purchase brand comparisons. To make matters even more difficult, the reports of such organizations as *Consumers Union* are quickly rendered obsolete by model changes or model number changes.

A third factor contributing to the problem of adequacy of product information is the language of advertising. From Martineau to Weir, many advertisers and copywriters have preached the sermon of *image*.

In the words of Pierre Martineau, "It is generally insufficient to convince a person on intellectual grounds. His feelings must be involved. And this we achieve by affective or esthetic suggestion and imagery, by the meanings behind the words and pictures."[4]

Consider also the "heretical" words of William D. Tyler, *Advertising Age* columnist: "Most advertising down the years has done little more than say sweet nothings about a product . . . It has contained the least information, the fewest facts, of almost anything ever written. We have relied mainly on adjectives, on charm, on manner of presentation, coupled with unspecific, unsupported claims of superiority."[5]

The question is how greater disclosure of product and terms-of-sale information can be achieved. The difficulties of attempting to provide greater information to consumers are substantial. The problem of communicating technical information to a nontechnical audience, the time and space limitations of the vehicle of communication, and the cost of the time and space used must all be taken into account.

On the other hand, there is the question of *methods*. Will the methods of information be voluntary or compulsory? Will they involve standards, labeling requirements, consumer-advisory services, consumer-education programs, or some combination of these?

---

[4]Pierre Martineau, *Motivation in Advertising* (New York: McGraw-Hill Book Co., 1957), p. 187.

[5]William D. Tyler, "Is Competitive Comparison Really Bad in Advertising? Reform With Care," *Advertising Age*, Vol. 37 (March 14, 1966), pp. 61–62, at p. 61.

VOLUNTARY DISCLOSURE

Private industry has made great strides in attempting to provide information to consumers and to forestall government activity. Consider the following:

1. Formation over the years of codes of ethics by various associations in the packaging field.

2. Adoption by the 50th National Conference on Weights and Measures (June, 1965) of a standard for conspicuous labeling, as an amendment to the Model State Regulation Pertaining to Packages. (The new standard defines officially and nationally for the first time what constitutes a "clear and conspicuous" statement of net contents on package labels.)

3. Adoption by the American Standards Association, the National Bureau of Standards, and many other groups of standards for the size, shape, or performance ratings (such as BTU output) of innumerable products and containers.

GOVERNMENT INTERVENTION

Of course, government regulations are sometimes unduly rigid, and create legal hazards for even the conscientious corporate citizen. (For example, the present standard of identity for butter was formulated at the turn of the century and does not permit the addition of emulsifiers or preservatives to butter, an unconscionable shackle to the butter industry's competition with margarine. Neither does it provide for the addition of vitamins to butter or the continuous-process method of manufacturing butter, both of which are common today.) Nevertheless, even more regulations probably are in prospect.

TERMS OF SALE

Aside from regulations pertaining to safety or gross misrepresentation, the greatest need for consumer protection is in regard to clarity of terms of sale. The least restrictive measure would require merely a statement of net contents on the package. However, mere knowledge of the weight or quantity of a product is an inadequate basis for intelligent choice; and if the statement of net contents is inconspicuous or the shopper unobservant, not even that much information will be known.

A further level of protection would be to provide for standardization of weights and quantities in which a consumer product may be distributed for retail sale. State laws already provide for standard package sizes for a few staple food products such as bread, butter, margarine, milk, cream, and flour.

Standardization of weights and quantities would provide informational gains to consumers. It would enable many shoppers to compare the price of equivalent amounts of alternative brands. In contrast, indications of price per ounce carried out to several decimal places would be no real improvement, and actually might distract consumers from making price comparisons of total amounts.

Standardization of weights and quantities would also call attention to price increases, which are otherwise hidden from some consumers in the form of a reduction in quantity.

It would be desirable, therefore, to establish standard weights or quantities in which selected consumer goods might be distributed. Provision for variations from these standards in multiples of 25 percent of the standard amounts would probably satisfy most consumer preferences for size of unit of purchase.

Establishment of standard weights and quantities might reduce the number of opportunities for using one size and style of container for packaging a variety of products as soup, cracker, and cereal companies now do. Considerable expense would also be involved in adjusting packaging machinery to the new weight or quantity standards. Nevertheless, the long-run advantages to consumers probably would exceed these disadvantages.

A still higher level of restriction, to regulate container sizes and shapes, is not only unnecessary but contrary to consumers' interests. It would severely inhibit package innovation. However, the International Organization for Standardization, whose standards may acquire the effect of law in over 50 member nations, has launched a program to develop retail package size standards that would affect *all* consumer products. Its program could, within a few years, force U.S. manufacturers to adopt similar standards for export purposes.

STANDARDS AND GRADE-LABELING

Compulsory standards of minimum quality or performance can be a useful form of consumer protection where health and safety is involved. Minimum standards can also serve to prevent consumers from being sold grossly inferior products.

Product standards usually impose minimum product requirements. On the other hand, grade-labeling involves an attempt to communicate in one or more symbols the relative quality of a product as influenced by a variety of characteristics.

Because grade-labeling requires a high degree of agreement as to what constitutes the best combination of product characteristics, its utility is limited to simple products having few attributes. Yet these products tend to be those which consumers are most capable of evaluating themselves. And even for these products, the whirlwind pace of product and package innovation occurring today would present an enormous grade-labeling task.

Furthermore, the effects of grade-labeling upon product research and innovation must also be considered. Grade-labeling would reduce product differentiation and thereby tend to promote price competition. As a result, smaller marketing margins would yield less research-and-development revenues.

CONSUMER ADVISORY SERVICES

As proposed by Donald Turner, Chief of the U.S. Justice Department's Antitrust Division, another means of communicating more information to consumers would be for the federal government to evaluate products and publish its evaluations, or to subsidize organizations such as Consumers Union.[6] Such publications as *Consumers Bulletin* or *Consumer Reports* provide a source of clear and continuing product information; and their evaluations can be both capsulized and detailed.

On the other hand, their value is limited by their remoteness from the point of purchase. A more serious disadvantage, were they to achieve widespread consumer influence, would be the power they would come to possess over the economic fate of individual companies. If the majority of consumers followed their brand recommendations, producers of lower-rated brands would be strongly induced to imitate the preferred brand as closely as possible.

Accordingly, product differentiation might be expected to decrease, and this would be to consumers' disadvantage. Simultaneously, a loss of product differentiation might lead to a reduction in the number of producers, another undesirable effect.

FULL DISCLOSURE

"Full disclosure" has a variety of implications. Most commonly, it is assumed to imply disclosure of the dangerous nature of a product. Such laws as the Flammable Fabrics Act (1953), the Hazardous Substances Labeling Act (1960), the Drug Amendments of 1962 (1962), and the Cigarette Labeling Act (1965) already impose this level of meaning.

A second level of meaning would compel disclosure of component ingredients, net contents, and other terms-of-sale information, such as interest and related charges. Laws such as the Food, Drug and Cosmetics Act (1968), the Wool Products Labeling Act (1939), the Fur Products Labeling Act (1951), the Textile Fiber Products Identification Act (1958), and the Automobile Information Disclosure Act (1958) are intended to provide legislative mandate for this type of disclosure. Disclosure of component ingredients is primarily useful in relation to determining the healthfulness, safety, value, or performance of a prod-

---

[6]"Anti-Trust Chief Urges Alternative to Advertising," *Advertising Age,* Vol. 37 (June 6, 1966), pp. 1 and 147–48, at p. 147.

uct. Over and above this, compulsion of such disclosure might be interpreted as protection for and responsiveness to the existence of individual preferences for certain products.

The next higher level of disclosure is the revelation of a product's performance characteristics. To some extent this level of disclosure is implemented voluntarily by manufacturers of above-average quality products who employ rational selling appeals. Horsepower ratings, BTU ratings, and lumber ratings are familiar voluntary disclosures by manufacturers and distributors of performance characteristics. But unfortunately, many voluntary performance descriptions are meaningless or unreliable and sometimes refer to inputs rather than outputs.

Most manufacturers prefer to avoid direct performance statements in favor of evocative expressions or episodes. This is especially likely to be the case where no substantial differences in performance exist among rival brands, because for these products disclosure of meaningful performance information would tend to reduce the apparent differentiation among brands.

The Drug Amendments of 1962 (1962), although passed in the wake of the thalidomide scare and applying to a narrow and emotionally-charged area of consumption, provide a legislative precedent for regulatory agency concern with product performance *even where health or safety are not involved*. Witness the FDA's attempt to require vitamins to be labeled with the statement: ". . . Except for persons with special medical needs, there is no scientific basis for recommending routine use of dietary supplements." A likely outcome of regulations pertaining to *nonperformance* would be regulations pertaining to *degrees* of performance.

As to the question of consumers' abilities to understand performance information, this problem will diminish over time in response to rising levels of education, the enormous capacity of consumers to learn informally, the effectiveness of media in informing consumers, and, most importantly, the challenge to learn presented by the availability of such information.

A still higher level of disclosure pertains to potentially derogatory information unrelated to health, safety, terms of sale, or performance of a product—illustrated by the FTC requirement of disclosure, where applicable, of the foreign origin of a product or component part. Conceivably, the FTC requirement could be extended to include disclosure, where applicable, of ratings by such groups as Consumers Union, production by companies not subscribing to voluntary codes of advertising practice, or production by nonunionized labor, etc.

The U.S. Supreme Court decision pertaining to disclosure of use of television mockups falls within this category of compulsory disclosure.[7]

---
[7]Same reference as footnote 2.

The Court took the extreme position that not only misrepresentations, but also deceptive presentations of valid claims, even if necessary to compensate for the technical deficiencies of communications media, are illegal.

IMPLEMENTATION

Note especially that the FTC may be capable of expanding its disclosure requirements without the aid of new legislation. FTC Commissioner Everette MacIntyre has been quite explicit on this matter.[8]

Furthermore, the position taken by the Commission is this: "The question . . . is not whether the Commission may declare substantive standards and principles, for it plainly may and must. The question is whether the Commission may . . . promulgate them only in the course of adjudication."[9]

In the Commission's opinion, it is also free to promulgate them in formal rule-making proceedings.

The issue is whether consumers have expectations of receiving some standard of product performance, say, average for that industry's product. If they do, then failure to disclose the fact that a particular brand is below that standard of expectation would appear to be deceptive. If, in addition, the performance factor in question is material to the consumer's purchase decision, its nondisclosure violates the FTC Act.

The principle that nondisclosure of material information constitutes a misrepresentation is well established in law.[10] Moreover, the U.S. Supreme Court made abundantly clear in the *Rapid Shave* case that reviewing courts should ordinarily accept the Commission's judgment as to what constitutes deception.[11] ". . . When the Commission finds deception it is also authorized, within the bounds of reason, to infer that the deception will constitute a material factor in a purchaser's decision to buy."[12] Accordingly, the opportunity for the FTC to widen its requirements for full disclosure is clear.

The selection of what additional disclosures should be required is admittedly a difficult administrative decision, particularly so the more complex the product involved.

Nevertheless, a reasonable compromise could be reached whereby certain information would have to be provided with the product, and whereby other, more extensive, information would have to be made readily available on request. Nothing in this proposal would prevent

[8]*The Packaging-Labeling Controls Bill* (Washington, D.C.: Chamber of Commerce of the United States, 1965), p. 14.

[9]Same reference as footnote 8, at p. 18.

[10]*P. Lorillard Co.* v. *FTC,* 186 F2d 52; *Raladam Co.* v. *FTC,* 283 U. S. 643. But see also *Alberty* v. *FTC,* 182 F2d 36, Certiorari denied, 340 U.S. 818.

[11]Same reference as footnote 2 at p. 1043.

[12]Same reference as footnote 2 at p. 1046.

a manufacturer from extolling additional characteristics of his products. Nor does this proposal imply that compulsory disclosures should be included in advertising or in promotion.

In short, this proposal would improve the functioning of the marketplace by increasing the amount of information therein. It would enable consumers to choose products rationally *if* they wished to do so.

IN CONCLUSION

The consumer-protection movement is definitely in the ascendancy. The issue is not whether consumers will be better protected, but what form the protection will take.

Better and more reliable product and terms-of-sale information on package labels is perhaps the most economical and least restrictive type of consumer protection. Moreover, *full disclosure* might help to dissuade current demands for additional restrictions on advertising.

D. Marketing research

Dik Warren Twedt explains the need for a code of ethics in marketing research. Though researchers generally have enjoyed a fine reputation, Twedt indicates some of the problem areas. The reader should examine the AMA Code carefully, noting deficiencies from the standpoints of the researcher, the user of research results and others intimately concerned with reputable marketing research.

18. WHY A MARKETING RESEARCH CODE OF ETHICS?*

Dik Warren Twedt

Marketing research is still enough of an art so that it is unlikely that any two practitioners, faced with the same problem, would proceed exactly alike. But the general principles of scientific method applied to marketing problems are quite well understood and practiced.

The stage has been reached where the term "marketing research" has certain specific connotations of method, technique, interpretation, and use and a fairly well defined set of professional standards. But deviation from these standards by marginal operators now has become a source of

---

*Journal of Marketing, October, 1963, pp. 48–50.

increasing concern to those who depend upon marketing research as a vital source of dependable information about the market.

The "interviewer" who conducts a "survey" that turns into a sales pitch is not a new phenomenon. In 1961, however, the attention of the American Marketing Association was drawn to the fact that large and highly respected business organizations were making use of the marketing research approach in order to disguise sales purposes. Personal and telephone interviews were being made under circumstances that could easily have led many respondents to assume that they were participating in a legitimate survey. In some cases, the real purpose of the interview was to sell books or magazines; and in others, the purpose was to obtain qualified leads for follow-up by salesmen.

It became clear to the Association's Committee on Standards that the time had come to establish a code of ethical conduct for marketing research. Without such a code, and general adherence to it, it seemed likely that marketing research abuses would soon lead to measurable loss of consumer cooperation with interviewers, and eventually to substantial deterioration of the marketing research function.

The Standards Committee, working closely with the AMA Central Office and its legal counsel, set up four major guideposts as it proceeded toward a recommended code:

1. It is appropriate that the American Marketing Association assume leadership in setting standards of marketing research, in accordance with the Association's prime directive—the advancement of science in marketing. Science advances only through truth, never through deception.
2. The public must be protected against marketing research abuses—both because the public has an inherent right to expect fair play, and because of a desire to maintain public confidence in procedures that are the principal sources of marketing information.
3. Once a standard of ethical conduct has been established, it will be helpful to those research practitioners who may have been quite capable of setting high standards for themselves, but who found that they were occasionally under pressure from employers or customers to deviate from these standards. Hopefully too, the code will discourage such reasoning as, "If I don't do it this way, somebody else will."
4. If marketing research fails to "keep its own house in order," it is probable that restrictive legislation will be enacted that could greatly hamper researchers in providing management with reliable data on which to base marketing decisions.

At the June, 1962, meeting of the American Marketing Association in Cincinnati, the Standards Committee made its formal recommendation to the Board of Directors to adopt the code as submitted. The Board voted to submit the code to the Association membership for ratification, and it was approved by a 98% majority of those voting.

A common complaint of the 2% who did not approve was that the code did not specify adequate penalties for infraction of its provisions. However, legal counsel has made it clear that the Association cannot set penalties—it can only establish minimum standards of professional conduct for its members. The "policing" of deviations from acceptable standards is legally the responsibility of such governmental bodies as the Federal Trade Commission.

The code also makes specific provision for its revision, "in an effort to reflect changes in the conditions governing the ethical practices of marketing research."

The importance of the present code to future marketing practice is clear. Efficient marketing requires information from consumers. In a nation of over 185 million people, the most appropriate way to obtain this information is through professional marketing research. It behooves all of us who work in this area to keep faith with the public, and thus ensure that we will be permitted to continue our contribution to the marketing process.

THE MARKETING RESEARCH CODE

Following is the complete Marketing Research Code of Ethics:

The American Marketing Association, in furtherance of its central objective of the advancement of science in marketing and in recognition of its obligation to the public, has established these principles of ethical practice of marketing research for the guidance of its members. In an increasingly complex society, marketing management is more and more dependent upon marketing information intelligently and systematically obtained. The consumer is the source of much of this information. Seeking the cooperation of the consumer in the development of information, marketing management must acknowledge its obligation to protect the public from misrepresentation and exploitation under the guise of research.

Similarly the research practitioner has an obligation to the discipline he practices and to those who provide support for his practice—an obligation to adhere to basic and commonly accepted standards of scientific investigation as they apply to the domain of marketing research.

It is the intent of this code to define ethical standards required of marketing research in satisfying these obligations.

Adherence to this code will assure the users of marketing research that the research was done in accordance with acceptable ethical practices. Those engaged in research will find in this code an affirmation of sound and honest basic principles which have developed over the years as the profession has grown. The field interviewers who are the point of contact between the profession and the consumer will also find guidance in fulfilling their vitally important role.

FOR RESEARCH USERS, PRACTITIONERS, AND INTERVIEWERS

1. No individual or organization will undertake any activity which is directly or indirectly represented to be marketing research, but which has as its real purpose the attempted sale of merchandise or services to some or all of the respondents interviewed in the course of the research.

2. If a respondent has been led to believe, directly or indirectly, that he is participating in a marketing research survey and that his anonymity will be protected, his name shall not be made known to anyone outside the research organization or research department, or used for other than research purposes.

FOR RESEARCH PRACTITIONERS

1. There will be no intentional or deliberate misrepresentation of research methods or results. An adequate description of methods employed will be made available upon request to the sponsor of the research. Evidence that field work has been completed according to specifications will, upon request, be made available to buyers of research.

2. The identity of the survey sponsor and/or the ultimate client for whom a survey is being done will be held in confidence at all times, unless this identity is to be revealed as part of the research design. Research information shall be held in confidence by the research organization or department and not used for personal gain or made available to any outside party unless the client specifically authorizes such release.

3. A research organization shall not undertake marketing studies for competitive clients when such studies would jeopardize the confidential nature of client-agency relationships.

FOR USERS OF MARKETING RESEARCH

1. A user of research shall not knowingly disseminate conclusions from a given research project or service that are inconsistent with or not warranted by the data.

2. To the extent that there is involved in a research project a unique design involving techniques, approaches or concepts not commonly available to research practitioners, the prospective user of research shall not solicit such a design from one practitioner and deliver it to another for execution without the approval of the design originator.

FOR FIELD INTERVIEWERS

1. Research assignments and materials received, as well as informa-

tion obtained from respondents, shall be held in confidence by the interviewer and revealed to no one except the research organization conducting the marketing study.

2. No information gained through a marketing research activity shall be used directly or indirectly, for the personal gain or advantage of the interviewer.

3. Interviews shall be conducted in strict accordance with specifications and instructions received.

4. An interviewer shall not carry out two or more interviewing assignments simultaneously unless authorized by all contractors or employers concerned.

Members of the American Marketing Association will be expected to conduct themselves in accordance with the provisions of this Code in all of their marketing research activities.

* * * *

The Code was approved by the Marketing Research Standards Committee of the American Marketing Association:

Chairman: Nancy C. Cooley, *President, National Certified Interviews, Inc.*

Richard Baxter, *Cunningham & Walsh*
James C. Becknell, *E. I du Pont de Nemours & Co., Inc.*
Donald A. Chase, *Kimberly-Clark Corporation*
Blaine Cook, *Lincoln-Mercury Division, Ford Motor Company*
Lester Frankel, *Audits & Surveys, Inc.*
Seymour Marshak, *Ford Motor Company*
Kimball Nedved, *S. C. Johnson & Son, Inc.*
A. C. Nielsen, Jr., *A. C. Nielsen Company*
Peter G. Peterson, *Bell & Howell Company*

E. Complex confrontations

The final two readings in Part III relate social issues to the confrontations in marketing. Lawrence G. Lavengood indicates the need for business values to enjoy social respect if our market system is to survive. How does American society attempt to transmit social values to business policy? How does American business respond? Are there adequate alternatives to law?

A number of the areas of confrontation in marketing have been set forth in this, the "Battleground," section. The final reading in Part III, by W. Arthur Cullman, raises the basic question of conflicts among our social norms. What is the proper way to define social responsibility on the part of the marketer? Different viewpoints (stockholders, employees, officers, researchers, consumers, etc.) clearly exist when social issues such as civil rights are raised. Relating responsibility to each segment of the public should not be so oversimplified.

19. THE LAW AND THE PROPHETS: AN INTELLIGENT BUSINESSMAN'S GUIDE TO RIGHTEOUSNESS*

Lawrence G. Lavengood

Since a professed priority of business leaders is to make American college students excited about modern business, a prize of some sort should go this year to the Dow Chemical Company. A Dow man recruiting at one of the better universities last winter invariably brought on several resolute job interviews—and an instant flood of moral philosophy. It is no fault of Dow's that on the whole the exercises in moral philosophy turned out to be less beneficial than the job interviews.

At my university the rusty state of moral discourse was exposed in two statements that condensed the thought of the day. An inflamed undergraduate, who obviously regarded Dow as the current equivalent of a press gang, declared that the speeches and demonstrations were not, after all, directed at the napalm manufacturer. "Why should they be?" he shouted. "Dow is in business to make money; it can't make a moral judgment." A graduate business student later added the commentary that the first student was correct at least in insisting that organizations cannot make moral judgments, because organizations as such do not make judgments of any kind. Men make them. Moral decisions and right conduct proceed, therefore, only from the conscience of individual persons.

No one rose at the time to point to the appalling fact that in a business society where large corporations abound, money-making and organizations had been excluded virtually by definition from the center of ethical inquiry. Poor Dow! There it stood, corporately unflinching— only to be barred from its own moral judgment day by clumsy philosophy. Many changes, to be sure, were rung that day on the theme of "conscience" and many more on that summary of abominations called "the system," but an interested listener never heard them connect conceptually. Conscience floated off to follow the sun, leaving the world to darkness and "the system"—an example of other-worldliness that

*From *Marketing and the New Science of Planning*, American Marketing Association, August, 1968, pp. 547–51.

might be amusing in this age of so-called secularity were it not so ominously irrelevant.

THEMES AND PROPOSITIONS

"Dow Day" at Northwestern, however, merely provides a vivid incidental backdrop for the burden of this paper, which aims at bringing value and policy (or "conscience" and "the system") into some useful relationship. The view is broad and rather lofty, attracting attention to the moral environment of marketing planning and other business functions. The line of discussion will be pragmatic, directed to a practical compound question:

In the social-historical experience of modern America how have changing social values and business policy been brought together, and have ethical standards and moral conduct been altered as a result?

The propriety of putting the matter this way is confirmed by respectable scholars in ethics and in politics. An answer from social-historical experience is something else. Hardly any of the influential work in behavioral studies or moral philosophy plumps exactly for the answer that will be advanced here. But, then, the study of how social value and business policy do or may connect to form an ethic suitable to a mature industrial environment is a newly opened field, and all positions in it are extremely tentative. My own research and reflection suggest a hypothesis from modern experience which involves elaboration of the following propositions:

1. Business corporations and the business system exert an influence of primary social significance in forming *and changing* the operational ethical standards, the conduct, and ultimately the conscience of persons. Corporations and business do this not as aggregations of autonomous individuals or units, but as social systems or institutions. Values are learned from policy.
2. The socially most effective force for change in the ethical direction of business policy has been the law (here considered as any serious, sustained expression of *public* policy). Values and morals are being legislated. Indeed, we legislate very little else.
3. Economic value is the central value through which public policy impinges on business morals. This is not to say that market calculation forms the fixed point around which all other values are subordinated in society, or even in business organizations. It is to say, however, that American business is a market institution, and that in practice it is usually through economic value that other social values have been asserted in business. Society changes the ethical direction of business by bending the market.

4. Much ethically influential market manipulation amounts to redefining through law the relationship between management and its constituencies. This being so, the essence of moral decency in modern business probably is not in the word "ethical," but in the ancient meaning of "righteousness."

5. Though it is possible to distinguish between genuine and expedient adherents to a "righteous" policy, when the two kinds of moral agents are observed from the social angle of vision (that is, from the viewpoint of the law), an "expedient" adherent seems to do as much good as a "genuine" one. The social effectiveness of the genuine, moreover, often seems dependent on the extent of expedient compliance. In short, the social utility of hypocrisy may be badly underrated.

THE PROPOSITIONS ELABORATED

This way of rendering the record admittedly has a perverse ring to it. Literature on the social role of modern management commonly does not conclude with propositions like these. Yet much of the literature points to these conclusions, even if it does not quite reach them. Something may be gained, therefore, by trying to press analysis and experience into sharper contact in the course of elucidating the five propositions stated above.

SYSTEMS AND ETHICAL STANDARDS

The opening assertion that business firms teach conduct and propagate social values rests on an arrangement of evidence from history, the psychology of learning, and management science. Each discipline today testifies, in its own rhetoric, that the system, be it a firm or a society, is not an abstraction, nor do an individual's personal and social ethics really operate as an autonomous moral force. Men's values and perceptions of themselves evolve in engagement with purposive organizations as well as with the broader social network of institutionalized rules, relations, rewards, and penalties. The human heart is not the independent variable that the old-time individualistic ethic likes to over-represent as the ultimate, sovereign, and only reliable seat of local government.

Scientific management missed the point at first. Its system concept originally showed up as entirely mechanistic, mostly, one supposes, because its early advancement by Frederick W. Taylor concerned efficient organization for mass production of standardized physical goods. Advocates of scientific management represented it as a regimentation not of men, but of time and kinetic units. Personality and most other intangible values in the main were outside the system, presumably as uninfluenced by it as they were uninfluential within it.

Social historians and other investigators long contested the notion that modern industrial organization is an amoral, impersonal abstraction. As they see it the early system concept, in denying emphasis to the influence of organization on men's lives, amounted to an intolerably narrow conceit of engineers. Latterly, organization theories and systems models have come to encompass far more than the manufacturing function; they have broadened their assumption about human nature in its work relationships; consequently they have moved a good way toward harmony with the old social critics of scientific management.

This is not to obscure the fact that organization theory owes a debt to Taylor and his disciples. Nor is it to imply that current theories and models are not still heavily mechanistic, probably in part because, as Neil Chamberlain points out, "However one may try to disguise the fact, the business firm as a system . . . attempts to become as machinelike as possible in the conduct of its everyday operation."[1] Yet, one distinction of contemporary thought is its appreciation of what could be called an organic conception of a system. Most significant for social ethics is the organic view that an organization's "strategy set" becomes a living, limiting constellation of pressures on personalities and social groups within the work organization.[2] Strategy becomes, in fact, a brooding moral force. It is not, of course, an unvarying parameter, impervious to personality or new ideas. But if it is successful at all, it lasts long enough to have a history. It gets established. And if established, the historical judgment is, it will operate on the "psychological fields" of individuals, affect behavior, and at length insinuate a meaning of "right" conduct.[3]

An organic, moral operation of organizations as systems is conveyed in the very term "organizational behavior." It is inherent in the designation of decision theory, a theory of organizational choice that shows how organizations select alternatives and choose among them. A recent behavioralist study of the business firm as a social institution, Alvar and Carol Elbing's *The Value Issue of Business*, draws out the implication:

Fixed value codes do not inhere in individual members of the business institution but are learned in social systems such as that of the business firm itself. The business institution is no mere arena where fixed value codes are displayed, but one important learning environment in which values [develop].[4]

---

[1]Neil W. Chamberlain, *Enterprise and Environment: The Firm in Time and Place* (New York: McGraw-Hill Book Co., 1968), p. 20.

[2]*Ibid.*, pp. 59–71.

[3]Frederick J. Teggart, *Theory and Processes of History* (Berkeley: University of California Press, 1941), pp. 281–90.

[4]A. O. and C. J. Elbing, *The Value Issue of Business* (New York: McGraw-Hill Book Co., 1967), p. 201.

In another new volume, Lynn Peters' provocative interpretation of source materials entitled *Management and Society,* the same point, enfolded in somewhat different diction, emerges from studies in economic history.[5] The Golembiewski study of organizational ethics reinforces the concept.[6]

A CONTRARY VIEW

Against these implications of theory and conclusions of history must be set a more conventional view, which apparently thrives in the very midst of formulations that would seem to undermine it. Thomas Petit's brisk but comprehensive survey of contemporary economic and behavioral theories applicable to management philosophy stresses a persistent, more abstractionist understanding of organizations, one echoing what was heard the day Dow came to Northwestern. A major statement from the book will make the point:

> The phrase "social control of the firm" implies that the enterprise is a living entity which can control its own behavior, and this, of course, is not true. Social control is a process by which behavior is influenced to conform to some set of norms. . . . [A firm] cannot do things necessary to control its own behavior: think, evaluate, make decisions, and implement policies. Only human beings do these things. Therefore, the firm . . . must indirectly be controlled through the manager, the controller of the firm.[7]

Every sentence in this statement is true enough in the sense that the writer intended. But regarded as a whole, the statement carries a questionable message. It imputes the legal fictional concept of the firm, which *is* an abstraction, to the behavioral concept of the firm, which is *not* disembodied. It thereby diverts attention from the fact that organizational life is itself "a process by which behavior is influenced to conform to some set of norms." Even so, with curious ambiguity the statement seems to admit that everyone in the firm *is* controlled in some lively way by the firm—except top management, who does the thinking and planning. This runs against reality in both directions. It implies too little room for play in the joints at lower echelons and too much free wheeling at the top. Management, though it has power to judge and act, is also constrained by what and whom it manages. If social control works, it works on the firm as a "living entity," a locus of value formation and change.

Economic theories of the firm, incidentally, assume the organic nature

---

[5]Lynn H. Peters, *Management and Society* (Belmont, Calif.: Dickenson Pub. Co., Inc., 1968), pp. 110–21, 128–41.

[6]Robert T. Golembiewski, *Men, Management, and Morality* (New York: McGraw-Hill Book Co., 1965), pp. 119–58.

[7]Thomas A. Petit, *The Moral Crisis in Management* (New York: McGraw-Hill Book Co., 1967), p. 119.

of an enterprise as a rule. In this respect economic theory has represented worldly experience with considerable accuracy.

LAW AS A TEACHER AND DISTRIBUTOR

There is method in taking pains to make explicit the broad moral meaning of the organic view of the firm implicit in ideas undergirding contemporary management science. Society all along has behaved as if these implications were true. To stimulate change in standards and values society often indirectly gets at individuals in business by directly affecting the policies and strategies of firms as organizations, rather than the other way around. The major instrument by which society injects value-teaching change into organizations is, of course, the law. But more than this, law often has been the *necessary* teacher and distributor of value, not just an alternative or a last resort.

Here it will be well to rely again on simple systems concepts, which seem to help new minds of a scientific turn get accustomed to some old facts of politics.

A business firm is an open social system; it is also a subset of the business system, which is a subsystem of society. This is a handy way of indicating that an enterprise is a social system with a purpose. The purpose is pursued in open encounter with pressures and signals generated in or transmitted through the market. The market itself is an institution related subordinately to society, or put another way, it is an arrangement of socially approved constructs such as property and profit. The business organization, as a subset of a subsystem of the body politic, has a single goal prescribed by society, the provision of goods and services. The organization, set by society in a socially sanctioned economizing system known as the market, translates the public's goal of provision into a so-called "private" goal of its own: the economically rational management of its assets. When the business organization is seen in its proper place in the complex social-political system, it can have no other basic commitment than the economic ordering of assets. If the organization uses its power to multiply commitments on its own account, it runs the risk of economizing poorly or of becoming, in one critic's term, "an imperialist."

Two corollaries emerge. The first concerns the conduct of men in business organizations. Conduct is constrained to meet the perceived imperatives of profitable management of assets in our market system. The second corollary relates to competition as a restriction on the social competence of individual enterprises. Given the American social preference for a decentralized, competitive system of economizing, there is no reason to expect that business organizations should voluntarily adopt strategies that impose competitive burdens on themselves. Even when managers wish to represent a new set of values in business operations, they customarily do so voluntarily only if the perceived benefits markedly exceed costs. Managers usually will not wait for a very long run before reckoning up accounts, either. And, understandably, the number of managers willing to make the same social experiment simultaneously on their own is unlikely to be socially significant.

But do not these stringencies force us to concede that the Dow Day moralists were right? Not at all. First off, we have reaffirmed the understanding of economic management of assets as a basic social function, and the market system as representing in itself certain fundamental social values. The style of business operations, moreover, tends to conform to a scheme of social expectations that have been internalized in well run organizations. Men in thriving enterprises of this sort already are doing considerable good while doing well. The organization impels them to do both.

Perhaps, however, not enough good gets done. That, in the end, rests with society to determine. Certainly many social values have no ready, natural connection with the microeconomic demands of rational management. Among the unready values are full disclosure, collective bargaining, racial desegregation, steadfast avoidance of cartels, limitation of market power, workmen's compensation for industrial injuries, and clean air.

The list contains, to be sure, several items that businessmen today would claim as business values with enormous influence on business ethics: full disclosure in securities transactions, collective bargaining, and workmen's compensation, for instance. Yet none of these became imbedded in the business system through the natural evolution of voluntary rational management. And none of the others is being or is likely to be so incorporated. In practice it would be systematically almost impossible to do so. When businessmen reach the desperate point where they say among themselves, "If we don't do it, government will," there are few occasions when they are not confessing that government *must* do something.

If society is earnest about incorporating non-market values and thus changing business ethics, it distributes the costs (a necessary societal act in a market system) and gives organizations something new to teach (a role organizations perform very well) by subjecting the market to the teaching-distributing power of the law.[8] Thus the system connects social conscience and business policy. When the connection is most successful, the business fraternity eventually comes to believe it thought up most of the resulting changes by itself.[9] There is no greater tribute to the law's civilizing influence.

[8]James A. Pike, *Beyond the Law* (Garden City, N.Y.: Doubleday & Co., 1963), pp. 71–73.

[9]An example of transformation is in Joseph W. Towle (ed.), *Ethics and Standards in American Business* (Boston: Houghton Mifflin Co., 1964), pp. 244–47.

ALTERNATIVES TO THE LAW

It is not universally acknowledged, however, that the law is the most reliable way of incorporating nonmarket values into the market system. Adolph Berle, of course, has advanced an elaborate, persuasive thesis giving the crown to professionalism.[10] Three most recent and sharply done studies of the social responsibilities of business—the previously cited works by Petit, Peters, and the Elbings—discuss the role of law hardly at all. They stress instead heightened managerial awareness of behavioral theories, enlarged skill in assessing and manipulating social forces, and general handiness in accommodating the direction of the wind. In much the same vein, the philosopher Albert Levi distinguishes three moral criteria—religious, legal, and professional—and argues that for the business community the professional criterion is most relevant. When law is the guide, Levi says the businessman "loses his moral autonomy"; the principle of conduct becomes fear, not a positive conception of duty.[11]

Levi concludes by observing that as an ethical standard, legality is not enough. By legality, however, he does not mean living the law; he means doing anything for which the law cannot punish you. Perhaps this view of the law as only the restrictive, tyrannical letter still holds sway to such an extent that the law as enabler, guide, and spirit seldom comes from behind the clouds. And one suspects that the current popularity of "situation ethics" has done much to thicken the clouds. If so, the search for moral motivation somewhere beyond the law becomes plausible. But it is not historical. Whether perceived or not, the law as public policy has worked as the dominant force, though not the only one, to establish *in the system* many of the conditions and values that make business managers look like professionals.

Two examples will have to suffice: labor relations and equal employment opportunities. Positive conception of duty on the part of managers did not plant the principle of collective bargaining in mass production industries. Nor, probably, could it have done so. Yet once the law declared encouragement of that principle to be public policy and specified the channels through which labor could negotiate with management, a great flow of changed conduct, conceptions, and values followed. Not least touched by the flow were firms that avoided actual unionization. Similarly, whatever professionalism exists in management, it had little to do with initiating *systemic* desegregaton of the work place. And, again, in a segregated society it probably could not have done so.

---

[10]Berle gives a swift summary of his view in Edward S. Mason (ed.), *The Corporation in Modern Society* (Cambridge, Mass.: Harvard University Press, 1959), pp. ix-xv.

[11]Towle, *op. cit.*, pp. 22–23.

RIGHTEOUSNESS AND HYPOCRISY

In both cases, however, a good deal remained, and still remains, for business organizations to do after the law was proclaimed. The law has to be brought to life. And, as in Aristotelian ethics, moral virtue here consists in applying reason and intelligence to making choices, in concrete circumstances, in order to *do* the law. What, for instance, is the operational meaning of "bargaining in good faith" or of "equal opportunity"? The enabling statutes do not specify a meaning. They establish a direction. What the new values come to mean in social life depends in no small measure on the intelligence, inventiveness, and spirit of business's practice of them.

Labor law and civil rights law rechanneled management prerogative and organizational operations by redefining relationships between business organizations and segments of society. In this they are like most policies forming our national economic constitution. Now the end of that sort of law is not simply legality, in the strict, grudging sense. We could not go on as a community if it were. The end of the law of relationships is righteousness, a prophetic Hebrew concept with surprising pertinence for modern organizational society.

Righteousness is the fulfilling of the obligations of a relationship arising from the demands of community.[12] In righteousness the legal and the ethical merge into one standard. The law, for instance, directs management to regard labor as a constituent interest rather than, as in other eras, a ward or a commodity. Businessmen today unhesitatingly insist that ethics require it, simply because it is right. Ethics now enforce the law, to a large extent, though in modern labor relations this was not always the pattern.

As the brief example from industrial history suggests, the relation of law to righteousness is instrumental: the law constrains and it proportions.

Because it carries sanctions, the law drives organizations to revise policies and strategies that fall short of the community's requirements for a particular relationship. The law does not wait until all hearts are changed. As in the Old Testament, the law's immediate concern is that righteousness be practiced regardless of whether all men love doing it. Guided by the law when it invades the market system, business organizations have a remarkable capacity for bringing men to conduct themselves as socially useful hypocrites. Hypocrisy often is a way-station on the journey to conversion. In any event, hypocrisy in the right direction releases righteous men for fuller effectiveness.[13]

    [12]E. R. Achtemeier, "Righteousness in the Old Testament," *The Interpreter's Dictionary of the Bible* (New York: Abingdon Press, 1962), pp. 80–81.
    [13]Harold L. Johnson, "Graphic Analysis of Multiple-Goal Firms: Development, Current Status and Critique," Occasional Paper No. 5, Center for Research, College of Business Administration, Pennsylvania State University (April, 1966).

The law also reduces the claims of righteousness to manageable proportions. Without proportionality, ethical claims might well become unbearably heavy and conflicting—or be dismissed as fantasies. But recognition that through public policy the community seeks to make right relations manageable ought to enlarge rather than diminish the sense of social purpose among men engaged in the modern arts of management.

20. SOCIETAL NORMS AND RESPONSIBILITY CONFLICTS AMONG VARIOUS PUBLICS SERVED*

W. Arthur Cullman

To find a group of marketing men who would agree completely on societal norms would be as hard as finding advertising experts who agree on the solution to an advertising investment problem. It will not be possible, in our opinion, to get agreement among those who contemplate the problems identified in the title. For this reason, no attempt will be made to find a consensus; rather we shall simply state some problems seen and some solutions which may alleviate or eliminate the problems.

One widely accepted societal norm, in our opinion, and the phrase "in our opinion" will be assumed from now on, is the high position held by education in our society. We hear increasing talk about the need for even high standards of education at all levels—including the doctorate. It is not held that all education is good but it is held that education is all good. The following are remarks made by Watson Washburn speaking at the annual meeting of Standard Oil Company (New Jersey) on May 23rd, 1962.

Your directors are giving millions of dollars of your corporation's money to charity. This seems wrong. Your company is supposedly run solely for the stockholders' benefit. It is not an eleemosynary institution. Many stockholders undoubtedly feel that charity begins at home. Others who can afford donations are certainly entitled to choose their own beneficiaries. The current practice is especially reprehensible when as here nearly $10,000,000 have been given since 1955 (it is now a larger sum) to educational institutions, many of which teach socialism and ridicule businessmen, savers, and investors as recently explained in the well documented best-seller *Keynes at Harvard*.

The management of the corporation defended the concept that philanthropic and educational contributions have become an integral part of

---

*From *Changing Marketing Systems*, American Marketing Association, December, 1967, pp. 153–55.

a corporation's business and civic responsibilities. Although there were some attempts to indicate that the company's interests were being served, the strongest defense came in the remarks of the former chairman of the board, Mr. F. W. Abrams, who said:

It has been said on occasion that corporate support of higher education should depend on the stockholders themselves, through the dividends they receive from their companies. This is a cynical, uninformed, and wasteful suggestion. In the first place the corporation would not be making any investment at all, much as it needs the products of education in its business. As a result it would be paying even higher taxes. The dollars paid by the individual stockholders would lose the benefit of the company's 52% tax bracket and each of these dollars would have to be taxed to a stockholder as income. It is fair to assume that the contributions to higher education by this means, if made, would lose more than half of their tax advantage.

In this exchange the conflict is clearly seen as management views its responsibility to society one way while the shareholder thinks of the corporation only as being a manufacturer of profits. No doubt, the antagonism to using corporate profits for education was heightened by the wide publicity given to the "pink" tinge on the campuses reported in 1961–62. Today, at least two major corporations—Motorola and Olin —are investing in paid advertising to question why some of the brightest products of our educational system seem to be shunning business as a career. In this case we see a conflict between the intellectual public, which is supported as well as served by business, and the managements of corporations who are serving so many varied publics—such as stockholders—that they have become less acceptable to an important public who should provide them with successors. The ideas which seem to reflect an emerging societal norm among what we have chosen to call the intellectual public have been articulated by Secretary of Health, Education and Welfare Gardner in his report as president of Carnegie Corp. To reflect this societal norm will take a major change in responsibility on the part of the management public. Labor, government, and consumers are some of the publics whose distrust in businessmen has been seen during the past five years; thus another conflict is surfaced.

It might interest those of us who are devoted to the advancement of science in marketing to think of the responsibility conflicts as reflections of market or public segments. A sophisticated marketing organization often aligns its thinking by markets to be served, and thus is able to influence the demand structure. Do we need to recognize the difference in demand and perception among the publics which must be served? We feel certain that many conflicts could be anticipated, ameliorated, and mollified if the publics were identified and analyzed as separable groups. The possibility of one appeal or approach being attractive to all is not overlooked. As a matter of fact, it is emphasized.

The problems arise when the essence of agreement is not found, and gratingly different appeals are used for various publics whose acceptance of the norm is limited or non-existent.

An example of differing societal norms causing conflict among two publics—the consumer and management—may be found in the seeming divergence between these two publics with respect to the proposed "Truth in Lending" legislation. Management has strongly opposed this legislation on the basis that the economy will suffer from less rapid expansion of consumer credit. Articles, speeches, statements and slogans have been developed to combat the proposed legislation. The societal norm assumed to be guiding managements is the importance of maintaining the economy and continuing this progress toward material well-being. The danger of the legislation seems to be ascribed to its short term affect on the consumer's purchasing habits. There is an underlying fear that the consumer will not increase his satisfactions by credit purchases if the total cost of credit is displayed in the form of a simple annualized interest. This fear seems to be based on the perception of the consumer, that rates above 6% are questionable.

The societal norm for the cost of money has long surrounded the mythical par of 6%. Yet on the international scene the devaluation of the pound sterling by the British on November 20th, 1967, forced "business loans" at the prime rate up to the magic 6% in the United States and higher in Britain. The societal norm for consumers is in conflict, in other words, with reality; yet another public, management, fears the power of this norm may blunt its drive for progress. The responsibility for serving the consumer in the long run must take precedence over every other societal norm in the American economic system.

Can management resolve this conflict? Massive doses of education to reduce the lag between consumer perception of the norm and realistic understanding of the price of money may be one answer. Until the consumer attitude change has been accomplished, management is forced to attempt to block passage of legislation which will divulge the "true interest" not because they are antagonistic to divulgence, but because they realize that consumers will misunderstand the divulged facts. The societal norm of management is thus given precedence over one perceived by consumers.

Looking at almost any of the various publics with which business deals, another taxonomic device highlights the divergence of societal norms. Responsibility conflicts arise from what we choose to call the "generation mix." The rather rapid demographic changes in the age groupings in American society are creating interesting conflicts with ramifications even beyond the confines of business. Within the ranks of labor the societal norm of a work week is changing for the non-senile group—those under thirty. Many jobholders over thirty have a norm of a workweek of approximately forty hours. Some management jobholders have a workweek concept of fifty or more hours.

What is the responsibility to each of these segments of the public which is perceiving itself as productive? Ignore for the moment those segments of the labor public who consider the workweek as "time to be served." We are talking about those who knowingly or unknowingly subscribe to Theory Y. The problem is resolved as one segment of the jobholder public accepts a norm. Dislocations of relative productivity among sections of the country, types of work, and various sizes of organizations are part of the price paid for lack of consistent norms. And even more noticeable is the norm among the younger segment of the productive workforce to accept restricted work opportunities. This is manifest as one looks at one organization, but, if one looks at the people, one frequently sees high productivity due to moonlighting. Has leadership shirked its responsibility in allowing the norm of a certain amount of work and/or time to become so accepted that moonlighting with its obvious uneconomic consequences is gaining acceptance as a norm? Conflict is seen here between various responsibilities for serving the varied publics even within one segment.

Can one discuss the segment of population under thirty without mentioning the "hippies" and their varied sub-cultural relations? Perhaps it should suffice to indicate that business has been sufficiently productive, satisfying the societal norm of material gain, that the "hippies" and their friends can survive. The norms of these publics have been explored by many and, to our knowledge, discovered by few, if any. Is it the responsibility of business to provide for this public, to stunt its growth, and to reduce or eliminate its recognition? The societal norm which we perceive does not permit us to condemn nor force us to espouse. Our overriding societal norm is growth with choice. Our growth has been so great that it allows room for people to choose a way which does not contribute to growth yet is permitted by it. Often defenders of television allude to the opportunity to change channels or turn off the set. If our system works correctly, commercials which are objected to will be withdrawn if a market segment does not select the product. Presumably, the sponsor is able to measure the effectiveness of the complaints. This is a large presumption. Our societal norm indicates that we should allow the objectors the right to complain.

Recognition of varying societal norms might have been helpful in reducing the conflict between business management and government during the past decade. In the eyes of those influencing governmental policy with respect to business, there seemed to be a norm that business should be willing to act as an agent of fiscal policy. Governmental authority ran head-on into societal norms of the rights of private property in at least two confrontations which are not yet completely resolved. In the case of the balance of payment problem, there was an expectation that business would perceive its responsibility to make major adjustments in long range global plans under persuasion from the government. In at least one notable case, Ford Motor's investment in Great Britain, the conflict, based upon differing norms, was patent. That Ford acted against the desires of the government is even more surprising in view of the close relationship between the Ford management and government leaders, including former Ford president, Robert S. McNamara.

When the Kennedy administration attempted to persuade the steel industry to stay within the price "guidelines," the government's perception of responsibility for "full employment" was confronted with a concept put forth by Roger Blough, Board Chairman of U.S. Steel. It was agreed that price increases were necessary to modernize production capacity so that U.S. Steel Corporation could produce adequate profits to compete successfully with foreign competition. Mr. Blough announced his price increases to President Kennedy on April 10, 1962 and rescinded them on April 13th. During those seventy-two hours, many pressures were used to forestall the price rise: public denunciation, pressure to split industry ranks, the threat of loss of government contracts, and moves toward criminal prosecution under the antitrust laws. Many publics were concerned in this situation and each seemingly perceived societal norms differently. Commentators referred to stockholders as being limited in their profits by government fiat, praised the government for "standing up to big business," questioned the meddling in the private sector, and reviewed Democratic party attitudes toward business. The labor public, rather surprisingly, seemed also to resent the new role of government. Secretary of Labor Goldberg's proposal to define and assert the public interest in collective bargaining drew a sharp retort from George Meany, president of the A.F.L.-C.I.O.

During the summer of 1967 the mutual fund industry was under pressure from the Federal Government to reduce its fees. This pressure was supported by a study made by competent researchers. Again we see the difference of opinion among various publics concerning price responsibility. The prevalent societal norm in the pricing area has been that our competitive economic system will tend to keep prices at an equilibrium between exorbitant profits and adequate quality of service or product. Exceptions exist with monopolies such as public utilities. The mutual fund industry has grown rapidly and is composed of a substantial number of firms. It cannot be called a monopoly situation. Again one can surmise that the government public views the societal norm for profit differently from the fund managements.

A minor digression illustrates the changing of societal norms when there is conflict. During the autumn of 1967 the mutual fund industry, which has blocked reduction in sales charges and management fees, has switched to supporting the bid by banks to enter the mutual fund industry. Normally competitive norms which have kept the mutual fund industry from supporting the entry of banks into their business have been supplanted by other norms which make it possible for mutual protection to replace competitiveness. At the end of November, 1967, the American Bankers Association spurned the offer and rebuffed mutual fund representatives. The bankers indicated that they had already made commitments to members of Congress to endorse major portions of the mutual funds' reform bill.

Another area where business responsibility seems to find conflicts among its publics is the area of civil rights. So much has been written about this problem that these comments may be repetitions, but they bear repeating nonetheless. Societal norms concerning the role of the Negro in society are changing. Business management has been pressured by many, including the government, to develop adequate roles for Negro employees despite difficulties of recruitment, selection, training and promotion. Many business men have responded cheerfully and with strong, exuberant idealism. Other publics have reduced the effectiveness of businessmen's efforts. By the end of 1967 conflicts within labor organizations were beginning to be resolved, but many unions are emotionally antagonistic to the civil rights concept. Despite the fears engendered by a succession of "summer riots" the overriding societal norm is distrust of the Negro as a person when large numbers are considered. Another public, the intellectuals, have espoused the Negro cause and have upbraided businessmen for their laggard role in aiding civil rights. Conflicts between publics which perceive the societal norm differently are dissipating much of the effort being expended to help the Negro find and secure equality of opportunity.

There are many other areas where substantial conflicts exist between various publics perceiving societal norms differently. More important than cataloguing the conflicts is suggesting ways of ameliorating them. There appear to be no magic wands or complex formulae which can be used. One of the current devices for helping to solve difficult problems —simulation of social interaction—seems to us not to hold any promise.

Education in its broadest sense will reduce these conflicts and permit man's wisdom to choose the most satisfying—or satisficing—solution. Each problem needs the white light of the torch of learning to illuminate the true issues and permit the societal norm to be adjusted to cover the majority view. This is the democratic way. It will make it necessary for some publics to be defeated in some conflicts. It will necessitate businessmen examining carefully those publics they serve. And most of all, it will permit the operation of a society in which the choice is made by the various segments of the population. Variations in service to differing market segments may be many, but the similarities will not be overlooked. As our techniques of education and commitment to education increase, the responsibility conflicts among various publics served will decrease in number and intensity.

Intellectuals will have to strain to include others in their public in order to minimize the danger that other publics will dominate society and force them to live under conditions which they abhor. There is a great need to reduce these conflicts lest a means other than education becomes accepted. Force, dictatorship and limited choice can be avoided if we all pull together to resolve conflicts by education.

Part IV

THE CHALLENGE

Marketing is a challenge when only the economic concerns of the firm are considered. When political, social, psychological, and other values are included, the challenge becomes even greater. Marketing has evolved slowly and it has always had the role of serving society in the sense of helping to distribute goods and services. Today, it has reached the point in society where broader issues are now challenging the firm and the marketer. The readings in Part IV suggest the breadth and depth of today's marketing challenge.

A. The impact of corporate planning

Bert Elwert discusses the relationship between marketing planning and social and ethical issues. Does the market function as a satisfactory mechanism of social control? Elwert also examines Galbraith's statements on marketing planning.

21. SOCIAL AND ETHICAL PROBLEMS OF MARKETING PLANNING*

Bert Elwert

All planning involves problems of a social and ethical nature. And every well planned study of planning includes, at least in a hat-tipping gesture, some attention to the wider social impact of the planning process. Unfortunately, hat tipping seems to be more common than earnest soul

---

*From *Marketing and the New Science of Planning,* American Marketing Association, August, 1968, pp. 133–38.

searching, and too often the outcome is rather like this: Planning is necessary but its effects cause some problems; we need to be aware of this fact; but the problems which arise certainly are not beyond our present capacity for solutions; therefore, we will go on doing what we have been doing but we should pay more heed to these problems and solve them or have someone else solve them; at the same time everyone should be more careful to practice the kind of personal conduct that we already know but tend to ignore.

Perhaps this tendency to treat social and ethical problems in a superficial way is a result of not truly knowing much about them. It would be a good deal closer to truth to say simply that planning is an essential part of business processes, and that some serious social and ethical problems arise along with it. In fact, very little is known about the ultimate consequences of these problems. For the moment they are either brushed aside or ignored. In the long run these problems may become so pressing as to result in fundamental changes in business practices and marketing planning but, until recently, we have been in a period when not much thought was given to that possibility.

Marketing planning, in its elaborated modern forms, certainly reaches beyond the ken of anything conceived in classical thought as the domain of the business firm. In the classic economic theory of the firm, a bloodless, soulless central agent, the entrepreneur, responded unerringly to data given by a market environment relatively so vast and inexorable in its workings as to be beyond entrepreneurial influence. In contrast is the modern managerial model, where management professionals make pricing decisions, plan new products and modify old ones, plan promotions and campaigns, evaluate alternative channels of distribution, organize sales units and dealer relationships, participate in trade associations, promote a favorable corporate image, and generally regard nothing in the firm's external environment as beyond their interest. It is worth noticing also that firms lobby in legislatures and promote their interests through other connections with government, although in many cases this activity is not conventionally classified as marketing planning.

A paradigm of the kind of firm in which marketing planning usually grows to its fullest flower would show these major characteristics:[1]

The firm is large relative to both the whole population of business firms and to the market it occupies.

As a sizeable organization relative to its market or markets the firm possesses sufficient market power to give it some influence over prices; for example, a unilateral price increase does not automatically result in zero sales.

The firm is a complex organization with an extensive product or service line, sales operations in several markets, and many widely scattered establishments.

---

[1]Carl Kaysen, "The Social Significance of the Modern Corporation," *American Economic Review*, May, 1957, pp. 311–19.

In the usual situation the firm exhibits vertical or conglomerate integration or some combination of the two.

Both mass marketing and mass production techniques are refined to a high level of sophistication.

The firm's size, history, and prospects generally give an impression of permanence and there is a general expectation that the firm will have a continuing place in both the present and future economy.

Stock ownership in the firm is widely dispersed and the management, which is generally professional, holds a stock interest that is relatively small or practically nil.

It is apparent that many of these characteristics provoke suspicion among segments of the economics fraternity and along the antitrust front—and not without reason. But our theory obviously is incomplete and we know painfully little about the possible imperatives for this type of firm. It is clear that precisely this type of organization bears the brunt of many social demands for security and stability. Legions of workers choose it for its size and seeming ability to resist the sudden squalls of shifting market activity. They acquire claims against it for pensions and a host of other benefits to come due in the future. This type represents firms bearing the broadest spectrum of fiduciary responsibility. Blue chip stocks now are in the asset portfolios of practically every conceivable type of non-government organization from churches to unions and from universities to old-peoples' homes. Hardly anyone involved with major social organizations escapes some form of dependence on "big business."

MARKETING PLANNING AND MARKET CONTROL

To contrast the modern scope of marketing planning with the time-honored role of the business firm in theory highlights the significance of marketing processes and draws attention to gaps in the theory, but it does not form a base for normative judgments. It is well recognized that the firm of theory never was intended as an accurate representation of the fully functioning real-world organization. Rather, it was conceived as a useful abstraction for explaining and sometimes predicting phenomena observed in markets populated by large numbers of firms. The classical problem was not to sell a product, but to describe why a certain amount was sold at a certain price.

It is a good estimate, moreover, that most persons seriously concerned with the social implications of marketing planning would still assume that conclusions of the accepted theory are viable. Although increasing administrative complexity and sophistication render the theoretical firm more unreal than ever, the tested results of market activity generally are interpreted as favorable to existing theory. Demand curves still hold to a negative slope; sellers produce more at high prices than low; users of resources incur costs, and firms whose costs are abnormally high exit the market impelled by the stiff winds of competition.

This line of reasoning takes the discussion onto relatively secure ground. For it supports the thesis that the market remains a dominant mechanism for social control and suggests the hypothesis that advancing organization, with its attendant planning process, will be constrained to serve what the consensus holds to be legitimate social wants. No matter how much marketing planning goes on, the market, so long as it remains intact, can be expected to allocate resources, ameliorate conflict, and generally even things up in ways acceptable to us all.

In this context marketing planning can be viewed as part of the essential rivalry of the marketplace. Obviously, competition restricted solely to the price variable would make the world a duller, less dynamic place than a world in which sellers vary the many dimensions of the market offering to give us things more useful, more attractive, better packaged, served by pleasant people, sold on credit cards and delivered to the door. And in some of its aspects surely marketing planning is directed toward these results. Much research and effort is aimed exactly at finding out what people would regard as useful, and worth paying for, what they like about market offerings, what they dislike, and so on.

Of course those especially sensitive to the social and ethical questions can point out that while marketing planning may lead to what is described here, it also represents an attempt to bend the demand curve, to insulate the firm from the full thrust of market forces. But those doubters can be countered by the impressive argument that the real world should present dynamic progress; it is better that way, of course. Every attempt by one planner to gain a market advantage—even if temporarily successful—only stimulates others to erode that advantage by improving their own offerings.

In its most elaborate form this theme clearly is the Schumpeterian ideal of competition primarily through innovation and improvement; in turn, they provide the motive force for an advancing material culture. Moreover, the essential precondition of this force is the temporary shelter of a protected market position from which the firm can carry on marketing planning, refine new products, and gather for its next assault on those sheltered harbors either held or sought by rivals. The theme holds understandable attractions, and it is not without some supporting data. Contributions such as those exemplified by cellophane, nylon, transistors, and color television are established benchmarks of industrial progress originated in firms whose market position and planning resources leave no doubt about the presence of substantial market power. They deserve their applause, and it is a safe bet that the applause will not subside soon, given the care and perseverance that go into advertising campaigns.

Advertising invariably raises thorny questions. The business of one man striving to influence the otherwise free choices of another necessarily contains serious ethical implications. But as a social problem advertising appears practically benign under the assumption that unadulterated market forces ultimately constrain the seller within the limits of social necessity. Indeed some of the long standing skepticism about advertising's usefulness is confronted with a newer and important development in economic thought that stresses the need for market information as a vital lubricant, if markets are to operate smoothly. Information is not a free good. On the contrary, it often is quite scarce and of high value. Although no one would argue for advertising as the perfect source of market information, it is information nevertheless, and as such it gains new consideration as a social value. The major social problems stem from the fact that advertising is controlled mainly by the seller, who has the strongest incentive to slant information toward his own purposes. However, a case can be made that competing messages tend to balance each other out and that buyers, with many alternatives from which to choose, will reward those sellers who combine reasonably accurate information with other market values of product or service.

For the broader ethical questions, the reassuring assumption of ultimate market control does not entirely relieve anxiety, but certainly it is comforting. Among students of business, and among many of its practitioners as well, there must be a good deal of dissatisfaction over the continuing divergence between what is said so piously and what is done so persistently. It becomes increasingly evident that we are not adequately describing an ethic that can be used to explain what happens in the business arena. There have been committees, conferences, commissions, boards, and councils and all have produced statements, codes, position papers, or policies. This excerpt is a good example: "While all relationships of an enterprise . . . are regulated in some degree by law, compliance with law can only provide a minimum standard of conduct. Beyond legal obligations, the policies and actions of businessmen must be based upon a regard for the proper claims of all affected groups."[2] The words may be weighty and even inspiring. But do they ring true if carried beyond the conference rooms into the marketplace? Is anyone really listening? Would a better proposition for explaining observed behavior be, "Take everything you can get away with and sometimes try for a little more?"

If the more skeptical, perhaps even cynical, alternative is better attuned to present realities, some recent writing may foreshadow a new look. An example appeared last winter in the *Harvard Business Review*, where an author argued that the true ethic of business is a game ethic

---

[2]Theodore L. Thau, "The Business Ethics Advisory Council," in *The Ethics of Business Enterprise*, Annals of the American Academy of Political and Social Science, September, 1962, p. 138.

oriented more to winning prizes than to ideals held up by the social order or religion.[3] The game, according to this writer, "calls for distrust of the other fellow . . . cunning, deception and concealment of one's strengths and intentions, not kindness and openheartedness are vital. . . ."

Should this description be accepted as an accurate reflection of what goes on in the minds that make up a market, there again is comfort in the assumption that in the end no one mind, or few minds, will prevail. Instead the anonymous, impersonal market will decide our destiny. If those who perform our business functions—marketing planners, first of all—are in fact practitioners of "cunning, deception and concealment," we may be spared the harsh transactions they intend because competition pits them against each other as well as against us. And if as individual buyers and sellers we muster our own cunning and beware deception and concealment, we may yet be satisfied with our bargains. But it is the manager who finally will owe most to the market. For without its sustained referee function, management actions guided by a game ethic would create intolerable social tensions. How long would society continue to play the game? Not long, without a belief that the market was an effective defense.

The thrust of these ideas is that social and ethical problems connected with marketing planning are softened when cast in the light of market regulation. The light is not always flattering and one may worry about what is concealed in the shadows. But market control can legitimatize an impressive range of planning strategies, tactics, and even subterfuges.

Once this point is grasped, it becomes an extreme irony that so many instances of socially abrasive planning strike at the very foundations of the market. The reference is to the fact that marketing planning, either studied or casual, has so often run afoul of the antitrust laws and other policies designed to preserve the market—the very market that, by the reasoning just followed, preserves social consent for marketing planning as we know it now.

It may be suggested that the statement is too strong, that, after all, these clashes with market-defending public policy are only a result of random planning blunders or the transgressions of small, poorly organized business under intense market pressures. The apology is dispelled by hard facts. If the violations are haphazard blunders, the market is being struck by a surprising number of random events. The Justice Department and Federal Trade Commission together are scarcely able to keep up with the enforcement workload, and there is no encouragement in the nature of their encounters. A majority of cases still involve simple price conspiracy which advanced planning personnel by now would regard as an exogenous constraint on the model rather than a relevant variable. Nor are small and perhaps misguided firms the prime source of the

---

[3]Albert Z. Carr, "Is Business Bluffing Ethical?" *Harvard Business Review,* January-February, 1968, pp. 143–53.

problem. If the record is examined over a few years, a fine list of large companies, admirably suited to the type described earlier as the most likely locus of advanced marketing planning, can be made up from recorded convictions, consent decrees, and pleas of no contest.

What should give pause for thought here is the question of whether planning can thrive, or even continue in its present form, if a significant part of its effort is in conflict with society's safeguards. The question deserves most serious consideration. Something obviously is out of phase in the market system when there are so many skirmishes and potentially larger combat between marketing planning and the system's authorized protectors.

Another side of market rivalry among large firms should be included to complete an examination of the more conventional problems associated with marketing planning. The Schumpeterian ideal of competitive innovation, which was cited earlier for its qualities as a possible defense of marketing planning, is not so well accepted as to belong in any professional consensus. On the contrary it has always engendered skepticism and recently it was cogently questioned by two writers who use data and examples drawn from the domestic steel industry.

The hypothesis says essentially that large firms have both greater incentives and greater resources for research and innovation, and thus will exhibit innovative market behavior. Adams and Dirlam contend that the hypothesis is completely unsupported by a test of data based on the invention of the oxygen steelmaking process and the reaction by dominant firms in the United States steel industry.[4] The oxygen process—an innovation of great technical and economic importance—was invented abroad, by a firm of minuscule resources compared to its American counterparts, and was adopted by American firms only after a considerable lag. When finally it was introduced in the United States, the innovators, ranked in order of innovation, were the twelfth largest company, followed by the fourth, the ninth, the nineteenth, the tenth, the thirteenth and the fifth. The three giants of the industry were practically at the end of the procession.[5]

There may be some dissatisfaction with this example because the role played by marketing planning obviously is not foremost. Maybe the link between marketing planning for final uses of steel and steel production processes is too remote. If so, the search for examples should move closer to the marketing function alone. Here the tested cases are harder to find since what is needed, ideally, is an example of some legitimate market

[4]Walter Adams and Joel B. Dirlam, "Big Steel, Invention, and Innovation," *The Quarterly Journal of Economics*, May 1966, pp. 167–89. See also Alan K. McAdams, "Big Steel, Invention and Innovation, Reconsidered," *The Quarterly Journal of Economics*, August, 1967, pp. 457–74.

[5]Walter Adams and Joel B. Dirlam, "Big Steel, Invention, and Innovations Reply," *The Quarterly Journal of Economics*, August, 1967, pp. 475–76.

demand that went unsatisfied. The best evidence would point not to something that happened, but to something that did not happen. There comes immediately to mind some needs that go unfulfilled in our society, but these may not be legitimate market demands since they are not backed by the necessary funds.

On a slightly different tack, however, there are respectable reasons for doubts about how well planning is serving what may be important market demands for variety and diversity. Take the United States auto market as an example. Would marketing planning ever have produced the small economy car if the domestic market had not been invaded from abroad? And how well is it serving demand for such a product now? The safety issue can be left aside for present purposes, because it is not clear that safety features are truly demanded by any large number of buyers. But the electric car raises interesting questions. Chances seem good that a relatively small electrically powered vehicle, with operating characteristics not dismally below those of present-day cars, would find a ready market if it offered price or other advantages. It would also help the air pollution problem. And it would also undermine some previous marketing planning done at no small cost by the big three automakers. What are the chances that the market will offer an electric car within the decade?[6] The answer certainly will add enlightenment concerning marketing planning and its social problems.

While the automobile market is in mind, it is pertinent to round out these considerations with a reminder of the criticism directed at some instances of product differentiation, a strategy heavily relied upon in contemporary marketing planning. The charge is that too often product changes create little or no utility and thus prove wasteful. The auto market is a prime source of the argument. Estimates of the factory costs of automobile model changes were made by Fisher, Griliches, and Kaysen for the late 1950's and the price tag came to more than $4 billion a year. For the years studied, the car buyer paid about $700 of the purchase price (over 25 percent) and about $40 per year in added gasoline costs to get his brand new model.[7] Of course, the data warrant no judgment on the utility of the changes, and the authors make none. Any reasonable observer would have to grant that the product has been improved as well as changed. In spite of Grandfather's complaint that "they just don't build them like they used to," practically no one would trade this year's model for, say, a new 1958 model at the same price.

But $4 billion per year is a very respectable sum and probably the

---

[6]For an interesting appraisal of the problem and its related marketing planning, see the statement of Professor Lloyd D. Orr in *Economic Concentration,* Hearings before the Subcommittee on Antitrust and Monopoly of the Committee on the Judiciary, U.S. Senate, 90th Cong., 1st sess., Part 6, pp. 2786–2800.

[7]Franklin M. Fisher, Evi Griliches, and Carl Kaysen, "The Costs of Automobile Model Changes since 1949," *Journal of Political Economy,* October, 1962, pp. 433–51.

price is higher now. Did the consumer want all that he bought, or does part of it represent a planner's preference? The nature and size of the problem depends upon how much consumer sovereignty is left in the market. And that turns the inquiry back to the issue of market control which, if raised again, runs the risk of being labored. A better choice now is to turn instead to the other side of the issue. How powerful are planner's preferences?

MARKETING PLANNING AND PLANNED MARKETS

Now that the inimitable and irrepressible Professor Galbraith once again has advanced the unconventional wisdom, the idea that marketing planning means planned markets must be met head on. Let it be crystal clear: What Galbraith is saying is that the market mechanism of our theory, and market control as we have been discussing it, now are irrelevant for the most important sectors of the economy. As Galbraith has it, planning controls markets and not the other way around.

For many years there has been a kind of underground literature about business—dependent almost entirely on assertion rather than reason—that viewed marketing practices essentially as part of a larger plot staged to manipulate the unsuspecting consumer. We have heard about persuaders, barons, wastemakers and all that. But Galbraith's work is of another genre so different in form and superior in quality as to make comparisons of this kind almost vulgar. Galbraith is not always right, perhaps not even most of the time, but currently there is no better candidate for first place among those "philosophers," if we may paraphrase Keynes, whose ideas "both when they are right and when they are wrong, are more powerful than is commonly understood."

Any attempt to isolate Galbraith's New Industrial State in its bare essentials requires some oversimplification; however, the following shows the main thread with special reference to marketing planning:

First, the large, complex organization is the industrial society's dominant economic unit. This fact grows inevitably out of advanced technology. Technology demands more specialized skills, greater interdependence within the organization, more careful planning, and thus more intricate coordination and direction by management. Most important, technology lengthens the planning period, from the time of first commitment to the time when returns are earned; and potential risk increases markedly because larger investments are committed more inflexibly for a longer time.

The decision-making process in this organization centers in a bureaucracy called the "technostructure" which pursues multiple goals, such as survival and antonomy, stability, status, professional development and opportunity to practice technical skills. These, in turn, require constant expansion of sales and an acceptable profit rate on the assets. But the foremost requirement is the greatest possible reduction of risk and uncertainty.

The reduction of risk and uncertainty is accomplished on the supply side by integration of assets, internal financing, and cooperation with labor unions. On the demand side, aggregate demand is stabilized by government fiscal and monetary policies. Just below that—and here is where marketing planning plays its key role—market demands are controlled and stabilized by the technical genius of marketing managers. All the tools of the marketing craft are brought to bear—research, advertising, public relations, product design, style changes, sales campaigns. The result is to shift the market initiative from the consumer to the marketing manager. In its quintessence marketing planning plans the market.

The marketing profession hardly can say that Galbraith has been unflattering. To hold that the techniques of planning now are so highly refined as to make possible this quantum leap in social control is, in a way, an immense tribute to those who develop and use the techniques. As might be expected, however, the marketing experts have not rushed to embrace the new thought.[8] No doubt they demur mainly on substantive grounds, although the marketing discipline hardly is noteworthy for sophisticated interest in the wider social impact of its work. But there must be relief, too, in a disclaimer that marketing planning is less than the central determinant of market demand. If the idea were to be accepted outright the social problems of marketing planning would loom bold and portentous, and none could say just where they would lead.

Again, as might be expected, economists have responded to Galbraith's contribution with less than widespread assent, although probably it is fair to say that they have viewed it seriously and with respect. For many, the problem is that Galbraith's work is so sweeping and encompasses so much that it is practically beyond empirical tests for truth. Perhaps history will be the test, but then all we can do is wait, and that is not very satisfactory at the moment.

Evaluations of the work attempted by some economists raise the usual questions and find the explanation flawed in the conventional ways. A major point of the criticism is that evidence is inadequate to support claims concerning the power and consequences of marketing planning. The evidence suggests to economists that advertising, product variation, and marketing campaigns are a less satisfactory explanation of total spending than reliance in more conventional ways on the traditional theories of supply and demand. At least the econometric models work better that way. Even so, many doubts about the models remain undispelled. Observed variations in demand functions for particular markets

---

[8]E. T. Grether, "Galbraith vs. The Market: A Review Article," *The Journal of Marketing*, January, 1968, pp. 9–13.

are explained in the models by such inferred influences as changes in tastes, rate of habit formation, and the like. What precisely is being observed here? Could this be the deft hand of marketing planning working unseen in the carefully specified edifice of the model builder? The answers are still in the future, but it is worth remembering that economists, like other highly trained specialists, sometimes suffer from a narrowness of vision induced by the depths of their insight. Some have been known to insist upon the invisible hand even when the hand was clearly visible to all around them.

Clearly no one, not economist, political expert, or marketing specialist, has yet come to grips fully with the large corporation. Should it turn out that Galbraith is essentially correct, a whole new range of issues arises for marketing planning. The planning function then is unprotected by the rationale of ultimate control under freely-choosing consumers and vigorous competitors striving to win the buyers' favor. It stands instead in the primary role of chooser, director, major arbiter of social values. Just how this power would be channeled to legitimacy also is unclear. While there are many who abhor the thought even of having the problem, Galbraith is neither pessimistic nor condemnatory. Although it seems that he, too, has yet to find a solid basis for a solution, he has suggested a basis for cooperation: ". . . the mature corporation . . . cannot plead its inherently private character, or its subordination to the market, as cover for the pursuit of goals of primary interest to its own guiding organization. [But] it can be expected to accept public goals—in matters of aesthetics, health, working conditions and hours, social tranquility—that are not inconsistent of course with its survival."[9]

MARKETING PLANNING AND THE NEW SOCIAL PROSPECT

In its fullest impact the Galbraithian thesis would herald a new era and the social problems inherent in planning would be upon us in forms never encountered before. At a minimum the impact would be to highlight some serious weaknesses in our understanding of the economy. It seems most probable, however, that Galbraith's contribution finally will be his identification and proposed explanation of powerful social forces affecting the economic order in ways far too little understood. The economy obviously is profoundly affected by technology, complex organization, demands for stability, and response to uncertainty. Galbraith tries, where others have lacked either the nerve or the imagination, to weave these together into a coherent whole. But there is no convincing case that these forces are on a course that sweeps away everything in their

---

[9]J. K. Galbraith, "The New Industrial State: The Cultural Impact" (No. 6 of the Reith Lectures delivered on the British Broadcasting Corporation), *The Listener and BBC Television Review*, December 22, 1966, p. 916.

path. It is especially difficult to see why the market should not survive in some form easily reorganizable by present criteria. The market is such a malleable and adaptable mechanism so readily fitted to many purposes that in all probability the free society will find it indispensable.

To what will it be adapted? The answer seems probable enough. The market as a concept of social organization will be adapted to serve the needs of the many among us who do not now share fully in its rewards. And it may also serve, with a measure of well planned intervention, as part of the means toward some public goals that now fall beyond our reach. In regard to the first point, a good case can be made that much of our current social tension results not from an overabundance of market activity—versus restricted public action—but from a failure to include enough of our people in market processes. In other words, too many people fall outside of the market. The aim of much social action is to correct just that problem. Job training should bring new market participants into the labor supply side, and also into the demand side, and income maintenance programs would bring new and more potent entrants on the demand side.

Marketing planning is guided not by some inexorable grinding of forces beyond our control, but by a comprehensible perception of opportunities and problems. It is a process of choice and the planners are choosers. Up to now perception has taken in the more obvious opportunities and the usual choice has been to serve conventional demands and also to nudge them along wherever possible. Who honestly can deny that planning in this form has helped more people enjoy more good things than ever before in history? All that is well and good. But does marketing planning also suffer from a narrowness of vision? If social change should broaden market participation in our society, will marketing planning perceive a wider agenda of opportunities and problems?

An easy answer is that marketing planning will perceive what is profitable, and that is the end of it. Perhaps so; surely few of us would expect planning to pursue what is not profitable. But how successfully will planning respond even to interesting profit opportunities if they require perception of something more than comfort and convenience consumption by the relatively affluent? Can the marketing planner comprehend anything beyond serving discretionary income, leisure activities, status-oriented consumption, and the joys of affluence? No judgment on these forms of consumption is intended here; they are part of the prized American standard of living. The question only asks whether marketing planning can achieve anything else.

The test will come when potential markets form around needs not now being met and around aspirations of some new arrivals to the market. Then we will find out whether marketing can adjust successfully to demands involving innovative combinations of public and private sector, and to life styles different from those regarded as the typical pattern. We will find out whether we can market new housing to middle-income families as well as we can sell swimming pools to suburbanites and whether we can sell aesthetic values as well as golf carts. At some future meeting these questions may be the subject for program discussion. How will it appear on the program? Will the title be something like "New Perspectives in Marketing Planning" or "Failures of Marketing Planning. . ."?

B. The need to communicate with government

The second article, by George W. Koch, examines the notion of joint responsibility for the consumer by business and government. Koch challenges marketers to communicate more effectively with the public policy makers in government and he describes ways in which the marketing profession has aided policy makers in the past years. The challenge to expand these efforts is clear.

22. GOVERNMENT–CONSUMER INTEREST: FROM THE BUSINESS POINT OF VIEW*

George W. Koch

In discussing "the business point of view" concerning government-consumer interests, it will be useful to consider a major concept, a suggestion for the avoidance of conflicts, and an important means by which the prospects for successful consumer-protection can better be assured.

The *concept* is that protection for the consumer is the joint responsibility of business and government. *Conflicts* can be avoided if businessmen will continue to improve their abilities to communicate effectively with the public policy makers in government who share the responsibility for consumer protection. *Prospects* for success in meeting this joint responsibility can be enhanced if both business and government will use more fully the valuable help of university educators and academic specialists.

The *concept* that consumer protection is a joint responsibility of both business and government is increasingly recognized as an important one. Examining the roots of this responsibility for each sector can clarify the concept.

---

*From *Changing Marketing Systems*, American Marketing Association, December, 1967, pp. 18–21.

Business becomes responsible for protecting its customers the minute it puts a consumer product on the market. However, business assumes this responsibility with research and development long before the product enters the market. The very existence of any business depends upon customers who are not only protected but pleased. For this reason business has been concerned in the past, as it is today, with protecting the buyers of its products. For example, the automobile industry invented four-wheel brakes and installed them on its cars without any government mandate. The lining of metal cans which prevents spoilage when food is left in the can after it is opened was developed by business to protect the health of its customers, without a bill being signed.

Today the responsibility of business for protecting the consumer is broadening, because the American marketplace is undergoing basic changes. Consumers and producers, and even consumers and retailers, are more and more remote from each other. In the past decade there has been an astonishing expansion in the array of products, price ranges and sizes from which consumers may choose. Today consumers must make buying decisions on new and often extremely complex products, such as stereo components for record players and aerosol can cheese spreads which need no refrigeration, some of which were unknown as recently as a year ago. The changes resulting from this remoteness, variety, and innovation have of course widened the responsibility of business to protect the consumer.

In addition, there has recently been a shift of emphasis in the area of concern for consumer interests. No longer is protection of the buyer limited to matters of health and safety, and the correction of an occasional flagrantly deceptive business practice. The focus in consumer protection is now on product prices, adequate information, and protection against confusion. It has shifted from production methods to marketing practices such as packaging, labeling, advertising and promotion, research and development, and the introduction of new products.

Considering this new stress on business marketing practices rather than simply on production methods, from a health and safety standpoint, it is evident that an essential part of the responsibility of business for consumer protection is the examination of its marketing practices by business itself. Government time and government money (which are after all the consumer's time and money) can be saved if *all* businesses will carefully review their marketing procedures, and then correct those procedures to protect the consumer if necessary, or gather the facts as to why the procedures should not be changed and then communicate those facts to the people concerned.

For instance, if the marketing experts had compared the number of cherries in the cherry-pie mix with the number of cherries in the piece of pie pictured on the package, or if the marketing men had examined the confusion and inconsistency in the use of such terms as "giant quart" and "jumbo quart," and if these procedures had been corrected, it might not have been necessary to spend government time and government money on the Fair Packaging and Labeling Act of 1966, nor to spend the industry money now being spent to change all labels.

On the other hand, the practice of advertising is being criticized today by those who feel that it adds unnecessarily to the price which the consumer pays for the product. Since careful review of advertising procedures by business is likely to show that the regulation of advertising could *increase* the price which the consumer pays for a product, business cannot cut down on or stop advertising just because it is being criticized. Therefore business is obligated to obtain the facts about advertising, and to communicate its reasoning about advertising to both government and consumers.

Thus businessmen, and especially those engaged in the manufacturing and marketing of consumer products, must respond to the new emphasis on the examination of marketing procedures as a part of consumer protection even more effectively than they responded to the interest in production methods, if they are to fulfill their responsibility to their customers.

Yet, much as some think business might wish to have the sole responsibility for consumer protection, that obligation is not the exclusive duty of business. Government clearly has a share in the responsibility as well. This idea is not new. It began with Section Eight of Article I of the Constitution of the United States, which placed the responsibility for "public welfare" with the government. Nor is the assumption of this responsibility by the government new. The Pure Food and Drug Law, for example, was enacted in the first decade of this century. And this responsibility of the government continues. Few people any longer question the idea that government should be concerned about seeing that the consumer gets adequate and understandable information.

Government has a continuing obligation in this aspect of public welfare, just as business has, and therefore the joint responsibility of government and business for the protection of the consumer is an increasingly important concept.

In the past, there have been *conflicts* in the broad province of business-government relationships. These have given rise to the old-fashioned stereotype of business as a sharp-fanged wolf lurking in the supermarket-forest to cheat and devour an innocent Red-Riding-Hood consumer, who can only be rescued by an honest woodsman—sent down from Washington, of course. And they have also given rise to the opposite cliché, which describes government as a bureaucratic, power-seeking knave who may kill, or at least sterilize, the free-economy goose that lays the golden eggs. Both these stereotypes are out-moded, and the conflicts they echo can be made out-moded, or considerably lessened, too.

Even in looking at this situation only "from a business point of view," it is evident that one significant step toward avoiding conflicts between government and business over consumer interests is to make certain that businessmen learn how to work effectively with public policy makers in government on those problems which concern them both.

Businessmen *are* learning. Back in the New-Deal Thirties, business fought the government. Then at the beginning of the Forties there was a shotgun marriage, because the war united government and business in a common cause. Working shoulder to shoulder with government taught businessmen that they could get along with government. So after World War II business decided to romance the makers of public policy in government, and sent its lawyers and public relations men to the state capitols and to Washington. But the conflicts did not dissolve. There was nearly a divorce between business and government. At this critical point, business realized that men in government did not want to talk with lawyers about the constitutional rights of business, nor did they want to hear the purity of business extolled by public relations men. The men in government wanted to talk about how public policy should be shaped for the public good. And they did not always believe that what was good for General Motors was good for the country.

Having realized that men in government were seriously concerned about public policy, top-level business executives themselves have begun to talk with government. Some of the activities and experiences of the Grocery Manufacturers of America will help to illustrate how businessmen are learning to work effectively with government on public policy problems.

Last year, about the time the Food and Drug Administration required the Borden Company to call back its powdered-milk product called "Starlac" because of the threat of salmonella infection, GMA established the GMA-FDA Council, composed of ten company chairmen or presidents and headed by C. W. Cook, Chairman of General Foods. It is the job of this council to meet quarterly or more often with Dr. James Goddard, Commissioner of the Food and Drug Administration. Discussions have been held with Dr. Goddard regarding such subjects as salmonella, labeling regulations, plant inspections, standards of ingredients, and good manufacturing practices. Through communication and cooperation, the Council has made progress in establishing a working relationship between business and government. In a speech this summer before the Federal Bar Association, Dr. James Goddard was reported as saying that his agency is "making good progress" with the food industry and that "the signs all point to a greater partnership of effort." He specifically cited cooperative work with GMA and the National Renderers Association and American Dry Milk Institute.

Another example of grocery-industry policy makers meeting with government policy makers to discuss mutual problems is the GMA-FTC Council. It is made up of six chief executive officers of small, medium, and large GMA member companies, and headed by Harry Dunning, President of Scott Paper Company and now Chairman of GMA, and it meets with Chairman Paul Rand Dixon of the Federal Trade Commission, and the four other commissioners. In four meetings thus far there have been discussions of such subjects as voluntary standards under the Fair Packaging and Labeling Law, "cents-off" promotions, private-label problems, and competition the manufacturer encounters in obtaining shelf space in the supermarket. Here are businessmen talking to government officials, each presenting practical information which can aid the other to understand and to work cooperatively on mutual problems. In testifying before the Senate Commerce Committee, Paul Rand Dixon, Chairman of the FTC, gave his views on the effectiveness of the GMA-FTC dialogues.

He described the FTC-GMA meetings, saying, "We sat around the table and discussed some of the problems they thought they saw, and we have eliminated them at the initial level." At one point, Senator Magnuson asked: "Would it be fair to say that you have had real cooperation from the industry in the carrying out of this Act?"

Mr. Dixon replied: "I think we have had excellent cooperation."
Senator Magnuson: "Particularly the food industry?"
Mr. Dixon: "Particularly the food industry, yes, sir."

In spite of the progress made through these and similar programs, it is still possible to hear an executive or two down along "Mahogany Row" say, "This corporation can't afford to get involved with government. The government is politics, and getting mixed up with politics will hurt our company image, or lose us some business." The fact is that this executive *must* become involved with the public policy makers in government, for they are in many ways his partners in his business, as well as his partners in the joint responsibility for the welfare of his customers. Conflicts can be minimized only if the presidents and chairmen of business corporations themselves learn how to work effectively with government, and take the time for the essential meetings with the public policy makers in government at which information can be exchanged, and mutually-satisfactory solutions to such problems as that of protecting the interest of the consumer can be worked out.

If businessmen and government officials will learn how to work together without conflicts, and will nurture the working relationships which have been developing, the *prospects* for cooperation which is successful from both points of view are enormously encouraging. Among many ways of enhancing the changes of prospective success, one important way is for both government and business to use fully the valuable help of university educator-experts.

When the truth is not wholly clear, the half-truth will be accepted. When the facts are missing, someone will make them up. In recent years, the biggest problems in the relations between the grocery industry and the government or the consumers have arisen simply because the basic facts of grocery manufacturing and marketing have not been made known. In many cases, the facts are not available because the necessary research has never been done. Last year, for example, housewives boycotted many supermarkets because they thought that grocery prices were too high. Yet it seems evident that this is the world's best-fed nation, with foods of greater variety and greater convenience available at lower cost than are available anywhere else in the world.

In such a confusing situation, properly-conducted research and widely-disseminated reports of research results could go far—for those on both sides of an issue—toward replacing misinformation with truth, and lack of information with facts.

The scholars and professors, the economists, sociologists, behavioral scientists, management-specialists and psychologists and other experts from fine universities can search out the truth and can provide, through their unbiased study, the facts. Surely that other old-fashioned stereotype, the one of the professor as an ivory-tower dreamer totally out of touch with the rude realities of politics and business, is dead, perhaps given its last farewell by the wide-ranging intellectual cosmopolitanism of the late President John F. Kennedy. GMA's experience has specifically shown that the objective, factual research reports prepared by educator-experts from the great academic institutions have both long-range theoretical and immediately practical values.

It is, for example, for this reason that the Consumer Research Institute of the Grocery Manufacturing Industry was recently formed. This Institute will sponsor and underwrite research investigations into the critical areas of consumer concern. The studies will be available to both business and government leaders, but most of the investigation will be undertaken by academic personnel which serves no faction.

In another instance, GMA chartered eleven outstanding professors to make five separate studies for submission to the National Food Marketing Commission. Professor Jesse W. Markham of Princeton University prepared a report on "Concentration in the Food Industry and Public Policy." A study of "Brand Competition in the Food Industry" was made by Professors Daniel M. Slate and Robert V. Mitchell of the University of Illinois. The problem of "Product Innovation, The Product Life, and

Competitive Behavior in Selected Food Processing Industries, 1947–1964" was researched by Robert D. Buzzell, associate professor, and Robert E. M. Nourse, research assistant, of the Graduate School of Business Administration, Harvard University; "The Cost Structure of Food Production and Distribution from Farmer to Consumer, 1954, 1958, 1963" by George B. Hegeman of Arthur D. Little, Inc. The problem of "Consumer Needs and Wants for Food Products" was researched by a project team headed by Dr. Gary A. Marple of the Arthur D. Little staff, and also consisting of Dr. Raymond A. Bauer of the Harvard Business School, Dr. Bruce Finnie of Harvard University, Dr. David Moore of New York State University, Dr. Cyril Sofer of Cambridge University, and three other associate members of the Arthur D. Little staff. These studies were used by several National Food Marketing Commission members in preparing their reports, were quoted extensively in the technical reports of the Commission, and furnished information which would otherwise have been unavailable either to business or to government.

Again, when President Johnson appointed the Food and Fiber Commission, GMA turned to the campus for objective and unprejudiced information. The Harvard Graduate School of Business was given a grant to make a study, the scope of which was agreed on in advance by the chairman and staff of the Food and Fiber Commission. The usefulness of this study, which was called "The United States Food and Fiber System in a Changing World Environment" and was prepared by Professors H. B. Arthur and Ray Goldberg of the Harvard University Graduate School of Business Administration and Kermit Bird on loan from the U.S. Department of Agriculture, is attested to by the fact that it was included as an appendix to the Food and Fiber Commission report.

Another example of the help the educator-expert can give business and government in meeting their shared obligation to the consumer is furnished by the House Interstate and Foreign Commerce Committee hearings on the Fair Packaging and Labeling Act in 1966. The Committee was making a detailed examination of the consumer's needs and problems in relation to the modern supermarket. It heard the testimony of government witnesses and of other spokesmen critical of industry. It heard testimony from man industry witnesses on the effects of the proposed legislation on the consumer and manufacturers. The statements conflicted, of course, largely because accurate information was lacking on both sides. In order to supply unbiased information on what was actually known about consumers' wants and needs, GMA asked Dr. John Howard of Columbia University to provide the Commerce Committee with material based on his studies of consumer behavior patterns. This information is included on page 843 of volume 2 of the records of the hearing, and thus the grocery industry is on record, in the literal sense of the word, as to its belief that the academic community can make a vital and valuable contribution to the solution of problems which government and business face together.

The firmness of our belief in the value and vitality of the contribution of educator-experts can also be judged by the fact that GMA has established an Educational Council as a part of its activities. Led by Alexander N. McFarland, Chairman of Corn Products Company, it will also be composed of chairmen or presidents of member companies. The Educational Council will re-examine the interaction of the grocery industry and the educational community, and will explore and develop new methods of making that interaction more productive.

The grocery industry is not, of course, alone in its belief that the professor can aid the government official and the corporation president in solving problems of public policy which affect them all. Nor is the grocery industry alone in its belief that the concept of consumer protection as a joint responsibility of business and government is an important one, or that conflicts between government and business can be minimized if businessmen will learn to work effectively with the public policy makers in government. The illustrations offered here are drawn from the field most familiar to me, and can be fairly said to be typical of the procedures and principles of all progressive businessmen. Indeed, the industry of which I can speak most knowledgeably, the food and grocery industry in the United States, is committed to the principle that what is good for the American consumer is good for American business.

What is good for the American consumer must be the joint responsibility of business and government. Business leaders must aid in the shouldering of this joint responsibility by learning to work with government in a way which helps to eliminate conflict to build an effective working team for the future. And both government and business must expand the use of the services of the university community as a valuable and vital means to improve the prospects of success in the discharge of this joint responsibility.

C. A proposal for private marketing ombudsmen

One of marketing's biggest challenges today is delivering an adequate standard of living to the low-income consumer. Walter A. Hamilton sets forth some do's and don'ts for ghetto marketing and poses the challenge of voluntary versus mandatory approaches in the ghetto area.

23. GHETTO MARKETING: VOLUNTARY VERSUS MANDATORY IMPROVEMENTS*

Walter A. Hamilton

Our subject is "marketing," not retailing or selling or just the moving of goods and services from point of origin to point of consumption. It is also the "ghetto," a particular kind of market, differing from other markets more in the way in which marketers have regarded it than in fact.

Ghetto marketing brings into focus all of the most common problems facing marketing today. What we do there may well be the precursor of what we will have to face up to doing everywhere sooner or later. Ghetto markets have some special characteristics, however. Many residents are heavily dependent on local stores in their own neighborhoods. Their income levels block them off from the means for greater mobility. The vast majority have neither cars nor access to adequate public transportation. They also depend heavily on the kind of high-cost low-volume credit—even for daily necessities—which is available at their income levels only at the neighborhood store. The money they get this week goes to pay for last week's groceries. They can never get even, let alone ahead. This means they often can't shop around outside their neighborhoods even if they go outside. Yet all the records and studies show that they pay their bills. If anything, they apparently are more conscientious about this than many outside the ghettos even though those bills are often far out of proportion to the value of the goods received.

Some students of the ghetto have observed that among the main differences between ghetto consumers and those elsewhere are the ways in which these consumers—or at least some small number among them— have come to evidence their displeasure. They throw things, burn things, and generally violate what others regard as the conventions of law and order. While none of us would endorse such civil disorder, we must also note that conformity and placidity have rarely, if ever, brought about change. Those who live in the inner city ghettos have chosen this way to force the "establishment" to stop and re-examine what it is doing, re-evaluate whether present practices are in fact either right, economically or socially healthy and constructive, or indeed even any longer tolerable in our society.

Many schemes and panaceas are currently in vogue. It is not my purpose to add to or even comment on these. Rather, let us reexamine mar-

---

*From a speech given at the American Marketing Association Conference, Denver, August, 1968.

keting practices in the ghetto and look at the basic alternatives open to us. From among these, hopefully, we can arrive at some new judgments for our common guidance.

Marketing embraces all of the connective tissue of our economic system—from identification of needs and wants to determination of how best to meet them. But marketing is part of business and business prospers and grows only insofar as it shows an attractive return on investment. The higher the risk, the higher the yield investors must see in prospect before they will make capital available. Many aspects of the ghetto market have been commonly *thought*—I stress that word *thought*—to make it a less attractive market than some others:

Land costs for business establishments are at a premium.
Crime and pilferage rates are high.
Insurance rates are high.
Average unit sales, especially in food, are low.
Personnel turnover rates, hence costs, are high.
Credit collection costs and bad debt ratios are high.

As the spotlight of serious market research has been turned on the ghettos in the wake of civil disorder, we have learned that some of these things either are not so or need not be. But they have nevertheless had most unfortunate consequences. Many manufacturers have simply chosen not to make any special appeal to the motivations and desires of the ghetto market. They have not sought to relate to it, as the psychologists would say. Responsible distributors have not focused on it either, except as a pool of low-cost labor for the heavier physical tasks involved in movement of goods, warehousing, longshoring and the like. And most important, many retailers have avoided seeking to serve the ghettos at all. That is not to say that many responsible retailers have not paid attention and done a good job. But most of the time, serving the local neighborhoods in the ghettos has been left to the marginal operators—those who have neither the skill nor the will to be part of the mainstream of marketing. It is among these fringe members of the marketing community that we find the unfair and deceptive practices to which ghetto residents object violently and with good cause. Even an abbreviated recital makes it clear why this is so:

Bait and switch promotions.
High pressure and coercive selling.
Almost exclusive recourse to the courts for bill collection.
Excessive markups on standard merchandise.
Misrepresentation of merchandise.
Intimidation of customers.

Other basic elements of sound marketing are often wholly absent, such as observance of basic local regulations on building safety and health, involvement in the community, and employment of people with whom customers can relate.

As long as ghetto residents tolerated these conditions, the vast majority of the marketing community felt that it could safely assume these problems were none of its business. Now we all know this is not so. Our whole economy suffers if the fundamental rules governing it break down and force any significant portion to suffer as a consequence. The discipline of the marketplace as the primary regulating force of our economy has broken down in the ghetto. How can it be restored, or if it cannot, what can we put in its place to serve these markets effectively?

Government and business, working together, are already doing something about it. A major attack on the problem of joblessness and discrimination among the low-skilled is underway. The Model Cities program is moving. A host of aid programs are focussed on correcting some of the basic things which make it possible for irresponsible and incompetent marketers to prey upon the poor. But these things all take time to have their effect—too much time for people to endure in silence.

The marketing community has some options open for its own initiative. Some are already being taken. Some of the burned-out supermarkets *are* being rebuilt. Some of the retailing members of the marketing community are getting together in ventures like the Social Development Corporation in New York. Almost every major city has one or more new thrusts underway to improve retailing and distribution services to its low-income areas. Government is cooperating. The Riot Insurance program has been enacted. The Small Business Administration has launched its program to promote minority entrepreneurship. But these things take time too.

And so we see another approach gaining public support in some quarters: Mandatory Federal controls in substitution for the discipline of the marketplace. Before we get too far down this road—and I mean the collective we of the nation, consumers and voters—we should make a conscious choice. How that choice is made and what it will be is a matter in which the marketing community can and should have a voice. For it is our marketing system as we have known it which stands to be changed the most if we change course now.

We have already seen some actions in the mandatory regulations direction. Failure on the part of the automotive industry to give sufficient heed to what the public adjudged to be safety resulted in the Auto Safety Act. And in its wake has come the Products Safety Commission with a charter to explore what other products involve safety problems and recommend what should be done about these. Inadequate local meat inspection procedures brought us the Wholesome Meat Act, and similar measures have been proposed in other areas. Such Federal regulatory approaches to protection of the consumer against what is felt to be excessive abuse by our competitive business system could bring about basic changes in the private enterprise system as we have known it. It has served us too well for us to allow its workings to be altered so drastically on an ever-widening scale without looking seriously at the alternatives.

There is a middle ground between Federal control and laissez-faire. It lies in Government-business partnership approaches which are also being actively tried in some equally critical areas. When it came to packaging proliferation, the nation chose to give voluntary standards a hard try. And I can report that this effort is working well, as every housewife will see for herself on grocery and drug store shelves in the next twelve months. When it came to air pollution, the Congress agreed to give the partnership approach a hard try: Federal criteria with state and local standards. After six years of trying to cope with training low-skilled unemployed, the Federal Government turned last winter to the National Alliance of Businessmen for a partnership approach which has put 145,000 people at work in less then six months and will more then double that number by year-end.

A third alternative is open—that of outright voluntary standards and codes. These have worked well in much of our marketing system in the past. Codes of ethics and standards of conduct and practice have been drawn by industry associations and have proved effective. But these reach only those in the responsible part of the community. They could be effective in helping correct the problems of the ghettos only if these same responsible marketers do commit themselves to serve the ghetto market directly.

Finally, there are both the beginnings of action and growing amount of talk about state and local government, business and academic cooperation to develop more effective codes, standards, and regulations at the local and state level. The Better Business Bureaus already have an extensive and detailed code of practices which addresses itself to all or most of the problems with which we are confronted in the ghettos. The Federal Trade Commission has already developed a model state statute— "Uniform Unfair Trade Practice and Consumer Protection Law." This is sometimes called the little "FTC" idea and is being promoted for adoption by states through the Council of State Governments. This model statute, or a variation on it, has been adopted by 16 states, but the adequacy of the measure adopted, as well as the capacity to enforce it, varies considerably.

The principle to which we are calling attention here is that of local level cooperative development of ground rules which, if properly enforced, could bring about major improvement in ghetto marketing quickly. Since the worst problems are in the major cities, and not state-wide, it is possible that some of you might get together with the Better Business Bureaus in your cities and with other responsible business associations and see what you could do about prompt enactment of such an ordnance in your cities. By utilizing the work that has been done, it would make it easier to assure compatability with state statutes which might eventually be enacted.

This sort of action is not adequate, however, unless equally vigorous and continued attention is given to the matter of enforcement. Here the Better Business Bureaus are also in the forefront. They are experimenting both with mobile vans and store front offices to give ghetto residents an action center to which they could bring their complaints and to which to go for counselling. We understand that the Better Business Bureaus are now developing an action plan to extend these experiments to as many of the major cities as is possible. They will need your help to do this, help which might come in part from some of your graduate students who certainly could profit in their educational development from this exposure. All of this approach obviously takes not only business leadership but also private money to put across and keep going. Private marketing ombudsmen in the ghettos need not wait on Government action. This seems like a very promising route to pursue.

Perhaps my own predilection shows through somewhat in this last statement, but I am convinced that this is a time for initiative and action, not more academic studies. There is much we do not yet know and need to know about ghetto marketing. But our efforts to get on with the job will certainly be better received if everything we undertake at this stage is action-oriented.

What we learn from the choice we make and the actions we take will shape the next evolutionary steps in the development of our entire marketing system. Out of the solutions to our ghetto marketing crisis can come productive and profitable improvements of wider applicability. Without your initiative and action, however, there could also come developments which could undermine the entire foundation of our marketplace discipline system of enterprise. And that is not a result any of us should regard with equanimity.

D. Marketing skills and developing nations

The key role which can be played by marketing and the challenge to marketing people in the development of the less-economically advanced nations is stressed by Walt W. Rostow. His observations are of particular interest because of the important positions in U.S. government planning he occupied over a period of years.

24. THE CONCEPT OF A NATIONAL MARKET
AND ITS ECONOMIC GROWTH IMPLICATIONS*

Walt W. Rostow

I

I can tell you—without flattery—that I believe the skills this organization commands and represents are going to prove critical in the generation ahead to the development of countries and regions which contain a clear majority of the world's population. I have in mind the developing countries of Asia, the Middle East, Africa, and Latin America. I also have in mind the Soviet Union and the countries of Eastern Europe. I would add, parenthetically, that should Communist China come, in time, to formulate a rational and effective development strategy—which it now lacks—marketing in all its dimensions must play there, too, a new and significant role.

II

To understand why this proposition is valid, one must look at the development theories and policies which have been applied to these regions over the past generation, examine where they now stand and where they must go as they move forward in their stages of development.

With a few exceptions, the developing nations of Asia, the Middle East, Africa, and Latin America began their first purposeful stage of modernization by concentrating their efforts in two areas: the production of manufactured goods in substitution for consumer goods imports and the creation of basic infrastructure; that is, roads, electric power, ports, education, etc. Agriculture and the modernization of rural life were systematically neglected, yielding now a dangerous decline in per capita food production in some major regions.

There was a certain legitimacy in these initial priorities. The development of an economy, at its core, consists in the progressive diffusion of the fruits of modern science and technology. Industry is the most dramatic form which modern science and technology assumes; and basic infrastructure is directly required for industrialization.

But there was also an element of irrationality. Agriculture was associated with the period of colonialism and/or with excessive dependence

*From *Marketing and Economic Development,* American Marketing Association, September, 1965, pp. 11–20.

on export markets in industrial countries. It appeared to be second order—and, even, faintly humiliating business, as compared to industrialization.

The combination of these two factors—rational and irrational—has led to a phase of development concentrated largely in a few cities, centered around a few industries, and, as I say, to a systematic neglect of what agriculture could and must contribute by way of food, industrial raw materials, foreign exchange, and enlarged domestic markets.

The start of industrialization varied in time as among the developing countries of the contemporary world. The Latin American countries generally began just before or during the Second World War, while many others began seriously only in the years after 1945. Some, indeed, have not yet launched their first phase of sustained industrialization. Nevertheless, it is broadly true that we have come to the end or are coming to the end of the phase when the initial, narrow postwar strategy for development can be regarded as viable.

In one developing country after another the perception is spreading that the next phase of development must be based on a systematic diffusion of the modern skills, now largely concentrated in urban areas, out into the countryside; on the making of efficient national markets; and, from this widened basis, on the generation of new lines of diversified exports which alone promise to earn the foreign exchange which the developing countries will need in the years ahead. Only this pattern of widened domestic markets and diversified exports promises to provide the foundation for that deepening of the industrial structure (from consumers goods down to capital goods and the heavy industry sectors) which a modern society requires.

If I may be permitted to use a somewhat private vocabulary,[1] it can be said that during the past generation we have had in many parts of the world a take-off in which the leading sectors have been import-substitution industries in consumer goods fields; and for these nations to move on into the drive to industrial maturity requires that they convert their somewhat isolated urban industrial concentrations into active, dynamic centers which purposefully diffuse the process of modernization out across the nation, while they generate the capacity, on this wider market foundation, to pay their way as they move to full industrialization of their societies.

This is a shorthand approximation of the task for the next generation that lies before the nations within the Free World, which contain most of the population of Asia, the Middle East, Africa, and Latin America; and it is also the problem which must be solved if a modern industrialized China is really going to emerge.

---

[1]Dr. Rostow refers here to his book, *The Stages of Economic Growth: A Non-Communist Manifesto* (New York: Cambridge University Press, 1960).

III

The problem in the Soviet Union and much of Eastern Europe is, of course, somewhat different. There the origins of industrialization generally reach back to the last quarter of the nineteenth century—in some regions even earlier. These nations (with certain exceptions) have moved forward in the postwar generation to complete the drive to industrial maturity. They did so under doctrines which made the expansion of heavy industry virtually an object in itself; that is, heavy industry was built either to supply military forces or to build more heavy industry. But they have now come to a stage in their development where Khrushchev was quite right in attacking what he called the "steel eaters." He asked, you may remember, 'What do you want us to do with more steel, eat it?' It is the inevitable—and predicted—slowing down in the heavy industry sectors which mainly accounts for the over-all sluggishness of these economies. They have exhausted the capacity of the heavy industry sectors to lead in the growth process.

Along this way, like the developing countries, the Soviet Union and the countries of Eastern Europe have neglected agriculture. In addition, they have kept it under forms of collective organization which were grossly inefficient in their use of capital and manpower, although collective arrangements are being diluted in parts of Eastern Europe in an effort to provide effective incentives to the farmer.

The next stage of development in the Soviet Union and Eastern Europe must, evidently, be based not merely on a correction of agricultural inefficiency but upon the turning of their relatively mature industrial complexes to supply the things which people want when average income levels reach the point at which they now stand in these countries.

If high rates of growth are to be resumed in the Soviet Union and in Eastern Europe, they will come about by some version of the economic and social revolution which we in the United States began in the 1920's and which began to grip Western Europe and Japan in the 1950's; that is, the revolution centered about the rapid diffusion of the automobile, durable consumers goods, suburban housing, and all the rest of the now familiar package.

I may say in passing that this revolution is not to be understood simply in terms of industrial gadgetry. Behind the desire for a private automobile, a television set, a suburban house with a little grass and a fence, are two profound human desires which, from all we can thus far observe, are universal; namely, a desire for mobility—for getting over the horizon—and a desire for privacy. The gadgets we command represent, simply, the ways modern industry has found to satisfy these deep, legitimate, and decent human desires.

Again, reverting to my own terms, I would say that, just as most of the developing world is in a process of adjustment from take-off to the drive to technological maturity, the Soviet Union and Eastern Europe are in a process of adjustment from their own version of the drive to technological maturity to the age of high-mass consumption.

IV

And here, of course, is where marketing comes in.

The modernization of the countryside in the developing countries evidently has many dimensions. We now know enough from practical experience to be able to say that, assuming roads and minimum basic education and assuming, also a certain backlog of relevant agricultural science, there are four necessary and sufficient conditions for an agricultural revolution.

First, the farmer must receive a reliable and fair price for his product.

Second, credit must be available at reasonable rates for him to make the change in the character of his output or the shift in productivity desired.

Third, there must be available on the spot technical assistance that is relevant to his soil, his weather conditions, and his change in either output or in productivity.

Finally, there must be available at reasonable rates two types of industrial products: inputs such as chemical fertilizers, insecticides, and farm tools; and incentive goods—that is, the consumer goods of good quality he and his family would purchase in greater quantity or work harder to get if they were cheaper or if their income were higher.

These four conditions can be satisfied in a good many ways. As I have wandered about the developing areas and studied the evidence available, I have been struck by the variety of institutional forms in which agricultural success stories appear—producers' cooperatives, food processing firms, large commercial farms, etc.; but they all have the characteristic of organizing around the farmer these four necessary and sufficient conditions.

You will note that marketing enters directly into these conditions both ways; that is, marketing from the farm to the city and from the city to the farm.

If the farmer is to receive a fair price for his product without a rise of food prices in the cities, there must be a modernization of marketing arrangements which permits this to happen. No aspect of the developing world troubles me more than the widespread situation where the farmer gets 15 or 20 percent of the selling price of his product—with the selling price in the city high and great wastage occurring along the way.

It is sometimes argued that the fragmented and expensive marketing arrangements which exist for many commodities in developing countries are, simply, an aspect of underdevelopment which will pass away with time and the progress of modernization as a whole. Specifically, it is sometimes pointed out that the modernization of marketing might remove from employment people who are now engaged, even at a low level of productivity.

Three considerations argue against this more complacent line of thought.

First, in many cases the marketing arrangements which confront a farmer in a developing country are what economists call monopsonistic; that is, the individual farmer is confronted with a situation where there is only one intermediary to whom he can sell his product. At the critical point of the harvest season the farmer is at the mercy of such intermediaries. That inequitable bargaining circumstance is often made worse because the purchaser of the farmer's products is often also the only available source of credit to the farmer. In short, traditional marketing arrangements are not only inefficient, they often do not have the competitive characteristics economists implicitly assume.

Second, the gap between prices on the farm and prices to the urban consumer constitutes a quite special barrier between the cities and the countryside, the effects of which must be measured not merely in terms of the alternative employment of labor but in terms of the whole urban-rural relationship. Specifically, archaic marketing arrangements make it unprofitable for the farmer to engage in higher productivity agricultural production; and they thereby reduce not only agricultural output but also the size of the market for manufactured goods. In modernizing marketing relations, we must take into account not merely the possible displacement of labor in the present marketing chains but the total effects on output and markets of what one Latin American president has called the Chinese wall they constitute between the city and the countryside.

Third, quite pragmatically, where modern marketing arrangements have been introduced (through producers' cooperatives, food processing firms, commercial farming, or other arrangements), the process of adjustment in employment in the maketing sector has not, in practice, proved difficult.

In short, I am confident that the modernization of marketing arrangements from the farm to the city is a crusade we can enter with a conviction that the benefits will far outweigh the costs in readjustment.

Looked at from the other side, that is, from the city to the countryside, the modernization of rural life demands new and effective ways of getting to the farmer both the things he needs to increase productivity and incentive goods.

With respect to chemical fertilizers, insecticides, seeds, and farm machinery, there is a role, beyond conventional marketing, to be undertaken by the salesman. It may be regarded as sacrilege by some, but it has generally proved true that the most powerful agent in the diffusion of new agricultural technology has been the commercial firm rather than public institutions set up for technical assistance purposes. I would not for a moment denigrate the role in the United States of the county agent nor of those who have followed in his tradition in the developing areas; but it is simply a fact that there are not enough county agents out working in the villages to do the job in contemporary developing areas. Among other reasons, too many trained agricultural technologists are to be found working in government offices in the capital city rather than in grass roots jobs. A good, pragmatic performance in the diffusion of technical knowledge can be and is being done in many parts of the world by those who have a straight commercial interest in selling their products. The salesman knows he must spend his time with potential customers.

With respect to incentive goods, we must begin by accepting the fact that people in the rural areas of the developing world are poor. Until their income rises, they may not be able to buy a great deal more than they are buying. On the other hand, it is also true that what they can buy in their villages by way of manufactured goods is often shoddy and expensive. We know from the history of rural areas in the United States—even the quite recent experience of the Tennessee Valley area—that the availability of attractive and inexpensive consumer goods can be an important stimulus to production and productivity. Lower prices can yield more purchases in the short run; lower prices and the availability of incentive goods of good quality can yield more output, income, and purchases in the longer run. The same lesson can be observed in Mexico and other developing areas where efforts to increase productivity on the supply side are combined with such incentives.

The technical marketing problem from the city to the countryside consists in finding ways to lower the unit cost of distribution under circumstances where rural markets are scattered and the volume of any one commodity to be sold at any one point is low. The most successful solution in developing countries is, of course, the marketing of beer and soft drinks. The volume of sales, however, is sufficient in this case to support regular truck deliveries even at low levels of rural income. What appears to be required is the development of unified marketing arrangements for a wide range of consumer goods so that the overhead distribution costs for each commodity are reduced.

As I have seen soft drink trucks roll into distant villages, I have often wished they had a trailer attached containing textiles, shoes, household equipment, flashlights, transistor radios, books and the other things the villagers would buy if prices were lower.

Producers' cooperatives, food processing plants, and other substantial institutions in rural areas can often serve as centers for the efficient assembly and distribution of such incentive goods, as well as the fertilizers, insecticides, etc., needed to increase productivity.

V

I have tried to indicate concretely the kind of marketing operations required if those engaged in distribution are to play their part in breaking down the Chinese wall between urban and rural life in developing countries and in assisting in the creation of national markets. The moderization of rural life, which lies at the heart of this structural problem, evidently involves elements which go beyond distribution itself. In our recent letter to the Presidents of the Latin American Republics and to the President of the United States, the Members of CIAP—the Inter-American Committee on the Alliance for Progress—listed seven major elements required to accelerate the modernization of rural life. Aside from more efficient distribution, these were: changes in land tenure in regions of many Latin American countries; changes in certain cases in government agricultural price policies; the expansion of production as well as distribution of chemical fertilizers; expansion and improvement of agricultural credit; the buildup of institutions such as producers' cooperatives and food processing firms; programs of popular cooperation and community development. Within this whole complex of actions designed to break the stagnation and apathy of life and production in rural areas, modern marketing arrangements have, however, a critical role.

The range of specific actions required in the Soviet Union and Eastern Europe is similar to that required in the developing areas; but the nations with Communist regimes confront their inherited commitment to collective institutions for production and distribution. Over the years these have proved generally inefficient and resistant to reform; although reform efforts have been made or are being made in several countries in the area. I know of very few government distribution operations anywhere in the world which have proved effective; and I know of a good many which have required massive subsidy to work at all. The reason is the lack of direct interest on the part of the bureaucrat in pressing for that extra margin of cost cutting and that extra margin of sales which make the difference.

Nevertheless, it is clear that there is a ferment in the Soviet Union and in Eastern Europe centered on the lack of incentives to productivity in agriculture and on methods for making the distribution system more responsive to the interests and tastes of the consumer. There is a growing awareness of the inner contradiction between the modes of organization which have been created in the past out of their ideological commitments and the imperatives of progress. No one can predict the outcome of these debates and the changes in policy that will ensue; but they constitute an interesting and important element for change on the world scene, which is essentially hopeful.

VI

The making of national markets through the more effective linking of urban and rural areas bears directly on the other great task of the developing countries in the years ahead; namely, their need to generate diversified exports. A whole range of special skills and special efforts is needed to market new products abroad. Potential markets must be studied with careful attention to local tastes; distribution channels must be established; regular and reliable flows of supplies must be moved and financed; quality controls must be built up; and efficient production must be generated if the exports are to be competitive. For countries whose first phase of industrialization has taken place internally, behind high tariff barriers which protected the local market, a quite revolutionary shift in mentality is required before business can generate the efficiency to face the winds of international competition. That shift is only beginning to take place in a few Latin American countries at the present time; although, in Asia, Taiwan has made the transition to diversified manufactured exports in good style, and South Korea is well on its way. In highly competitive international markets it does not take many cases of supplies that fail to arrive on time or of uncertain quality for the export effort to be set back.

That branch of the art of distribution concerned with the export trade will evidently be increasingly important in the developing areas in the years ahead.

But there is a further connection worth noting. Historically the export of manufactured goods has usually followed or paralleled the development of a national market. The classic case was that of cotton textiles. Starting with Great Britain, one country after another entered the textile export trade as a kind of reflex to learning how to produce and distribute efficiently within its own national market; for cotton textiles are the first modern manufactured product likely to develop a mass market in a relatively poor country. Other manufactured goods, in turn, have flowed into international channels as they took hold in domestic markets—right down to Japan's booming export of transistor radios. In concentrating in the years ahead on the development of national markets, therefore, the developing countries will also be laying the foundations for the export of those diversified manufactures on which their future foreign exchange earning capacity will substantially rest.

VII

The argument I have tried to lay before you today has a particular significance for the development of economic thought as well as for public policy. Whether we are conscious of it or not, our ways of thinking about the economy are still colored by ideas that go back to the classical economists of the nineteenth century and, indeed, back to the eighteenth century world of the physiocrats. They began to organize their thoughts by focusing of the physical factors of production, notably land and labor. The concept of the widening of the market was introduced and effectively dramatized, of course, by Adam Smith. But what it took to widen the market, beyond physical means of transport, was not generally taken seriously by the founding fathers of modern economic thought. In fact, distribution (and services generally) tended to be ignored or regarded, somehow, as an inferior kind of economic activity. Down to the present day it is difficult to get development economists and policy makers to accord to problems of efficiency in distribution the same attention they give automatically to problems of production, investment, and finance.

For Communists the problem is compounded by the nature of Marxist economics. Karl Marx was, as an economist, rooted in the classical tradition. His propositions perpetuated in a particularly strong form the tendency to denigrate distribution—so much so that it is formally excluded from Communist concepts of national income.

Thus in facing now the tasks of widening the market, both in the developing areas and in the Soviet Union and in Eastern Europe, governments must overcome those most insidious of pressures; that is, the pressures created by the sometimes unconscious acceptance of ideas from the past that obscure the character and priority of current problems.

If I am correct that men must, in the generations ahead, diffuse the process of modernization out over long neglected rural regions, creating new efficient networks of distribution, we shall see not merely new and challenging tasks for those who command the skills of distribution but a new theoretical respect and appreciation for the art of that widening of the market which, for so long, was taken for granted.

E. Closing the communications gap

The final article is an appropriate conclusion to this book of readings which have been concerned with marketing's responsibilities to society. The needs for better understanding, improved communications, and even dialogue have been suggested in many of the articles. Raymond A. Bauer and Stephen A. Greyser explain why dialogue is difficult, why it "never happens." Their stimulating article poses the challenge of communication: What can be done?

25. THE DIALOGUE THAT NEVER HAPPENS*

Raymond A. Bauer
and Stephen A. Greyser

In recent years government and business spokesmen alike have advocated a "dialogue" between their two groups for the reduction of friction and the advancement of the general good. Yet, all too often, this is a dialogue that never happens. Rather, what passes for dialogue *in form* is often a sequence of monologues *in fact*, wherein each spokesman merely grants "equal time" to the other and pretends to listen while preparing his own next set of comments. Obviously, this is not always the case; and, if taken literally, it tends to minimize some real progress being made.

Our aim here is to try to facilitate and stimulate that progress by exploring what lies behind the dialogue that never happens and by suggesting what can be done—on both sides—to develop more meaningful and effective business-government interactions.

In this context, we link "government spokesmen" with "critics." Naturally, not all in government are critics of business, and vice versa. However, almost all critics seek redress of their grievances via government action and seek government spokesmen to present their views "in behalf of the public."

Our primary focus will be in the field of marketing—particularly selling and advertising—which is perhaps the most controversial and most frequently criticized single zone of business. Marketing seems to be the area where achieving true dialogue is most difficult and where business and government spokesmen most seem to talk past each other.

Before examining why this takes place, let us look at two comments on advertising that illustrate the lack of dialogue. The first comment is that of Donald F. Turner, Assistant Attorney General in charge of the Antitrust Division of the Justice Department:

Harvard Business Review, November–December, 1967, pp. 2, 3, 4, 6, 8, 10, 12, 186, 188. Based on speech given by Raymond Bauer at the 1967 American Marketing Association Conference, Toronto, June, 1967.

Authors' note: We gratefully acknowledge the assistance of Robert D. Moran. Harvard Business School Doctoral Candidate, in the development of and research for the article.

There are three steps to informed choice: (1) the consumer must know the product exists; (2) the consumer must know how the product performs; and (3) he must know how it performs compared to other products. If advertising only performs step one and appeals on other than a performance basis, informed choice cannot be made.[1]

The other comment is that of Charles L. Gould, Publisher, the San Francisco *Examiner*:

No government agency, no do-gooders in private life can possibly have as much interest in pleasing the consuming public as do . . . successful companies. For, in our economy, their lives literally depend on keeping their customers happy.[2]

DOUBLE ENTENDRES

Why do business and government spokesmen talk past each other in discussing ostensibly the same marketplace? We think it is because each has a basically different model of the consumer world in which marketing operates. This misunderstanding grows from different perceptions about a number of key words.

The first word is *competition*. The critics of business think of competition tacitly as strictly price differentiation. Modern businessmen, however, as marketing experts frequently point out, think of competition primarily in terms of product differentiation, sometimes via physical product developments and sometimes via promotional themes. The important thing is that price competition plays a relatively minor role in today's marketplace.

Some of the perplexity between these two views of competition has to do with confusion over a second word, *product*. In the critic's view, a product is the notion of some entity which has a primary identifiable function only. For example, an automobile is a device for transporting bodies, animate or inanimate; it ordinarily has four wheels and a driver, and is powered by gasoline. There are variants on this formula (three-wheeled automobiles) which are legitimate, provided the variants serve the same function. Intuitively the businessman knows there is something wrong with this notion of the product because the product's secondary function may be his major means of providing differentiation (an auto's looks, horsepower, and so on).

Then there is the term *consumer needs*, which the business critic sees as corresponding to a product's primary function—for example, needs for transportation, nutrition, recreation (presumably for health purposes),

---

[1]Statement made at the Ninth Annual American Federation of Advertising Conference on Government Relations held in Washington, D.C., February, 1967.
[2]*Ibid.*

and other things. The businessman, on the other hand, sees needs as virtually *any* consumer lever he can use to differentiate his product.

Next, there is the notion of *rationality*. The critic, with a fixed notion of "needs" and "product," sees any decision that results in an efficient matching of product to needs as rational. The businessman, taking no set position on what a person's needs should be, contends that any decision the customer makes to serve his own perceived self-interest is rational.

The last addition to our pro tem vocabulary is *information*. The critic fits information neatly into his view that a rational decision is one which matches product function and consumer needs, rather circularly defined as the individual's requirement for the function the product serves. Any information that serves that need is "good" information. To the businessman, information is basically any data or argument that will (truthfully) put forth the attractiveness of a product in the context of the consumer's own buying criteria.

Exhibit I summarizes our views of these two different models of the consumer world. We realize that we may have presented a somewhat

EXHIBIT I

TWO DIFFERENT MODELS OF THE CONSUMER WORLD

Key Words	Critic's View	Businessman's View
Competition	Price competition.	Product differentiation.
Product	Primary function only.	Differentiation through secondary function.
Consumer needs..	Correspond point-for-point to primary functions.	Any customer desire on which the product can be differentiated.
Rationality	Efficient matching of product to customer needs.	Any customer decision that serves the customer's own perceived self-interest.
Information	Any data that facilitate the fit of a product's proper function with the customer's needs.	Any data that will (truthfully) put forth the attractiveness of the product in the eyes of the customer.

exaggerated dichotomy. But we think the models are best demonstrated by this delineation of the pure views of contrasting positions, recognizing that both sides modify them to some extent.

VIEWS OF HUMAN NATURE

A review of our "vocabulary with a double meaning" and the two models of the consumer world shows that the critic's view is based on a conviction that he knows what "should be." In contrast, the businessman's view is based on militant agnosticism with regard to "good" or "bad" value judgments which might be made (by anyone) about individual marketplace transactions.

The businessman's view of human nature may be the more flattering, perhaps excessively so. Certainly, the marketer's notion of "consumer sovereignty" compliments the consumer in attributing to him the capacity to decide what he needs and to make his choice competently even under exceedingly complex circumstances. It also sometimes challenges him to do so. This perhaps undeserved flattery glosses over some obvious flaws in the market mechanism. It is rooted in the belief that this mechanism, even though imperfect in specific instances, is better than administrative procedures for regulating the market.

The critic takes a far less optimistic view of human nature—both the consumer's and the seller's. He thinks that the seller often (sometimes intentionally) confuses consumers with a welter of one-sided argumentation. Such information, in the critic's eye, not only lacks impartiality, but usually focuses on secondary product functions and is not geared to consumer needs.

Both sets of assumptions are, we think, at least partially justified. Customers do have limited information and limited capacity to process it. This is the way of the world. Furthermore, there is no reason to believe that every seller has every customer's interest as his own primary concern in every transaction, even though in the long run it probably is in the seller's own best interest to serve every customer well.

All of this disagreement comes to focus on a point where both business and government are in agreement; namely, modern products are sufficiently complex that the individual consumer is in a rather poor position to judge their merits quickly and easily. The businessman says that the customer should be, and often is, guided in his judgment by knowledge of brand reputation and manufacturer integrity, both of which are enhanced by advertising. The critic argues that the customer should be, but too seldom is, aided by impartial information sources primarily evaluating product attributes.

These conflicting views of vocabulary and human nature are reflected in several specific topic areas.

BRANDS AND RATING SERVICES

One of these areas is the relationship of national branding to consumer rating services, the latter being a traditional source of "impartial information" for consumers. Somehow the crux of this relationship seems to have escaped most people's attention: consumer rating services are possible only *because* of the existence of a limited number of brands for a given product. In order for a rating to be meaningful, two conditions are necessary:

1. *Identifiability.* The consumer must be able to recognize the products and brands rated.
2. *Uniformity.* Manufacturers must habitually produce products of sufficiently uniform quality that consumer and rating service alike can learn enough from a sample of the product to say or think something meaningful about another sample of the same product which may be bought in some other part of the country at some later time. This is a seldom-realized aspect of national branding.

It is generally assumed by both groups that the "consumer movement" is basically opposed to heavily advertised branded goods. The stereotype of *Consumer Reports* is that it regularly aims at shunting trade away from national brands to Sears, to Montgomery Ward, or to minor brands. Yet the one study made of this issue showed that, contrary to the stereotype, *Consumer Reports* had consistently given higher ratings to the heavily advertised national brands than to their competitors.[3]

Ideological blindness. What we have here is an instance of the consumer movement and brand-name manufacturers being ideologically blinded by different models of the market world. The consumer movement concentrates on the notion of a product having a definable primary function that should take precedence over virtually all other attributes of the product. True, some concessions have recently been made to aesthetics. But, on the whole, the consumer movement is suspicious of the marketing world that strives to sell products on the basis of secondary attributes which the consumer movement itself regards with a jaundiced eye.

The evidence available to the consumer movement is that, in general, national advertising is *not* accompanied by poorer performance on primary criteria. But the consumer movement fails to realize that it *takes for granted* the central claim for advertised branded products—namely, that by being identifiable and uniform in quality, they offer the customer an opportunity to make his choice on the basis of his confidence in a particular manufacturer.

But the manufacturers of nationally branded products and their spokesmen have been equally blind. First of all, we know of none who has pointed out the extent to which any form of consumer rating must be based on the identifiability and uniformity of brand products. The only situation where this does not apply is when the rating service can instruct the consumer in how to evaluate the product—for example,

---

[3]Eugene R. Beem and John S. Ewing, "Business Appraises Consumer Testing Agencies," *Harvard Business Review*, March-April, 1954, pp. 113-26, especially p. 121.

looking for marbleizing in beef. However, this is limited to products of such a nature that the customer can, with but little help, evaluate them for himself; it cannot apply to products for which he has to rely on the technical services of an independent evaluator or on the reputation of the manufacturer.

Moreover, except for such big-ticket items as automobiles, consumer rating services usually test products only once in several years. In other words, they rate not only a *sample* of a manufacturer's products, but also a sample of his performance *over time*. Thus, if one "follows the ratings" and buys an air conditioner or a toaster this year, he may buy it on the rating of a product made one, two, or three years ago. Similarly, if one buys a new automobile, he depends in part on the repair record (reported by at least one rating service) for previous models of that brand.

In large part, then, consumer rating services are devices for rating *manufacturers!* This is not to say they do not rate specific products. Sometimes they even draw fine distinctions between different models from the same company. But in the course of rating products, they also rate manufacturers. What more could the manufacturer ask for? Is this not what he claims he strives for?

Basic dichotomy. More to the point, what is it that has kept the consumer movement and brand-name manufacturers from paying attention to this area of shared overlapping interests? Neither will quarrel with the exposure either of factual deception or of product weaknesses on dimensions that both agree are essential to the product. This is not where the problem is. The problem is that the manufacturer *sells* one thing and the rating service *rates* another.

The concept of a "product" that dominates the thinking of rating services and the thought processes of those who suggest more "impartial evaluation information" for consumers (e.g., Donald Turner of the Department of Justice and Congressman Benjamin Rosenthal of New York) is that a product is an entity with a single, primary, specifiable function—or, in the case of some products such as food, perhaps a limited number of functions, e.g., being nutritious, tasty, and visually appealing. The specific goal of many proposed ratings—with their emphasis on the physical and technical characteristics of products—is to free the customer from the influence of many needs to which the marketer addresses himself, most particularly the desire for ego-enhancement, social acceptance, and status.

The marketer, oddly enough, tends to accept a little of the critic's view of what a product is. Marketing texts, too, speak of primary and secondary functions of a product as though it were self-evident that the aesthetic ego-gratifying, and status-enhancing aspects of the product were hung on as an afterthought. If this is true, why are Grecian vases preserved to be admired for their beauty? And why did nations of yore pass sumptuary laws to prevent people from wearing clothes inappropriate to their status?

We shall shortly explore what may lie behind this confusion about the nature of products. First, however, let us examine another topical area in which similar confusion exists.

MATERIALIST SOCIETY

The selling function in business is regularly evaluated by social commentators in relationship to the circumstance that ours is a "materialist society." We could say we do not understand what people are talking about when they refer to a materialist society, beyond the fact that our society does possess a lot of material goods. But, in point of fact, we think *they* do not understand what they are talking about. Let us elucidate.

At first hearing, one might conclude that criticism of a materialist society is a criticism of the extent to which people spend their resources of time, energy, and wealth on the acquisition of material things. One of the notions that gets expressed is that people should be more interested in pursuing nonmaterial goods.

The perplexing matter is, however, that the criticism becomes strongest on the circumstance that people *do* pursue nonmaterial goals—such as ego enhancement, psychic security, social status, and so on—but use material goods as a means of achieving them. Perhaps the distinctive feature of our society is the extent to which *material* goods are used to attain *nonmaterial* goals.

Now there are many ways in which societies satisfy such needs. For example, there are ways of attaining status that do not involve material goods of any substance. Most societies grant status to warriors and other heroes, to wise men who have served the society, and so on. Often the external manifestation of this status is rigidly prescribed and involves signs whose material worth is insignificant: a hero wears a medal, a ribbon in his lapel, or a certain type of headdress, or he may be addressed by an honorific title.

However, in societies that value economic performance, it is not uncommon for material goods to be used as status symbols. Indians of the Southwest, for example, favor sheep as a symbol even to the extent of overtaxing the grazing lands and lowering the economic status of the tribe. As a practical matter, this might be more damaging to the welfare of the Navaho than is the damage that many low-income Negroes do to their own individual welfares when, as research shows, they insist on serving a premium-priced brand of Scotch.

Many of the things about which there is complaint are not self-evidently bad. Art collecting is generally considered a "good thing." But take the worst instance of a person who neurotically seeks self-assurance by buying art objects. Clinically, one might argue that he would do himself a lot more long-run good with psychotherapy even though, when one considers the resale value of the art objects, he may have taken the more economical course of action. Similarly, it is not self-evident that the promotion of toiletries to the youth as a symbol of transition to manhood is inherently cruel—unless the commercials are especially bad! It is clear, however, that there is no societal consensus that the transition to manhood should be symbolized by the use of toiletries.

What seems to be the nub of the criticism of our society as a materialist one is that simultaneously a great number of nonmaterial goals are served by material goods, and there is no consensus that this should be so. Behind this is our old friend (or enemy): the concept of a product as serving solely a primary function. In the perspective of history and of other societies, this is a rather peculiar notion. Who in a primitive society would contend that a canoe paddle should not be carved artistically, or that a chief should not have a more elaborate paddle than a commoner?

Much of the confusion over the words on our list seems to be a residue of the early age of mass production. The production engineer, faced with the task of devising ways to turn out standardized products at low cost, had to ask himself, "What are the irreducible elements of this product?" This was probably best epitomized in Henry Ford's concept of the automobile, and his comment that people could have any color they wanted so long as it was black. Clearly, Ford thought it was immoral even to nourish the thought that a product ought to look good, let alone that it should serve various psychic and social functions.

But all this was closely related to the mass producer's effort to find the irreducible essence of what he manufactured. This effort broke up the natural organic integrity of products, which, at almost all times in all societies, have served multiple functions.

Many writers have called attention to the fact that in recent times our society has passed from the period of simpleminded mass production to that of product differentiation on attributes beyond the irreducible primary function. As yet, however, we do not think there is adequate appreciation of the impact of the residue of the early period of mass production on thinking about what a product is. In that period even very complex products were converted into commodities. Since each performed essentially the same primary function, the chief means of competition was pricing.

PRODUCTS AS COMMODITIES

At this point, we shall argue that the thinking of those who criticize the selling function is based on a model for the marketing of commodities. This factor does not exhaust the criticisms, but we believe it is at the core of present misunderstandings over the concepts on which we have focused our discussion.

On the one hand, to the extent that products are commodities, it is possible to specify the function or functions which all products in that category should serve. It follows that a person who buys and uses such a commodity for some purpose other than for what it was intended has indeed done something odd, although perhaps useful to him (for example, baseball catchers who use foam-rubber "falsies" to pad their mitts). In any event, it is possible both to specify the basis on which the commodity should be evaluated and the information a person is entitled to have in order to judge that product. A person searching for a commodity ought first to find out whether it serves this function and then to ask its price.

On the other hand, to the extent that products are *not* commodities, it is impossible to expect that price competition will necessarily be the main basis of competition. Likewise it is impossible to specify what information is needed or what constitutes rational behavior. Is it rational for a person to buy toothpaste because its advertiser claims it has "sex appeal?" Presumably people would rather look at clean than dingy teeth and presumably people also like to have sex appeal—at least up to the point where it gets to be a hazard or a nuisance.

But it does not follow, insofar as we can see, that ratings—or grade labeling—should discourage product differentiation or the promotion of products on a noncommodity basis. If the consumer were assured that all products in a given rating category performed their primary functions about equally well, could it not be argued that those attributes which differentiate the products on other functions would then become increasingly interesting and important? Or, to be more specific, what makes it possible for "instant-on" TV tuning to be promoted—other than a presumed agreement, by both manufacturer and consumers, that the TV set performs its primary function little better or worse than its competition?

This is a facet of competition not appreciated by the opponents of grade-labeling, who have argued that it would reduce competition. Perhaps it would be more helpful if the opponents of grade labeling first gathered some evidence on what has actually happened to competition in countries where grade labeling has been introduced. (The head of one major relevant trade association recently told one of us that he knew of no such research.)

TOWARD MORE INFORMATION

Readers will note that we have indulged in considerable speculation in this article. But most of the issues on which we have speculated are researchable. Relatively little, for example, is really known about how businesses actually see themselves carrying out "the practice of competition," or even about the actual competitive mechanisms of setting prices. Furthermore, in all of this, there is no mention of the *consumer's* view of these various concepts or of his model of the marketing process. To be sure, we can be reasonably certain of some things. For example, we know that consumers do regard products as serving needs beyond the bare essentials. Yet it would be helpful to know far more about their views of the overall marketing process.

What we propose as a worthwhile endeavor is an independent assessment of the consumer's view of the marketing process, focusing on information needs from his point of view. Thus, rather than businessmen lamenting the critics' proposals for product-rating systems and the critics bemoaning what seem to be obvious abuses of marketing tools, both sides ought to move toward proposing an information system for the consumer that takes into account *his* needs and *his* information-handling capacities while still adhering to the realities of the marketing process.

For those who have the reading habit, it will be obvious that this proposal is but an extension of the conclusions reached by members of the American Marketing Association's Task Force on "Basic Problems in Marketing" for the improvement of relations between marketing and government.[4] In brief, along with suggested studies on the influence of government policies and programs on corporate marketing decisions, a special study was recommended in the area of consumer-buyer decision making and behavior:

> It is of the highest importance to investigate the impacts of the host of governmental regulations, facilities, aids, and interventions upon the quality and efficiency of consumer-buyer decision making.[5]

The report went on to state that, particularly in light of the generally recognized drift from *caveat emptor* toward *caveat venditor,* "abundant basic research opportunities and needs exist" in the area of government impact and consumer-buyer behavior.

WHAT CAN BUSINESSMEN DO?

Certainly there is a crying need for more information and, as we have tried to illustrate, for fresh analytic thinking on almost all of the issues on which government and business are butting heads. We have elaborated on the different models of how the marketplace does, and should,

---

[4]See E. T. Grether and Robert J. Holloway, "Impact of Government upon the Market System," *Journal of Marketing,* April, 1967, pp. 1–5; and Seymour Banks, "Commentary on 'Impact of Government upon the Market System,'" *Journal of Marketing,* pp. 5–7.

[5]Grether and Holloway, *op. cit.,* p. 5.

work because we think their existence explains the largest part of why marketers and their critics often talk past each other, even when they have the best intentions of engaging in a dialogue. The other part is explained by the relative absence of facts. As we have noted, the consumer's view of the market-advertising process and his informational needs represent an important (and relatively unprobed) research area.

Returning to the "dialogue," we should add a further problem beyond that of business and government spokesmen talking past one another. Inasmuch as many on both sides see themselves as representing their colleagues' views, partisanship becomes mixed with the aforementioned misunderstanding. Since such partisanship is likely to address itself to stereotyped views of "the other side," the comments become irrelevant. That many well-qualified first-hand commentators are regarded as self-serving by their critics is a point aptly made by Denis Thomas. Equally apt is his corollary observation that those "who view business . . . from a suitably hygienic distance lose no marks for partiality even if their facts are wrong."[6]

How then can effective interactions take place? Obviously, the key parts will be played by:

1. Thoughtful business and government leaders.

2. Marketers and their critics who take the time to consider and to understand (even if they do not agree with) each others' premises and assumptions.

3. Those who engage in meaningful dialogue oriented to fact finding rather than fault finding.

4. Those on both sides who address themselves to solving the problems of the real, rather than the presumed, public.

These constructive parts are not easy to play, but there are many who are trying, and succeeding, as these three examples illustrate:

1. The Department of Commerce has taken a series of measures, including the formation of a National Marketing Advisory Committee, to play a positive "activist" role in business-government relations; marketers are involved in what goes on rather than, as has occurred in many previous government situations, being informed after the fact.

2. William Colihan, Executive Vice President of Young & Rubicam, Inc., proposed at the University of Missouri's Freedom of Information Conference that marketing undertake a major consumer education job to "make the marketing system benefit the nonaffluent, the undereducated."[7] This 20% of adult consumers represents, he feels, both a public responsibility and a marketing opportunity.

3. John N. Milne of Toronto's MacLaren Advertising Company Lim-

---

[6]Denis Thomas, *The Visible Persuaders* (London: Hutchinson & Co., 1967), p. 11.

[7]William Colihan, *Freedom of Information in the Market Place* (FOI Center, Columbia, Missouri, 1967), pp. 140–48.

ited spelled out eleven specific major economic, social, ethical, and communications research projects to provide a "factual basis for an objective assessment of advertising, to replace emotional pleas." Business, government, universities, and projects in other nations would serve as sources and beneficiaries of data "so that advertising's usefulness to all segments of society can be assessed and improved."[8]

Beyond the parts played by thoughtful business and government people, we see a distinctive role for schools of business in bringing about meaningful interaction. Business schools are a unique resource both in their understanding of the business system and in their capability to conduct relevant research. Other faculties, at least equally competent and objective in research, generally do not have the depth of understanding of why things are the way they are—a necessary precursor to relevant study. We hasten to add that grasping how something *does* operate implies no consent that this is how it *should* operate, now or in the future.

Both in research and as participants (or moderators) in dialogue, business school faculties can play a significant role.

Business and government should sponsor the necessary research. The particular need for business is to recognize that the era of exclusively partisan pleading must end. In our judgment, the American Association of Advertising Agencies' sponsorship of research on consumer reactions to advertising and advertisements is a splendid model.[9] The findings are by no means exclusively favorable to advertising. But they make more clear where problems do, and do not, lie. And academic "insurance" of the objective conduct of the research and presentation of findings should bring about a degree of governmental acceptance and set the standard for any subsequent research.

We can use more of this, and more of it is beginning to take place. A dialogue is always most profitable when the parties have something to talk about.

---

[8]Speech given at the Annual Conference of the Federation of Canadian Advertising and Sales Clubs, Montreal, June 1967.

[9]For a description of the research and a review of the major results, see Stephen A. Greyser (ed.), *The AAAA Study on Consumer Judgment of Advertising—An Analysis of the Principal Findings* (New York: American Association of Advertising Agencies, 1965); and Opinion Research Corporation, *The AAAA Study on Consumer Judgment of Advertising* (Princeton, N.J., 1965); the findings and their interpretation are the subject of the authors' book, *Advertising in America: The Consumer View* (Boston: Division of Research, Harvard Business School, 1968).

Suggested additional
AMA readings

Adelman, Morris A. "The 'Product' and 'Price' in Distribution," in *Adaptive Behavior in Marketing* (ed. Robert T. Buzzell), pp. 126–34. Chicago: American Marketing Association, 1956.

Alderson, Wroe. "The Marketing Viewpoint in National Economic Planning," *Journal of Marketing*, Vol. 7 (April, 1943), pp. 326–32.

Barron, J. F. " 'Normal' Business Behavior and the Justice Department," *Journal of Marketing*, Vol. 27 (January, 1963), pp. 46–49.

Bartels, Robert. "Marketing as a Social and Political Tool," in *Marketing: A Maturing Discipline* (ed. Martin L. Bell), pp. 210–16. Chicago: American Marketing Association, 1960.

Bauer, Raymond A., Cunningham, Scott M., and Wortzel, Lawrence H. "The Marketing Dilemma of Negroes," *Journal of Marketing*, Vol. 29 (July, 1965), pp. 1–6.

Beckman, Theodore N. "A Challenge for a Reappraisal of the Basic Nature and Scope of Marketing," in *Emerging Concepts in Marketing* (ed. William S. Decker), pp. 3–15. Chicago: American Marketing Association, 1962.

Belasco, James A. "The Salesman's Role Revisited," *Journal of Marketing*, Vol. 30 (April, 1966), pp. 6–8.

Berridge, William A., and Paris, James D. "Reflections on Marketing Responsibilities—A Research Viewpoint," in *Marketing: A Maturing Discipline* (ed. Martin L. Bell), pp. 219–39. Chicago: American Marketing Association, 1960.

Blank, David M. "Some Comments on the Role of Advertising in the American Economy—A Plea for Revaluation," in *Reflections on Progress in Marketing* (ed. L. George Smith), pp. 145–53. Chicago: American Marketing Association, 1964.

Blankenship, A. B. "Some Questions of Ethics in Marketing Research," *Journal of Marketing Research*, Vol. 1 (May, 1964), pp. 26–31.

Borum, Rodney L. "An Activist Approach to Government-Business Relations," in *Marketing for Tomorrow . . . Today* (ed. M. S. Moyer and R. E. Vosburgh), pp. 11–13. Chicago: American Marketing Association, 1967.

Brown, William F. "The Protection of the Consumer and Competition, Some

Fundamental Issues," in *Effective Marketing Coordination* (ed. George L. Baker, Jr.), pp. 426–38. Chicago: American Marketing Association, 1961.

Bymers, Gwen J.   "New Responsibility for the Consumer as Seen by a Home Economist," in *A New Measure of Responsibility for Marketing* (ed. Keith Cox and Ben M. Enis), pp. 18–23. Chicago: American Marketing Association, 1968.

Colihan, William J., Jr.   "Ethics in Today's Marketing," in *Changing Marketing Systems* (ed. Reed Moyer), pp. 164–66. Chicago: American Marketing Association, 1967.

Cook, James V.   "1970—Can Marketing Measure up?" in *Effective Marketing Coordination* (ed. George L. Baker, Jr.), pp. 21–27. Chicago: American Marketing Association, 1961.

Coolsen, Frank G.   "Marketing and Economic Development," in *Emerging Concepts in Marketing* (ed. William S. Decker), pp. 26–37. Chicago: American Marketing Association, 1962.

Copeland, Morris A.   "A Social Appraisal of Differential Pricing," *Journal of Marketing*, Vol. 6, Part 2 (April, 1942), pp. 177–84.

Cron, Theodore O.   "Easy Street," in *Changing Marketing Systems* (ed. Reed Moyer), pp. 178–79. Chicago: American Marketing Association, 1967.

Dowd, Laurence P.   "Social Responsibilities in Distribution—An Integral Part of Marketing Education," in *Marketing: A Maturing Discipline* (ed. Martin L. Bell), pp. 204–9. Chicago: American Marketing Association, 1960.

Firestone, Raymond C.   "National Aims and Business Responsibility," in *Marketing Precision and Executive Action* (ed. Charles H. Hindersman), pp. 11–18. Chicago: American Marketing Association, 1962.

Goodman, Charles S.   "Do the Poor Pay More?" *Journal of Marketing*, Vol. 32 (January, 1968), pp. 18–24.

Grether, E. T.   "Galbraith Versus the Market: A Review Article," *Journal of Marketing*, Vol. 32 (January, 1968), pp. 9–13.

Harper, Marion, Jr.   "The National Conscience in the Decade of Incentive," in *Dynamic Marketing for a Changing World* (ed. Robert S. Hancock), pp. 3–11. Chicago: American Marketing Association, 1960.

Hertz, David B.   "Marketing as a Social Discipline," in *The Social Responsibilities of Marketing* (ed. William D. Stevens), pp. 212–18. Chicago: American Marketing Association, 1961.

Hirsch, Leon V.   "The Contribution of Marketing to Economic Development— A Generally Neglected Area," in *The Social Responsibilities of Marketing* (ed. William D. Stevens), pp. 413–18. Chicago: American Marketing Association, 1961.

Hollander, Stanley C.   "Teaching and Research Implications of a Public Policy Approach," in *Changing Marketing Systems* (ed. Reed Moyer), pp. 363–67. Chicago: American Marketing Association, 1967.

Hovde, Howard T.   "The Marketing Viewpoint in Planning for Community Betterment," *Journal of Marketing*, Vol. 7 (April, 1943), pp. 337–41.

Jackson, Hugh R.   "Notes on Social Responsibilities of Advertising," in *The Social Responsibilities of Marketing* (ed. William D. Stevens), pp. 98–100. Chicago: American Marketing Association, 1961.

Kanter, Donald L. "The Myth of the Long-Suffering Consumer," in *Marketing for Tomorrow . . . Today* (ed. M. S. Moyer and R. E. Vosburgh), pp. 130–33. Chicago: American Marketing Association, 1967.

Kelley, Eugene J. "Marketing and Moral Values in an Acquisitive Society," in *Marketing: A Maturing Discipline* (ed. Martin L. Bell), pp. 195–203. Chicago: American Marketing Association, 1960.

Kloepfer, William, Jr. "The New Publics—Professionals, Consumers and Government," in *Innovation—Key to Marketing Progress* (ed. Henry Gomez), pp. 586–91. Chicago: American Marketing Association, 1963.

Knopp, Jacky, Jr. "What Are 'Commodities of Like Grade and Quality'?" *Journal of Marketing*, Vol. 27 (July, 1963), pp. 63–66.

Lande, Irvin M. "Consumer Marketing Development in Emerging Economies," in *Marketing for Tomorrow . . . Today* (ed. M. S. Moyer and R. E. Vosburgh), pp. 251–53. Chicago: American Marketing Association, 1967.

Lazer, William. "Changing Societal Norms and Marketing Implications," in *Changing Marketing Systems* (ed. Reed Moyer), pp. 156–160. Chicago: American Marketing Association, 1967.

Loevinger, Lee. "The Social Responsibilities of Marketing," in *The Social Responsibilities of Marketing* (ed. William D. Stevens), pp. 3–6. Chicago: American Marketing Association, 1961.

Lowe, John W. "An Economist Defends Advertising," in *Journal of Marketing*, Vol. 27 (July, 1963), pp. 16–19.

Lucas, Darrell B. "Public Policy Relating to Marketing Subject Areas," in *A New Measure of Responsibility for Marketing* (ed. Keith Cox and Ben M. Enis), pp. 102–4. Chicago: American Marketing Association, 1968.

Manischewitz, D. Beryl. "Government Attitudes and Marketing Image," in *The Social Responsibilities of Marketing* (ed. William D. Stevens), pp. 41–52. Chicago: American Marketing Association, 1961.

————— and Stuart, John A. "Marketing under Attack," *Journal of Marketing*, Vol. 26 (July, 1962), pp. 1–6.

Marks, Norton E., and Scott, Richard A. "Ethics for Marketing Executives: The Educational Environment," in *Changing Marketing Systems* (ed. Reed Moyer), pp. 379–81. Chicago: American Marketing Association, 1967.

Mason, John L. "The Low Prestige of Personal Selling," *Journal of Marketing*, Vol. 29 (October, 1965), pp. 7–10.

Mauser, Ferdinand F. "The Social Obligations of Marketing Research," *Journal of Marketing*, Vol. 15 (July, 1950), pp. 74–76.

Mayer, Charles S. "Requiem for the Truth-in-Packaging Bill?" *Journal of Marketing*, Vol. 30 (April, 1966), pp. 1–5.

Mazur, Paul. "Soliloquy in Marketing," in *Marketing: A Maturing Discipline* (ed. Martin L. Bell), pp. 10–17. Chicago: American Marketing Association, 1960.

Miller, Richard Lee. "Dr. Weber and the Consumer," *Journal of Marketing*, Vol. 26 (January, 1962), pp. 57–61.

Millican, Richard D. "Is a Marketing Man Just a Marketing Man?" *Journal of Marketing*, Vol. 28 (April, 1964), pp. 8–9.

Morse, Richard L. D. "Are Consumer Grades Needed?" *Journal of Marketing,* Vol. 30 (July, 1966), pp. 52–53.

Murphy, Daniel J. "The Ethics of Retail Pricing," in *The Social Responsibilities of Marketing* (ed. William D. Stevens), pp. 109–20. Chicago: American Marketing Association, 1961.

Patterson, James M. "Business-Government Relations: An Alternative View," in *A New Measure of Responsibility for Marketing* (ed. Keith Cox and Ben M. Enis), pp. 46–52. Chicago: American Marketing Association, 1968.

————. "What Are the Social and Ethical Responsibilities of Marketing Executives?" *Journal of Marketing,* Vol. 30 (July, 1966), pp. 12–15.

Petit, Thomas A., and Zakon, Alan. "Advertising and Social Values," *Journal of Marketing,* Vol. 26 (October, 1962), pp. 15–17.

Preston, Lee E. "Advertising Effects and Public Policy," in *Marketing and the New Science of Planning* (ed. Robert L. King), pp. 558–65. Chicago: American Marketing Association, 1968.

Quinn, E. C. "Marketing, a Corporate Viewpoint," in *Marketing: A Maturing Discipline* (ed. Martin L. Bell), pp. 240–47. Chicago: American Marketing Association, 1960.

Sandage, C. H. "Ethics and the Philosophy of Advertising," in *Emerging Concepts in Marketing* (ed. William S. Decker), pp. 128–31. Chicago: American Marketing Association, 1962.

Schutte, Thomas F. "Marketing Implications of Executive Perceptions of Business Ethics," in *Toward Scientific Marketing* (ed. Stephen A. Greyser), pp. 186–99. Chicago: American Marketing Association, 1963.

Shepard, Albert. "Ethics, Legality and Profitability," in *Marketing Precision and Executive Action* (ed. Charles H. Hindersman), pp. 31–37. Chicago: American Marketing Association, 1968.

Stoller, Martin. "The Character and Dimension of the Marketing Problem in the Developing Countries," in *A New Measure of Responsibility for Marketing* (ed. Keith Cox and Ben M. Enis), pp. 27–35. Chicago: American Marketing Association, 1968.

Voorhis, Jerry. "Marketing and the Consumer," in *The Social Responsibilities of Marketing* (ed. William D. Stevens), pp. 34–40. Chicago: American Marketing Association, 1961.